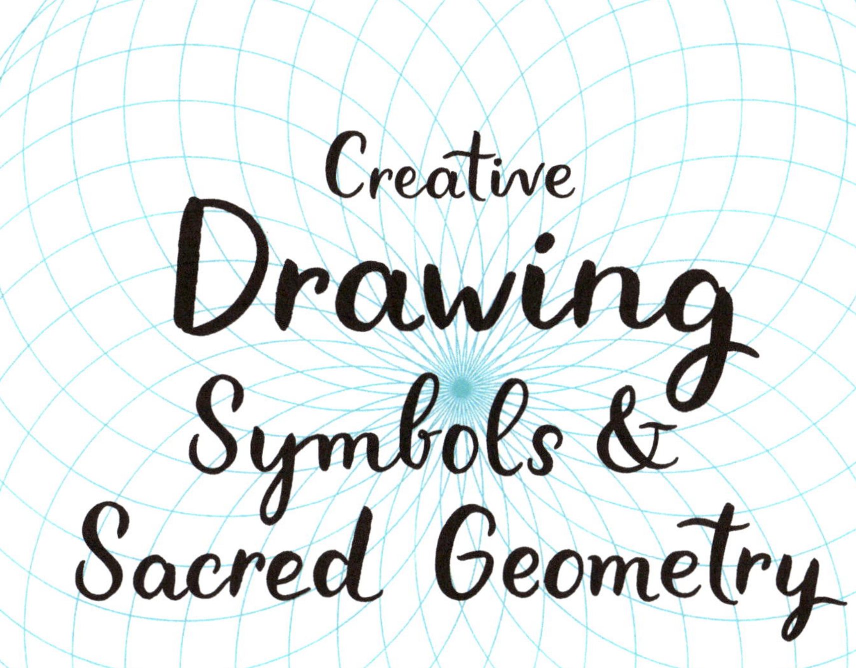

Creative Drawing Symbols & Sacred Geometry

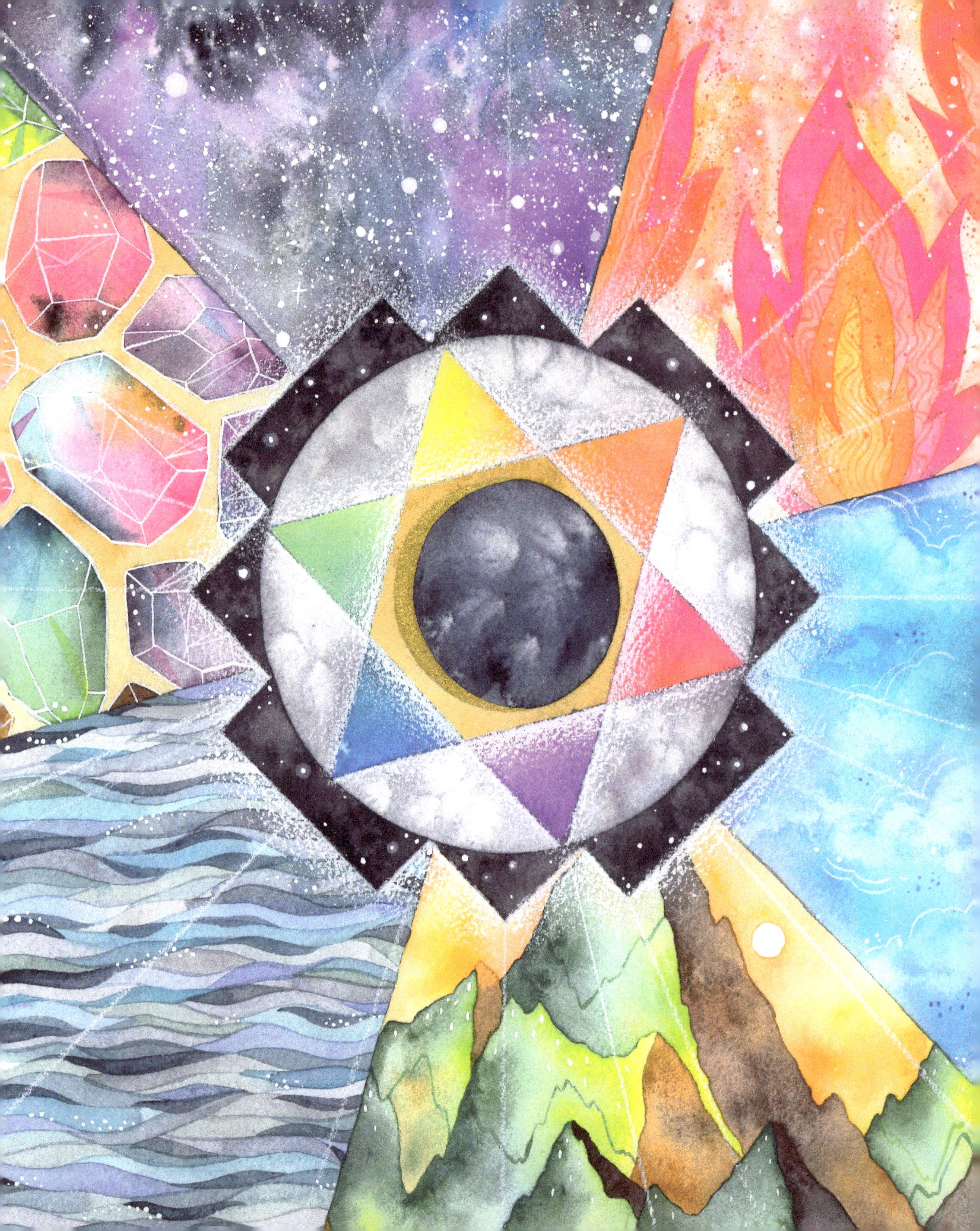

Creative Drawing Symbols & Sacred Geometry

A BEGINNER'S STEP-BY-STEP GUIDE TO DRAWING AND PAINTING INSPIRED MOTIFS

Ana Victoria Calderón

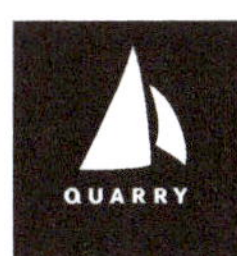

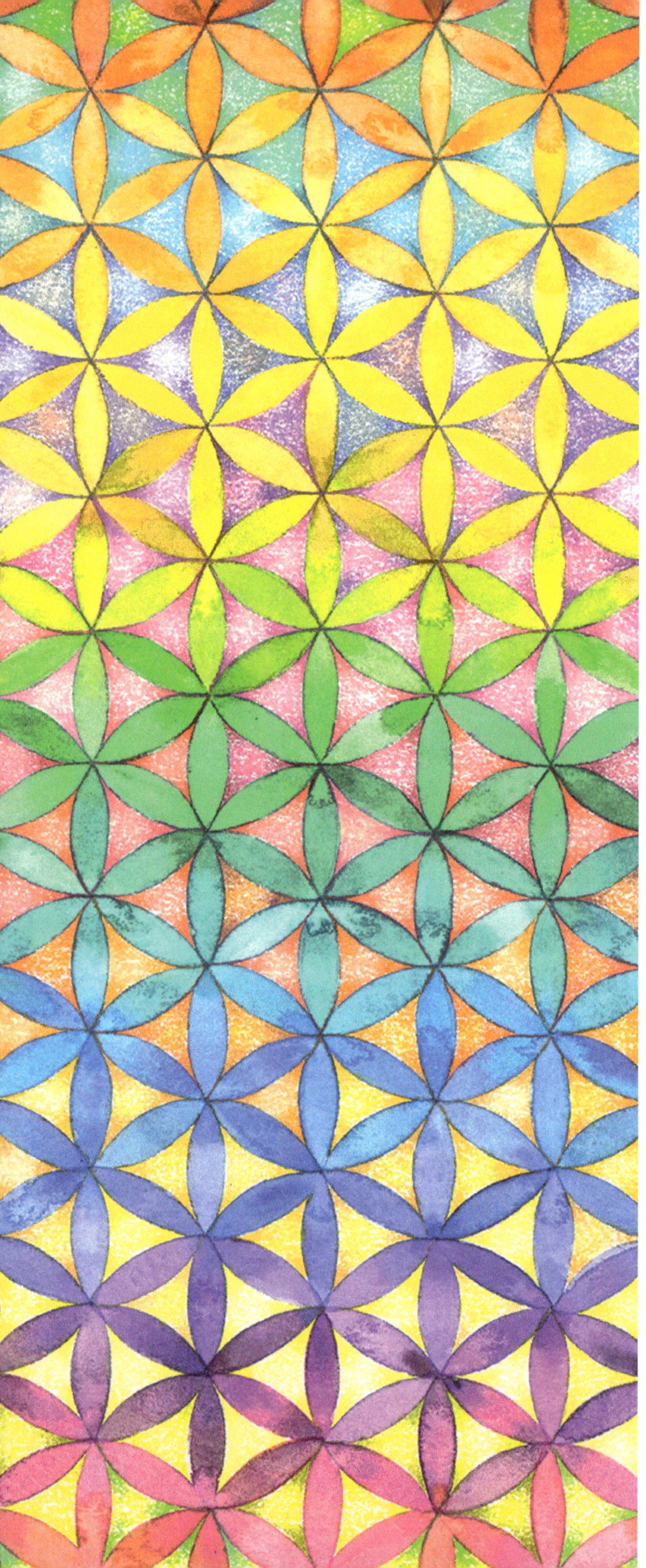

CONTENTS

INTRODUCTION

My Discovery of Sacred Geometry and Meditative Art Making

As artists, our personal life experiences are directly related to our creative evolution. A few years back, I found myself in need of spiritual growth; my mind was scrambled, and I was desperately longing for inner peace. I began exploring, going to regular acupuncture sessions, learning about Ayurveda, journaling, and practicing an ancient form of mantra-based meditation. As I went deeper into my inner world, my mind began to heal, and a new form of curiosity began to bloom that fueled my creative practice.

I can't recall the exact moment I became captivated with the magical theme of perfect shapes and forms; they simply began to appear in my consciousness. The words *sacred geometry* kept coming up in my writing exercises. At the time, I didn't even know what that meant, but somehow this concept had been waiting for me, buried deep in my psyche. I had no idea what kind of creative exploration was about to follow; all I knew was that it was extremely charming.

Follow the charm, my meditation teacher would say.

But where to start? When my fascination with sacred geometry began, I embarked on a long and sometimes bewildering journey of investigation. I purchased multiple books, watched hundreds of videos, took any course I could find, and started drawing these shapes on my own. Sacred geometry is such a broad concept that it was hard to even figure out where to begin, but once I got started, I simply couldn't stop drawing these shapes. During my quest of discovery on this topic, to say I became overwhelmed with the amount of available material is an understatement.

"Mighty is geometry—joined with art, resistless."

—EURIPIDES

While there is endless information to discover, in all my research I never found a practical guide that would explain the basic concepts behind these shapes in simple terms or how they worked as a system. It was even more difficult as an artist in a sea of complex mathematical textbooks, psychology papers, and, frankly, quite a few eccentric spiritual interpretations. I was not looking for this. I wanted my journey with sacred geometry to be a personal one, a pure one, where I could experience the beauty of drawing these shapes and discover meanings I found in them through the process.

I did end up figuring it out, and with that came a delightful creative experience.

Geometry = Truth = Beauty = Goodness

As more and more of my students became curious about these shapes and my fascination with sacred geometry, they came to me with daily questions, wanting to know more about this topic and specifically whether there were any books I could recommend to learn how to draw these timeless formations. I honestly had no books to suggest because I had not found one that explained this subject matter in simple terms. In order for me to suggest anything at all, I would have had to send them a complex document with at least one hundred resources and wish them luck.

This is how the idea to put together a simple guide for artists came forth. This book is more than an instructive manual; it's the beginning of a journey of creative discovery.

There was one other aspect that led me to write a book on this topic. While I am not opposed to sharing this information online, I knew this knowledge had to be protected somehow. Sacred geometry is an entire drawing system, with much meaning and room for personal interpretation. The only other format I have shared my learnings in has been during intensive painting retreats where my students are in a contained space, learning, meditating, and drawing together. With this book, I felt the need to put out a proper guide for beginners who are curious about the topic and wish to get an overview of the beautiful universe of sacred geometry without being overwhelmed. My goal is to simplify this topic, make it easy to follow, and share the basic concepts of drawing sacred geometry through the artist's perspective.

"Geometry is knowledge of the eternally existent."

—PYTHAGORAS

After you have read this book, you may find yourself engaged in this subject and wanting to know more. I will be clear: There is much more to learn beyond what is shared here, including technical information, history, and theoretical knowledge. Take it as a mere starting point with an entire universe to discover ahead. This book will keep the topic of sacred geometry and symbols simple while sharing fun ways to interact with them artistically using my favorite painting and drawing techniques.

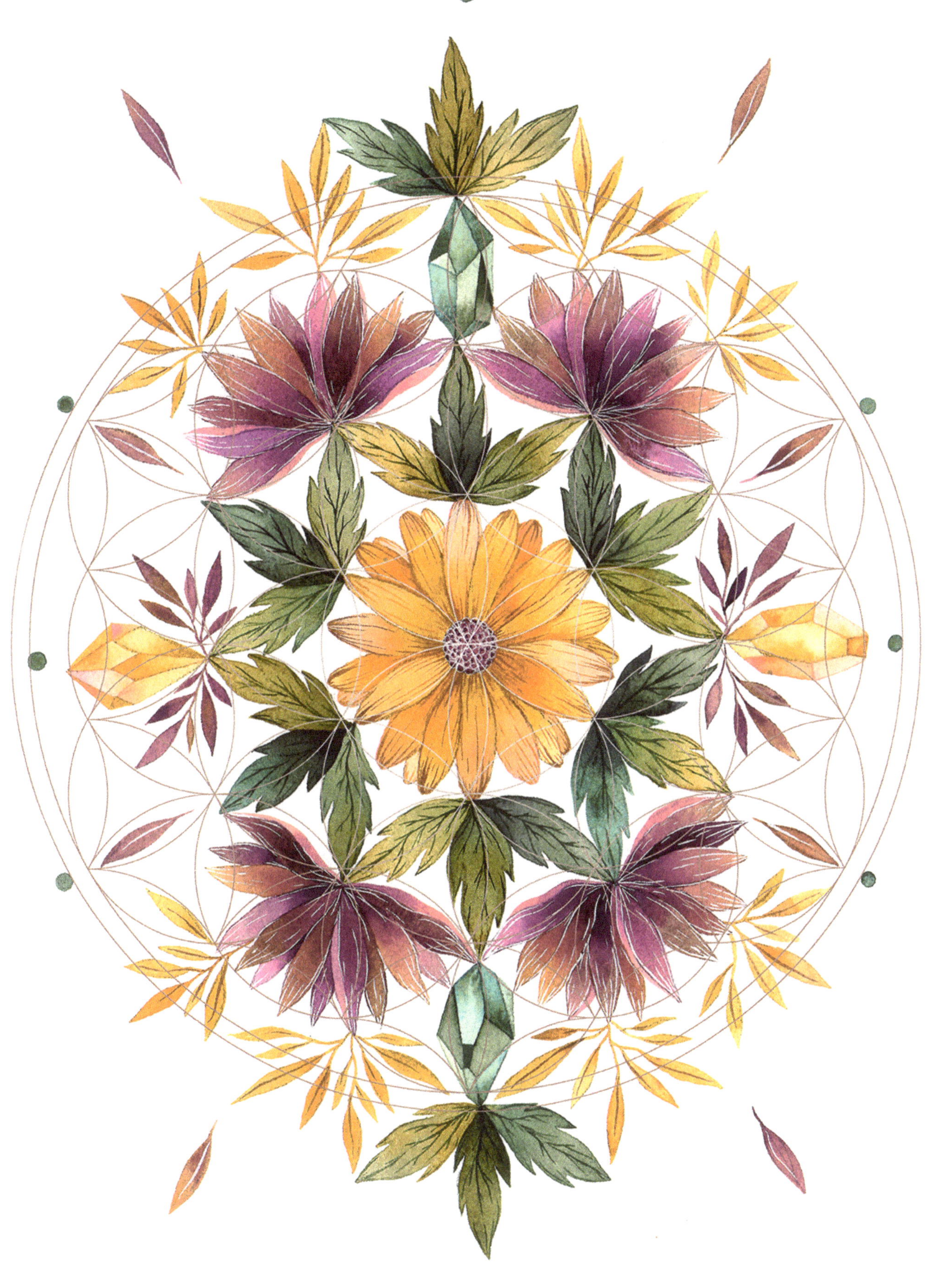

What Makes Sacred Geometry Sacred?

It is no wonder that sacred geometry is so attractive to us as humans, and it is common to find ourselves mysteriously drawn to this topic before we even hear the term or know what the symbols represent. That is because sacred geometry is an intrinsic part of our inner and outer world. When we begin to discover the world of sacred geometry, it becomes more apparent that these symbols are a part of absolutely everything that makes us us. While sacred geometry does not correspond to one specific culture, it is adopted by many, just as nature does not belong to us because we are a part of nature itself.

Sacred geometry can be found in a variety of topics and interpretations, including:

- Alchemy
- All forms of art throughout the ages, including painting, drawing, architecture, and music
- Ancient civilizations
- Astronomy
- Chemistry
- Diverse religions
- Human conception and anatomy
- Mathematical calculations
- Mysticism and symbolism
- Numerology
- Patterns in nature
- Philosophy
- Sacred temples
- Shrines
- Spiritual practice

"Geometry will draw the soul toward truth and create the spirit of philosophy."

—PLATO

Sacred geometry is even encoded in us—and in our world—at a biological level. So, what is our relationship to geometry? Without exception, everything in the universe is geometrical, including all internal structures. Every single geometric shape that exists is part of a growing formation that begins with the most primal shape, the circle, and builds on that. To understand why these shapes are so powerful, I will explain the basics of geometric shapes along with metaphors to accompany each. Some of these shapes we see every day; others are not so obvious. See the opposite page for just a few examples.

What makes this even more interesting is the process the artist goes through while discovering these shapes. It is said that it is not enough to simply observe sacred geometry; you must create these shapes on your own for a complete experience.

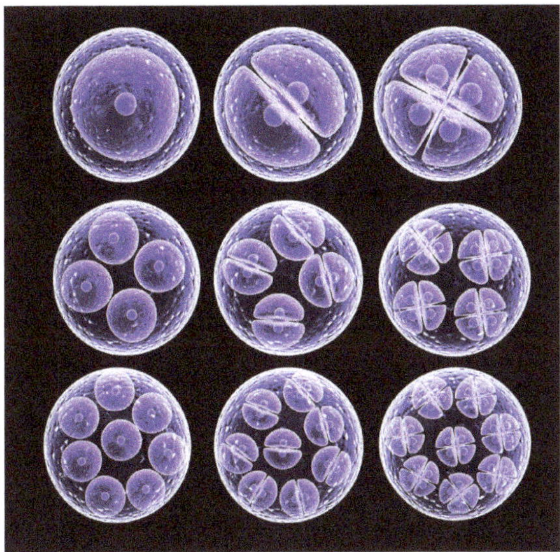

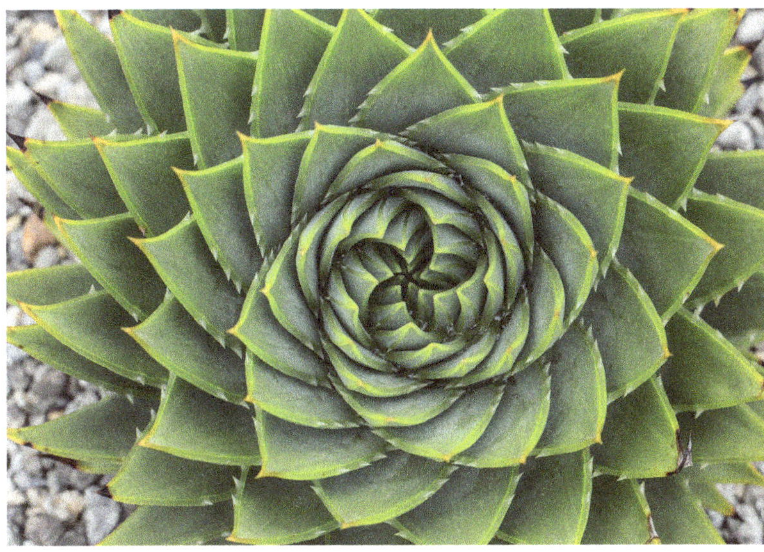

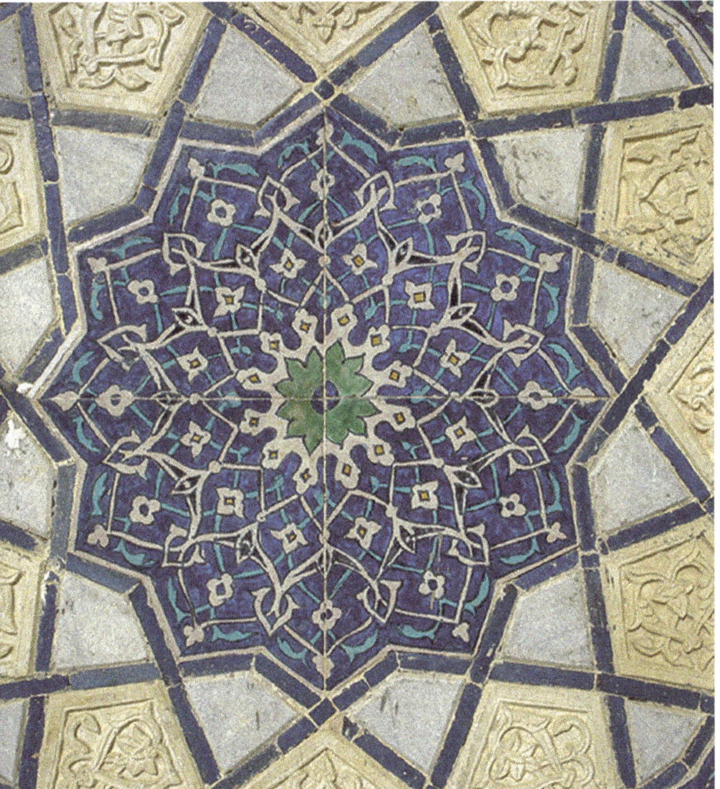

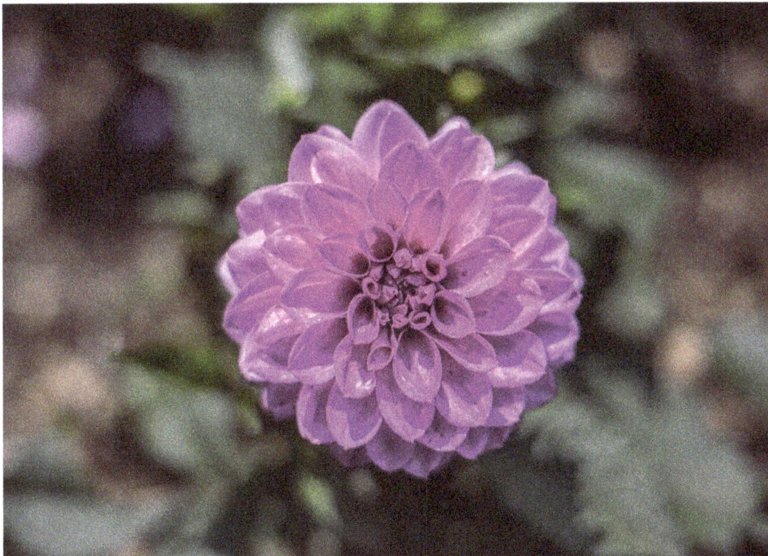

Clockwise from top left: An illustration of the process of cell division; the *Aloe polyphylla*, which grows in a distinctive spiral shape; a variety of dahlia plant with concentric florets; a detail of a blue tile floral and geometric star design on a wall of the ancient landmark Bibi-Khanym Mosque in Samarkand, Uzbekistan.

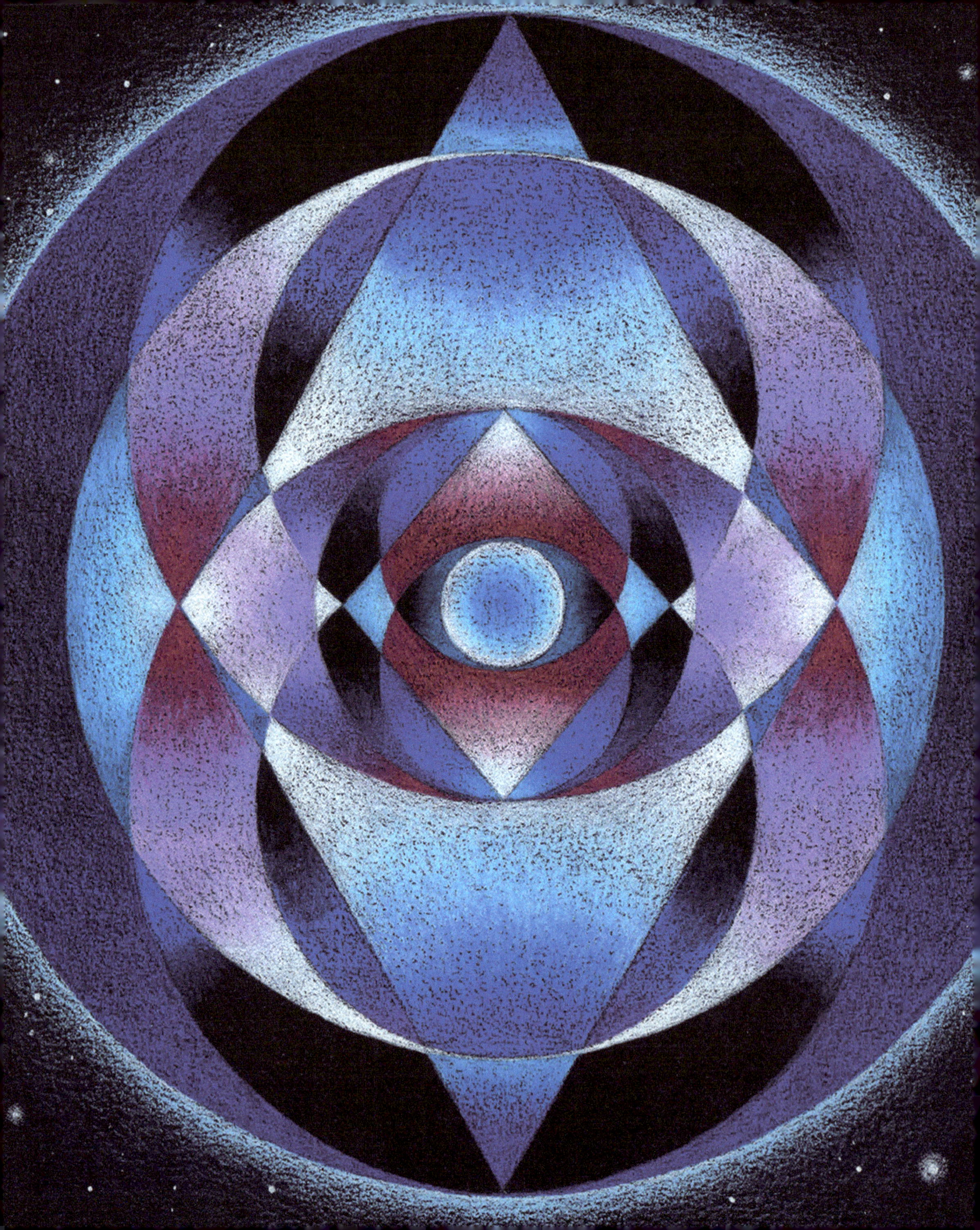

1

GEOMETRY TOOLS AND ART SUPPLIES

Geometric artwork is composed of two phases that integrate the union of our logical and creative brains, which is why creating this work results in such a powerful experience.

THE RELATIONSHIP BETWEEN MATHEMATICAL PRECISION AND ARTISTIC FLUIDITY

On one hand, we have our technical drawing. This is where you figure out how to draw each shape using specific steps and logic. This process satisfies our analytical brain by making something that is completely perfect and true. All intersections match up exactly where they are meant to be, and the drawing is perfect from a mathematical perspective. Our drawing is created in perfect universal order.

Once our base drawing is complete, our creative brain takes on the intuitive mission of discovering new shapes and patterns within the original grid. We are free to explore artistic interpretations, stories, colors, and techniques and be fully immersed in the joy of art making.

GEOMETRIC ARTWORK EXPERIENCE

LOGIC	CREATIVITY
Your starting point, drawing with a ruler and compass	Permission to be creative with your geometric drawing
Mathematical	Artistic
Masculine energy = straight line	Feminine energy = curve
Linear thinking	Abstract thinking
Focus	Emotions
Rational	Intuition
Order	Holistic
Facts	Visualization
Reasoning	Expression
Control	Play
Precision	Imagination
Perfection	Experimentation

When following the activities in this book, you will participate in both areas. For this, you will need two sets of art supplies: those for technical drawing and those for creative interpretation.

TECHNICAL DRAWING TOOLS

Compass

The most common types of compasses include those with either a lead tip as your drawing tool or a holder that allows you to insert your preferred drawing tool, which could be a pencil, pen, marker, or colored pencil. As with all supplies, there is a wide range of quality, from student to professional grade.

Ruler or Straightedge

In reality, you will not need specific measurements to create these drawings, which is why the term *straightedge,* as opposed to a ruler, is usually used in sacred geometry.

Protractor

A protractor is optional and not necessary for true sacred geometry shapes, but it can come in handy in certain situations.

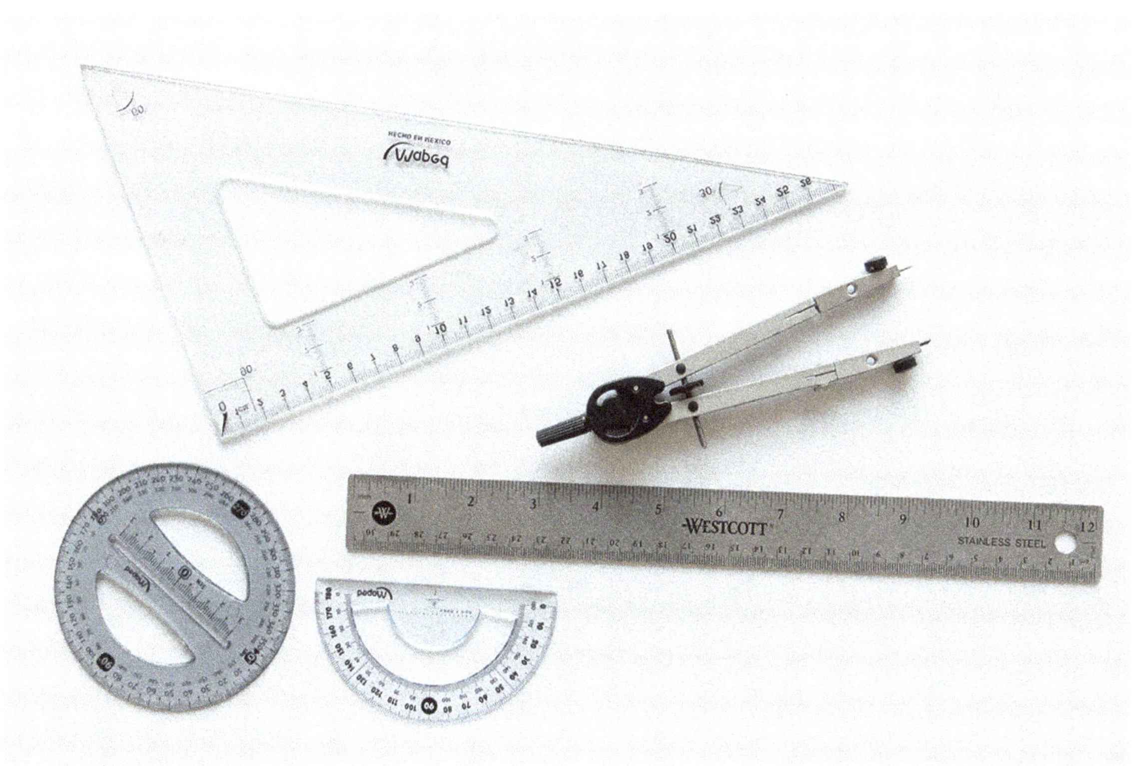

Mixed Media, Drawing, Black, and Watercolor Paper

All kinds of paper are suitable for tracing artistic geometry, but these are some types I've used in this book. Feel free to experiment! However, I suggest avoiding paper with too much texture, as it can be hard to maintain precision.

TOOLS FOR CREATIVE INTERPRETATION

The artistic medium is completely up to you. The projects in this book focus on drawing and include a few inspirational painting projects, but you are completely free to explore with the medium of your choice.

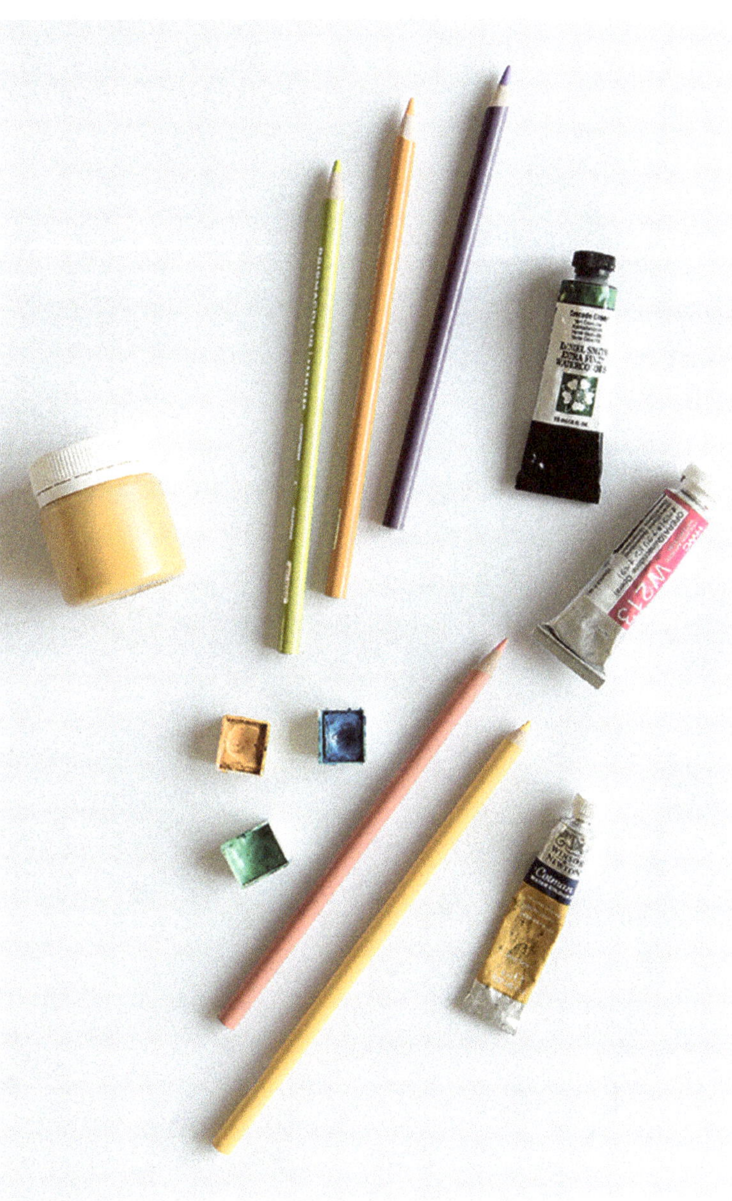

Colored Pencils

There is a wonderful world of colored pencils available! The professional brands I prefer are Prismacolor Premier, Caran d'Ache Luminance, and Faber-Castell Polychromos.

Paint

You can use watercolor pans, liquids, or tubes. You'll also need gouache or any opaque paint as well as metallic paints. My preferred brands are Winsor & Newton, Sennelier, Daniel Smith, Schmincke, Kremer, and Holbein.

Brushes

Synthetic brushes work best for precision. Princeton and Winsor & Newton have great options. I find it easier to use rounder, smaller brushes with pointy tips for precise shapes.

Basic Supplies

You'll need a pencil, an eraser, scissors, adhesive, and a pencil sharpener.

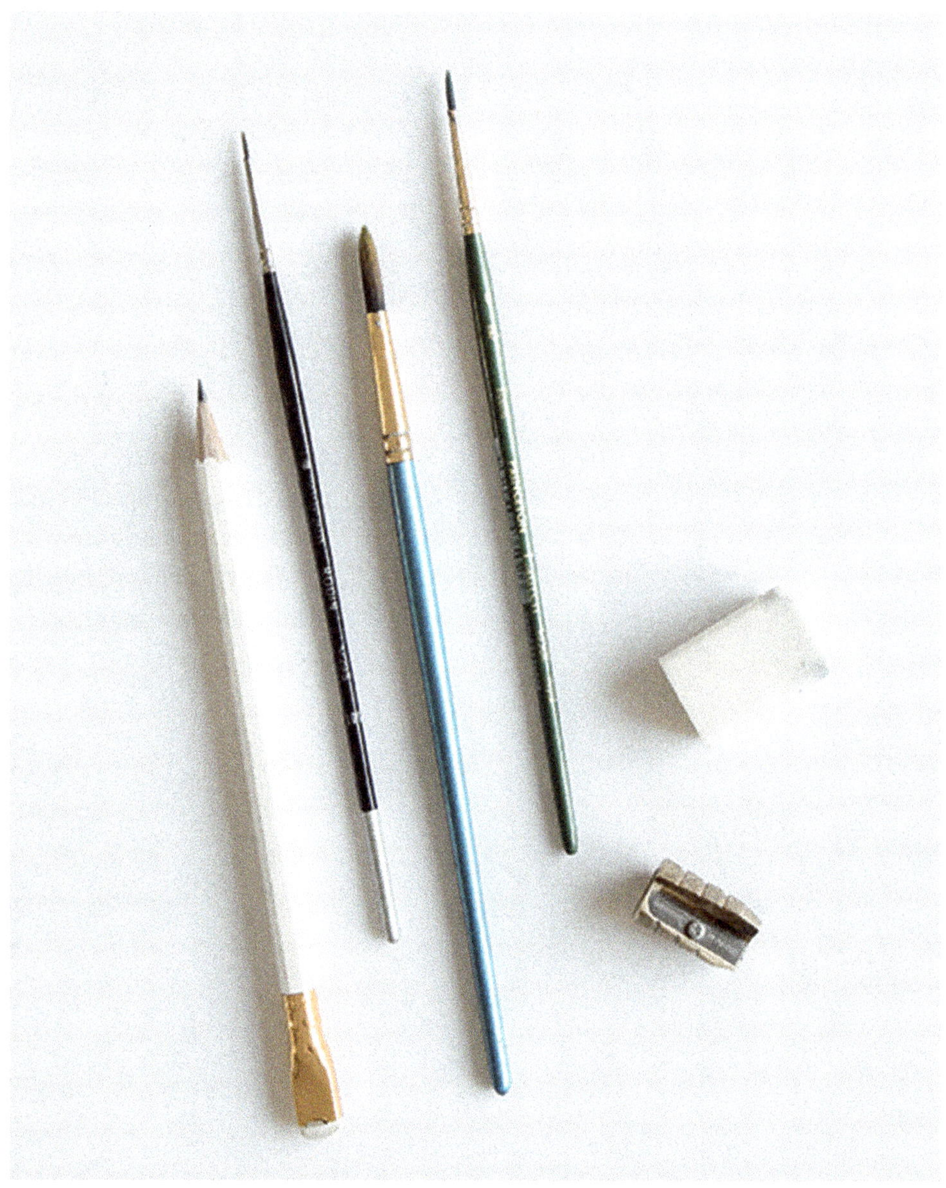

Embellishments

It's fun to use pressed flowers, cutouts, or stickers in your artwork. I always encourage experimenting with your personal art practice!

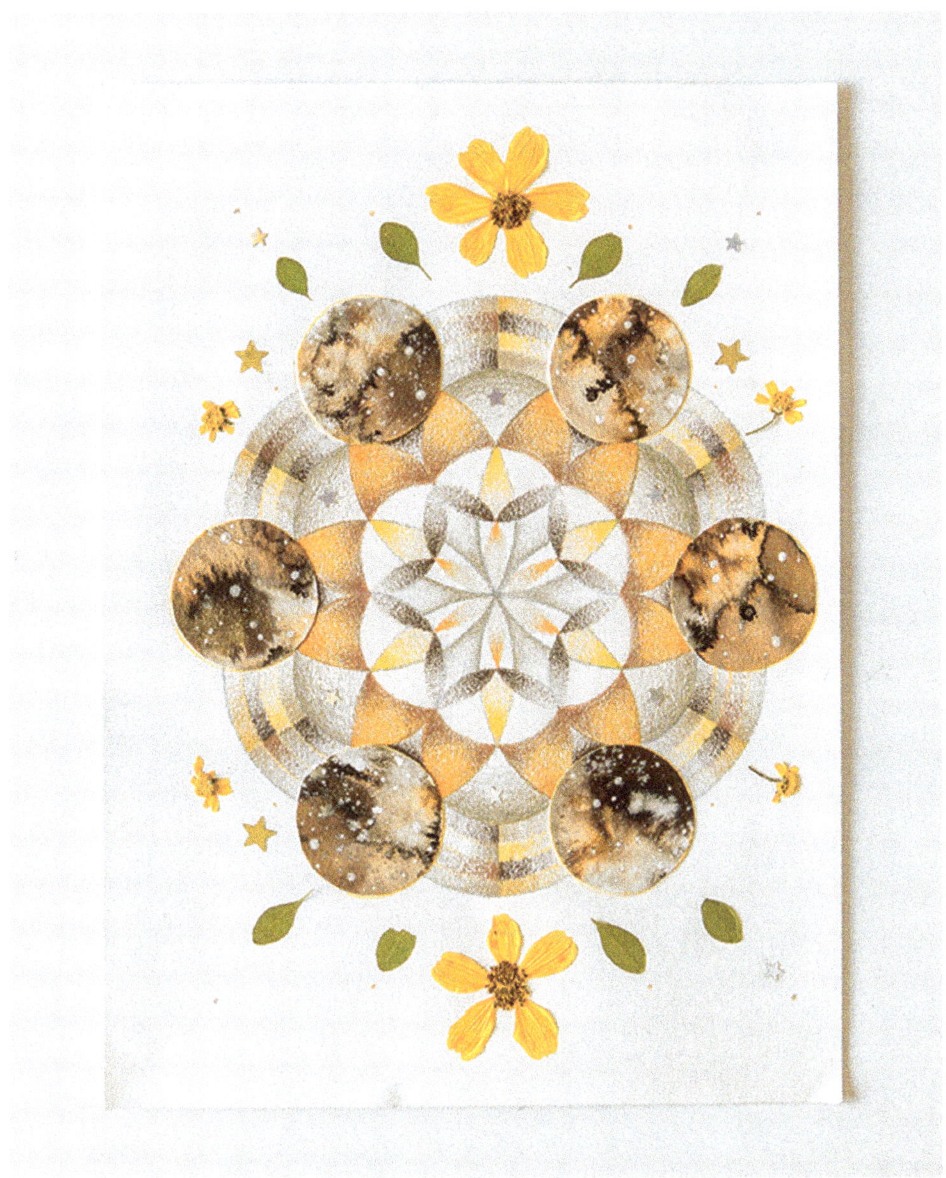

I embellished the piece above with pressed flowers, leaves, petals, and collaged watercolor circles.

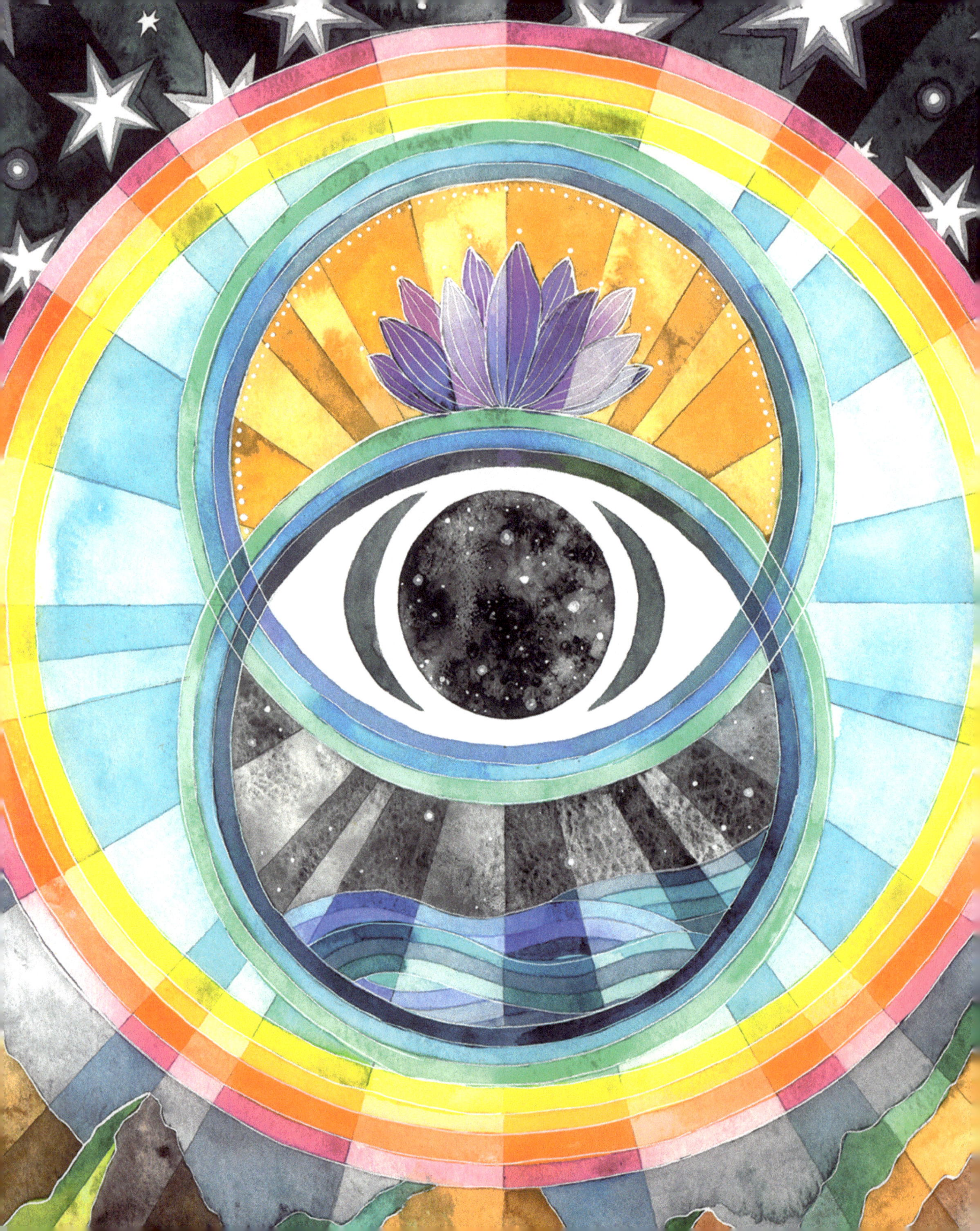

2

BASIC SHAPES AND SYMBOLISM

In each chapter, I share peeks into philosophical meanings that have been associated with geometric shapes by us humans. This is one of the aspects that makes sacred geometry sacred, because we have had a fascination and relationship with these shapes throughout the ages.

As I mentioned in the Introduction, this book will pique your curiosity about meanings associated with shapes. I will keep these interpretations at a logical level: our relationship with nature and historical uses. This is just the tip of the iceberg. Continue exploring deeper meanings if this is something that calls you.

THE CIRCLE

To speak of sacred geometry is to speak of the circle. This universal shape is at the core of every single formation we create in this book. For the series of drawings in this chapter, we must start at the very beginning.

The circle is a universal shape used in most cultures and religions and is the most common shape in nature. It is recognized as a divine sign, including halos and spiritual symbols. Its perfection will lead us to a series of captivating formations. To draw a circle, we ourselves must be centered as we create.

"Circles, like the soul, are neverending and turn round and round without a stop."

—RALPH WALDO EMERSON

THE CIRCLE: INTERPRETATIONS

Here are some symbolic meanings associated with the circle.

- Infinity, as the circle has no beginning and no end
- Totality
- The source of creation
- Symbolizes the number 1
- The sun, the moon, our planet, all planets
- A single cell
- A boundary represented by the circumference
- Perfection, wholeness, completion

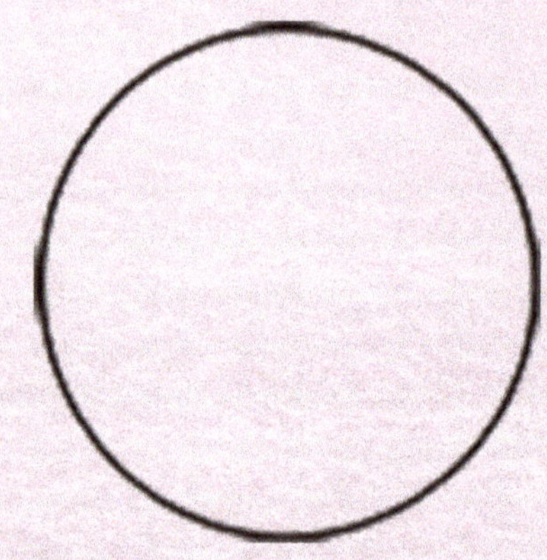

TIPS FOR USING YOUR COMPASS

A compass is the most treasured instrument in the art of geometry.

It's important to take good care of your technical instruments, as precision is of the utmost importance in this style of drawing. Treating these tools gently and having patience with them is part of the process. This specific instrument facilitates the drawing of perfect circles and arches and measures distance between intersections and specific points.

A compass consists of two arms and a movable joint. On one arm is a needle; on the other, a drawing tool. The needle will be the center of your circle while the drawing tool creates the circumference. As detailed in the supplies chapter, there are compasses that come with a pencil lead point integrated into one arm, while others have the option for you to insert whichever drawing tool you prefer, securing it tightly with the adjustable nut on the arm. The hole through which the drawing tool is placed is called the *aperture.*

To properly draw a circle, always hold the compass from the top so you don't shift the distance between arms accidentally. Even the slightest change of distance between the two arms can ruin the types of shapes and patterns we will be drawing in this book, as circles must be identical in radius for these to work.

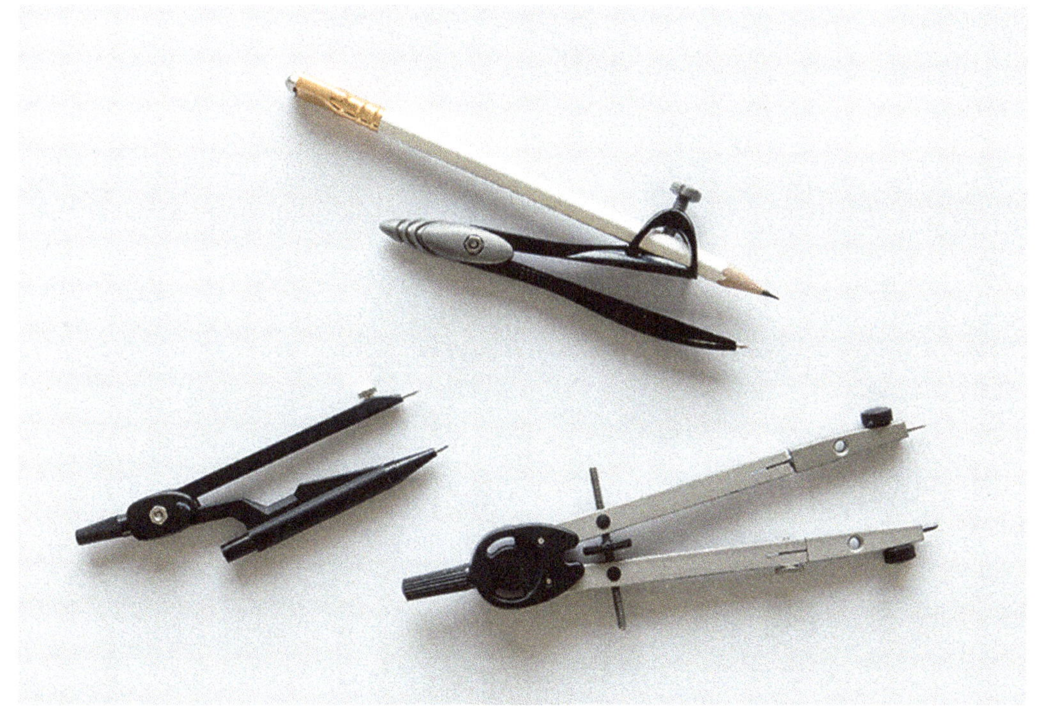

VESICA PISCIS

The moment a circle duplicates itself, intersections start to form. This is the true starting point of sacred geometry, the vesica piscis.

The vesica piscis is at the center of all other shapes in the universe. The more you explore sacred geometry, the more you will find this to be true, as it is the first step in a series of overlapping circles that initiates an expansive drawing system.

VESICA PISCIS: INTERPRETATIONS

Here are some symbolic meanings associated with the vesica piscis.

- The starting place of sacred geometry, where an intersection is born.
- The original source (circle) duplicates itself; knowledge is gained with motion and movement as interlocking circles are formed.
- Duality coming together to represent the first stage of creation.
- The divine feminine, the womb of the universe. Every shape can be made from the vesica piscis, a metaphor for the womb equaling creation itself.
- Representation of our biological shape as a two-cell embryo.
- Universal shapes found within the vesica include a human eye, a crescent moon, an almond, and a lens.

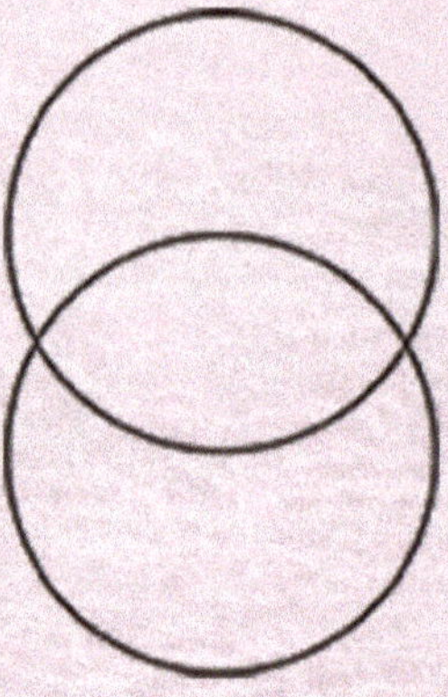

Drawing Technique

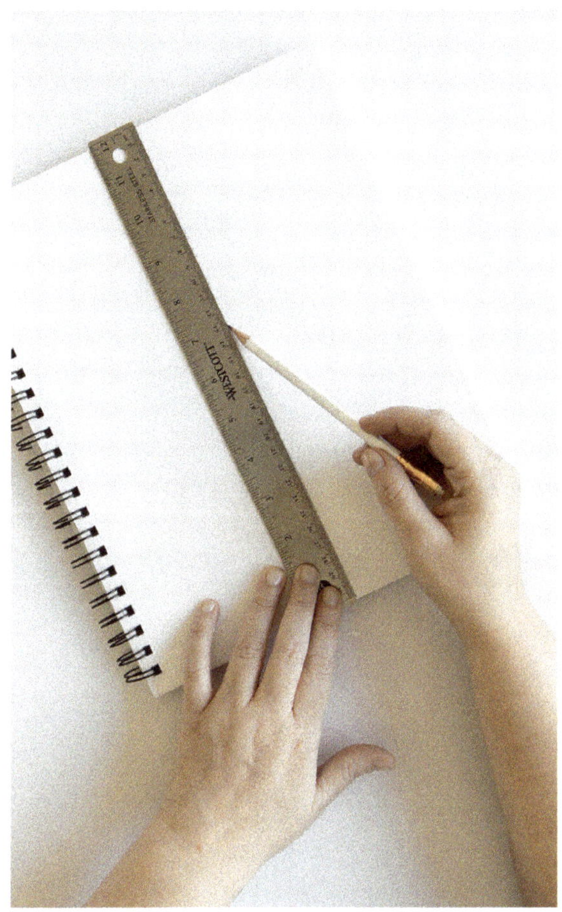

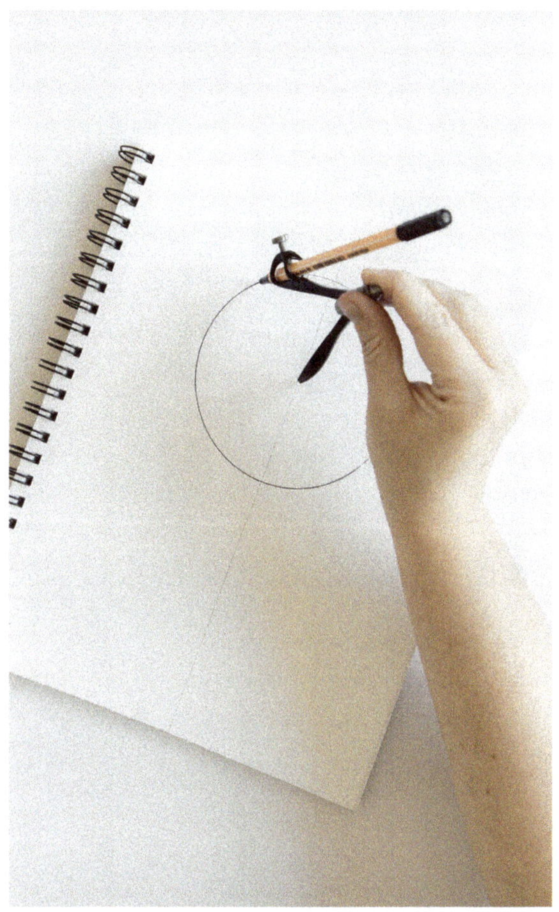

1 Begin by drawing a vertical line at the center of your page.

2 Place the needle of the compass on this line, slightly above the center. Rotate your compass to create a circle.

(continued)

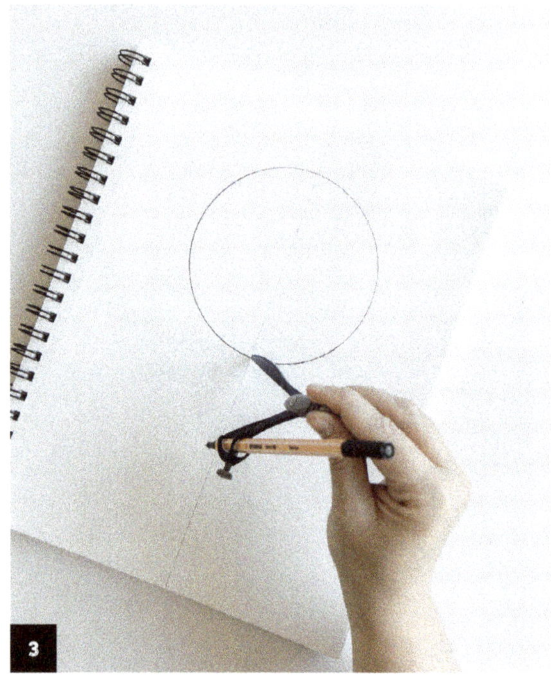

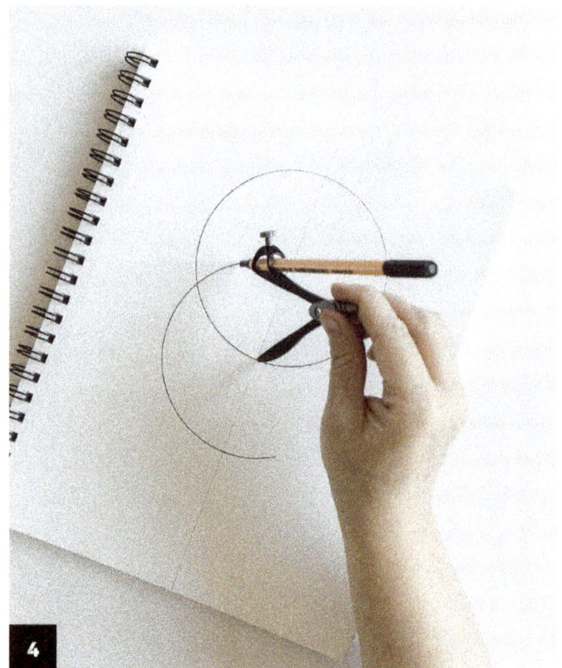

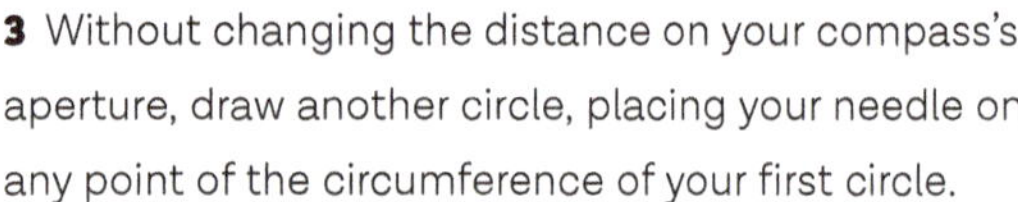

3 Without changing the distance on your compass's aperture, draw another circle, placing your needle on any point of the circumference of your first circle.

4 In this case, we will be using the vertical guideline as a reference for an orderly drawing.

5 Congratulations! You have created your very first sacred geometry drawing.

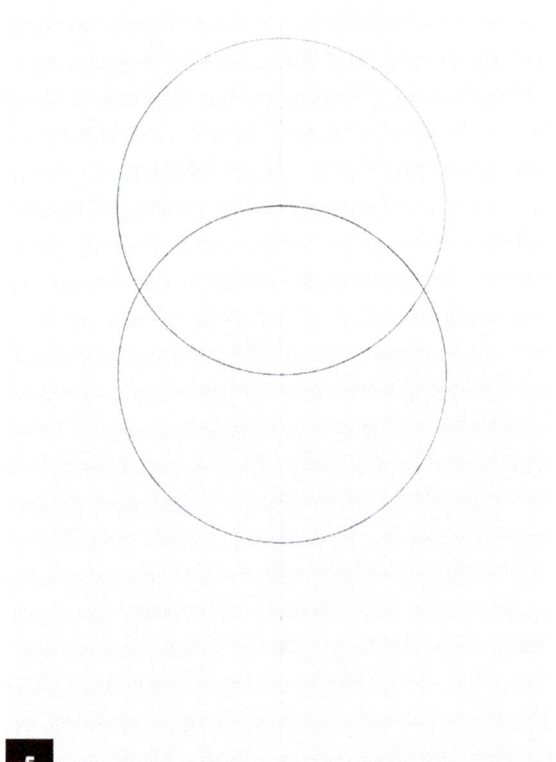

5

ARTISTIC EXPLORATION: SHAPES WITHIN THE SHAPE

Now comes the fun part. Your creative mission is to discover symbols, shapes, and patterns within this simple shape. Here is a method to get you started:

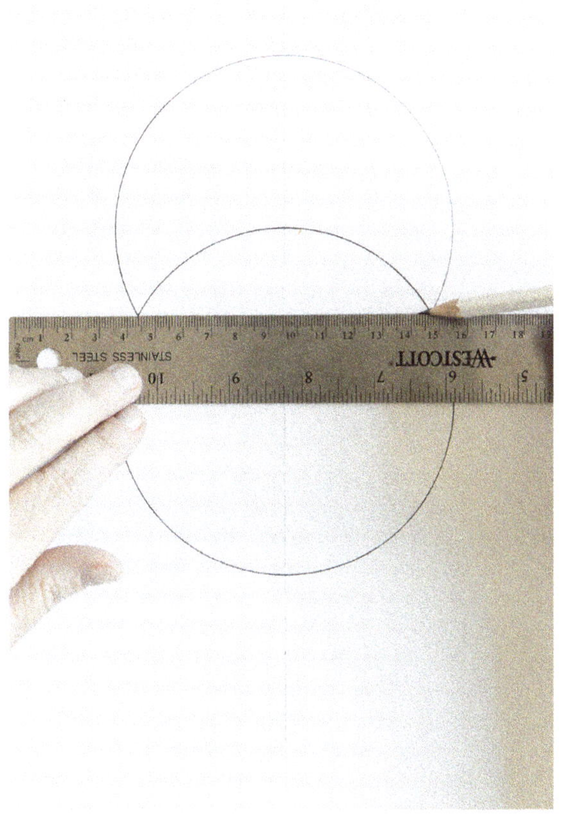

1 Using your straightedge, draw a horizontal line between the two intersections of your circles.

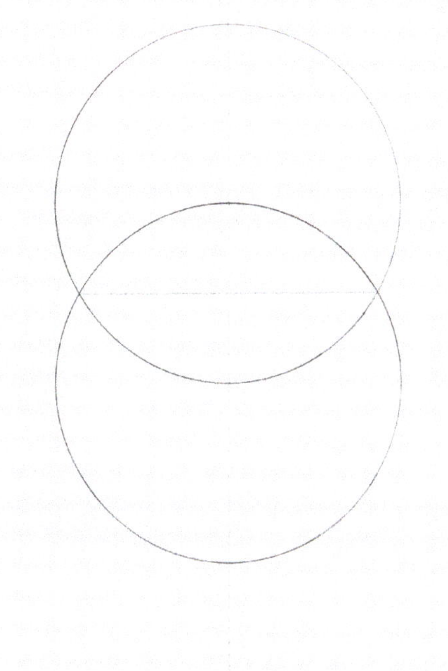

2 The cross that is formed from your vertical and horizontal line now indicates the very center of your shape.

(continued)

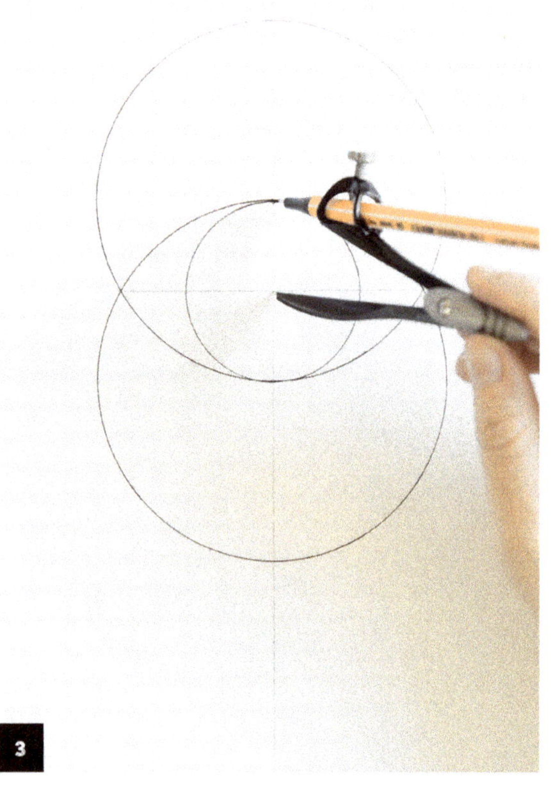

3

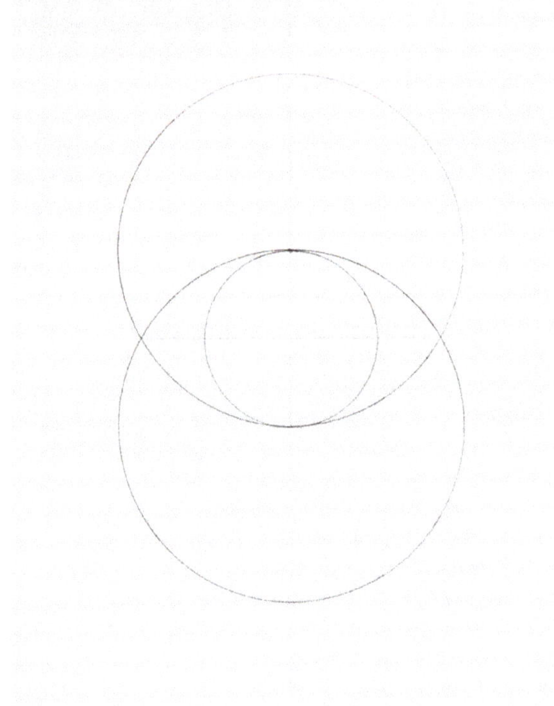

4

3 Place the compass needle at this cross point and adjust the width of your compass to the distance between the center and the top of your almond shape. Trace a new circle.

4 You have now created the perfect symbol for the human eye.

5 Feel free to erase any unwanted pencil guidelines or have fun integrating them into your drawing as you please.

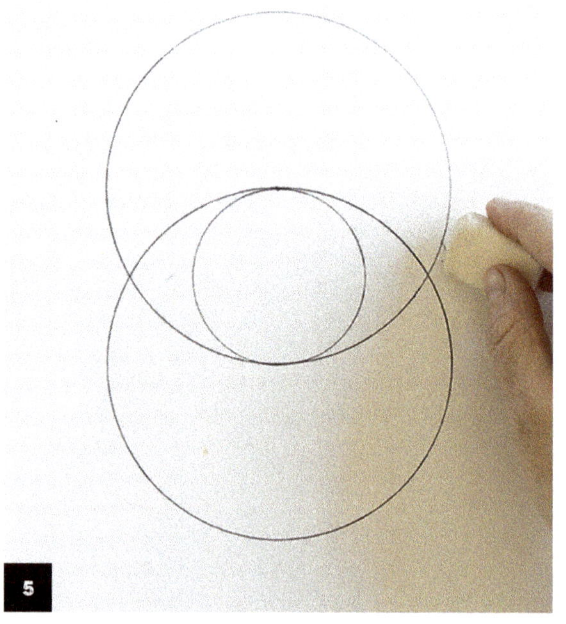

5

Here are some other examples of the endless possibilities you can explore by using a vesica piscis as your guide.

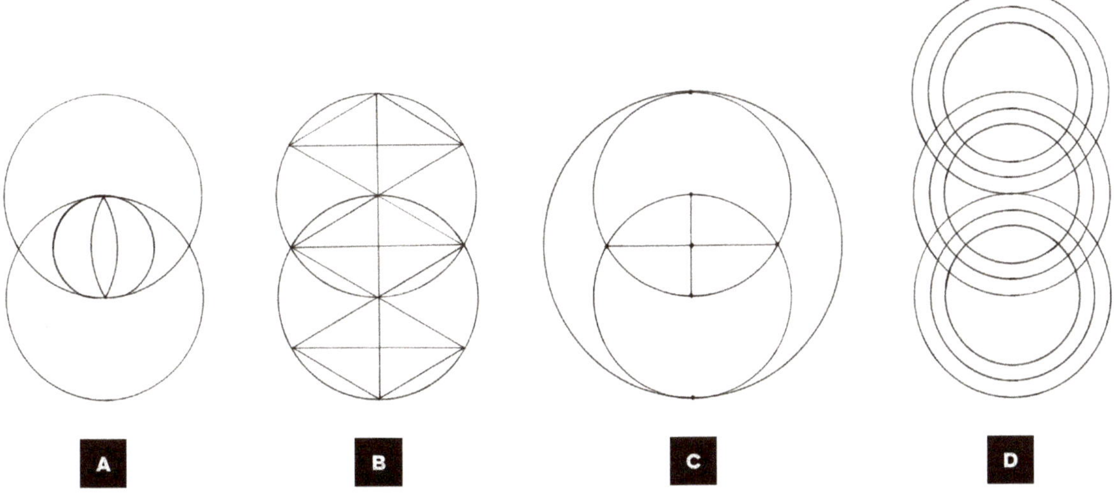

- **Eye of the tiger.** Once you have a basic human eye shape traced, open the compass to the original radius of the vesica piscis circle and place your needle at the circle intersections on each side and draw two arches, which will fit perfectly inside your smaller circle **(A)**.
- **Three diamonds.** Using the original cross explained in step 3, place your straightedge along the side intersections on the circles and connect them with the intersections at the center of your almond shape. You will begin to uncover X shapes and eventually diamonds **(B)**.
- **Encompassing circle.** Using the cross from step 3 on page 28, erase unwanted guidelines and trace a new large circle by opening your compass from the cross center point to the top edge of one of your circles. Trace a new circle that will fit both circles. I added little dots at each intersection for an interesting design element **(C)**.
- **Interlocking circles.** Double your vesica piscis by adding an extra circle at the bottom of your shape. You can also close your compass angle a few different times and create a series of inner circles for each original circle **(D)**.

Can you think of new ways to explore the wonders of a vesica piscis? Remember, the beauty lies in merging your creativity with each technical drawing, so don't be afraid to play, use your intersections with curiosity, and explore possibilities with the rest of your drawing tools and art supplies.

TRINITY KNOT

The trinity knot, also known as the triquetra, is a triangular figure composed of three interlaced arcs or overlapping vesica piscis, often drawn with an additional center circle.

TRINITY KNOT: INTERPRETATIONS

Here are some symbolic meanings associated with the trinity knot.

- Generally thought to represent the mind, body, and spirit
- Common ornament in medieval architecture, literature, and legends
- Representation of the divine trinity in religious symbolism
- Widely associated with the Celtic tradition representing the triple goddess (maiden-mother-crone) or three phases of a woman's life cycle
- Associated with the triskelion motif, consisting of a triple spiral, which has been found on artifacts in a variety of cultures throughout the ages

Drawing Technique

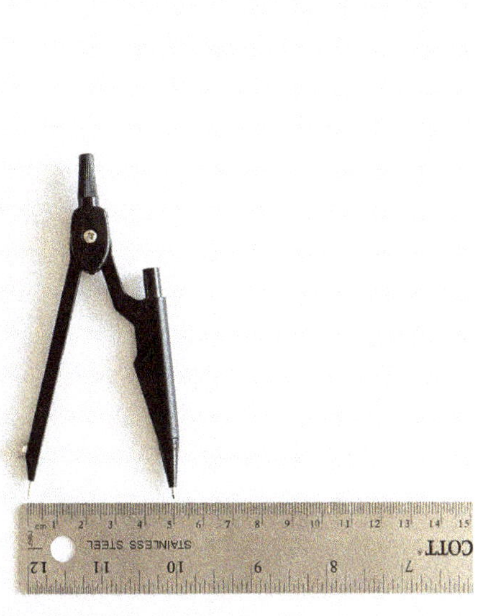

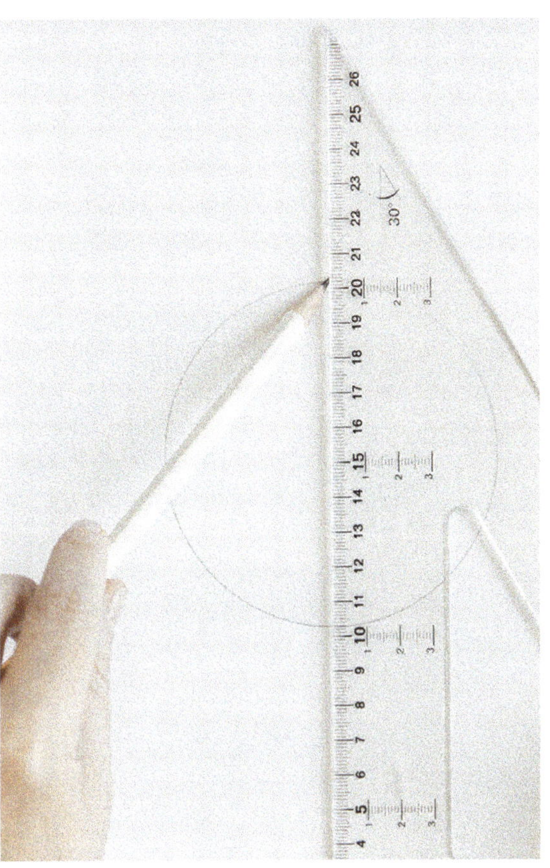

1 For instructive purposes, I will share measurements in this specific case to keep things simple. I am using a 2-inch (5 cm) radius for my original circle. Once you get the hang of it, feel free to use any measurement proportion you please.

2 Find the middle point of your paper and draw a circle using that 2-inch (5 cm) aperture. Make a small mark at the top center point of your circumference. You can do this easily using a square or an L-shaped ruler and placing it at a 90-degree angle at the bottom of your page in alignment with the center point of your circle.

(continued)

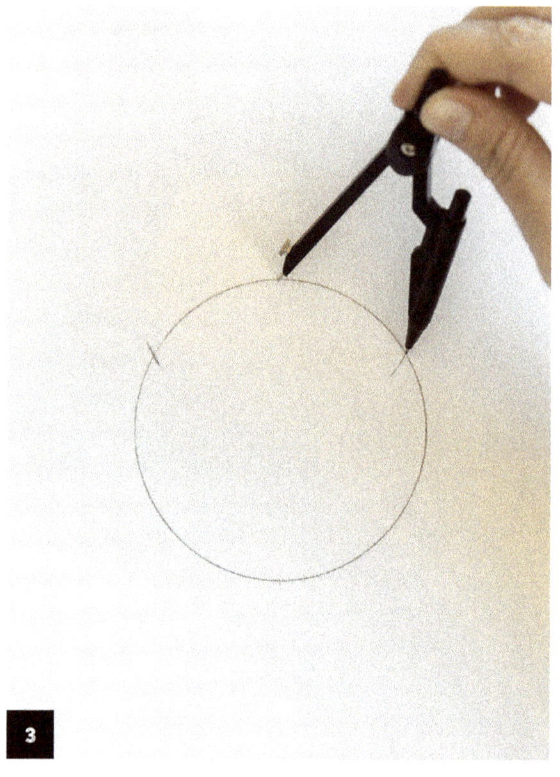

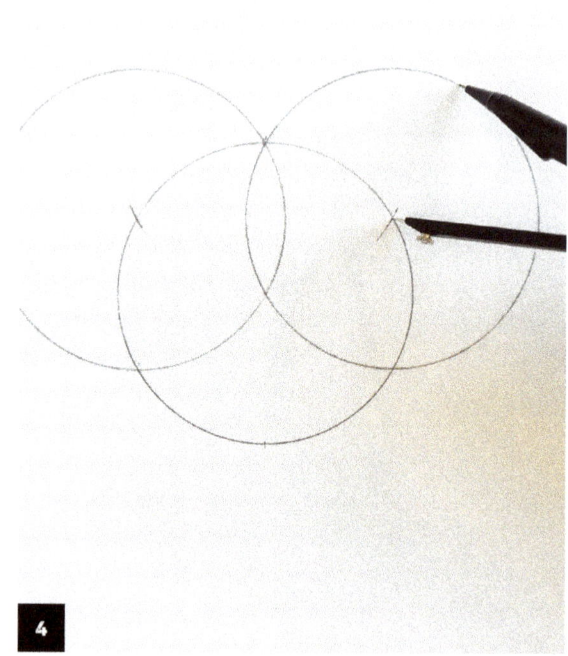

3 Place the needle at that top point and draw two small intersecting lines around the circle. Make sure you keep the original 2-inch (5 cm) radius the same. Even a ¼-inch (1 mm) shift of your compass can set the entire design off.

4 Once you have these two marks, trace two circles using each intersecting point as your center. I am using a lead pencil at this time because there will be lots of erasing later on.

5 To find the bottom point where you will trace your third circle, you can simply place your compass needle on one of the points where your original circle intersects with the second or third circle. Then place a small mark and draw your third circle using that point as your center. You can also trace the bottom point of your circle using the method in step 2, but using your compass will always provide more precision.

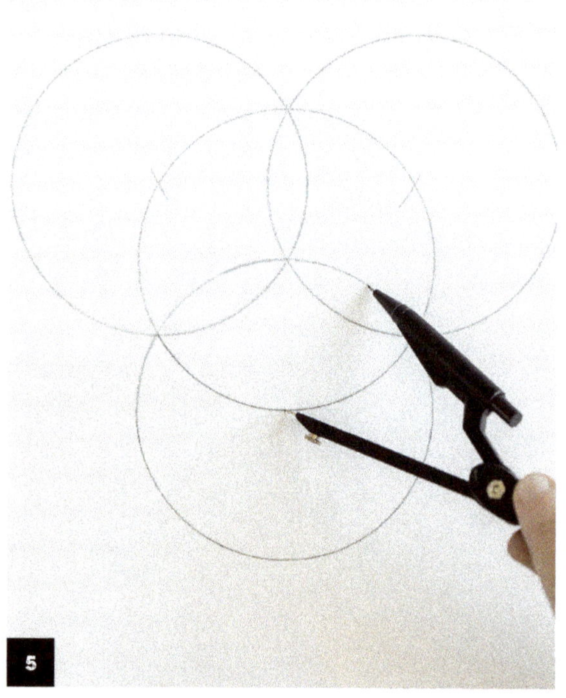

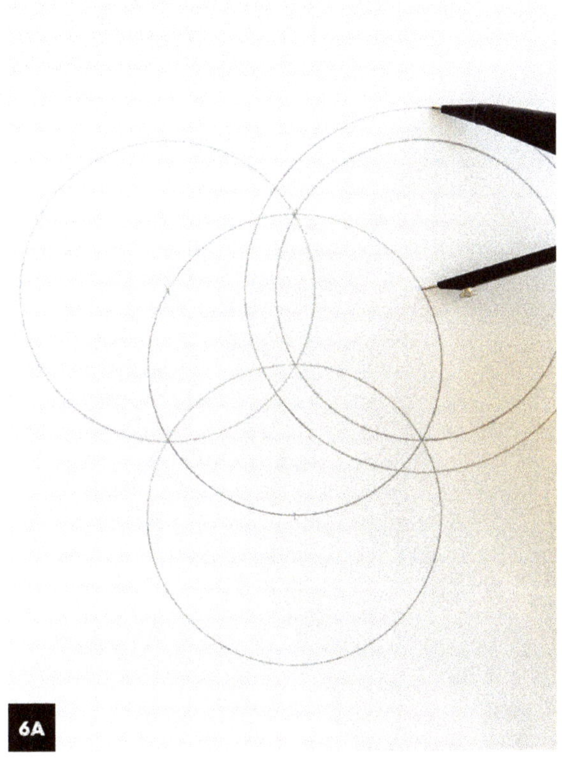
6A

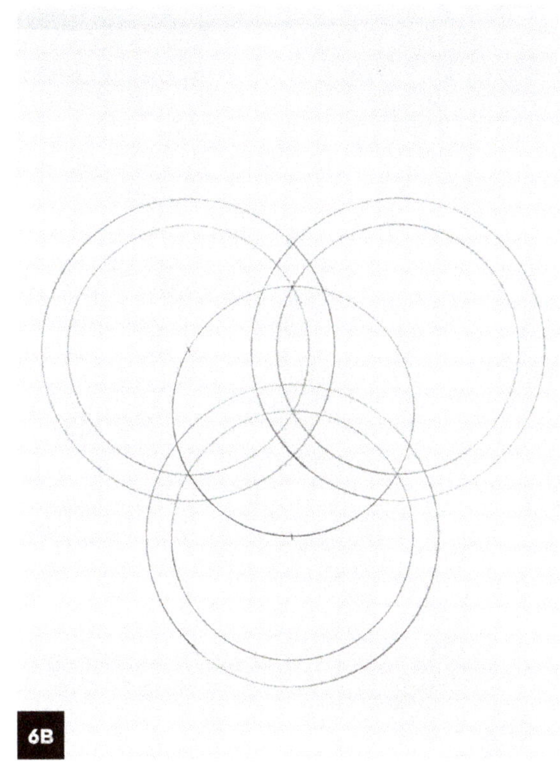
6B

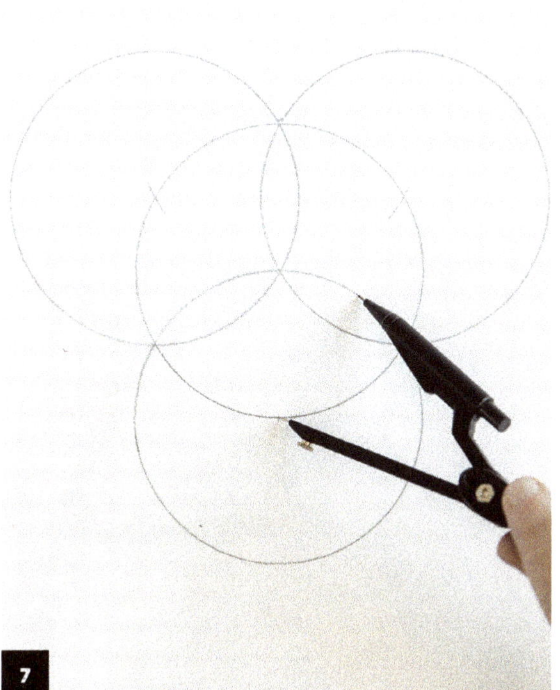
7

6 Open your compass to 2½ inches (6 cm) and trace new circles using the same center points to create the appearance of rims.

7 Now close your compass aperture to 1½ inches (4 cm) and trace a circle in the original center. If you wish, you can close the circle one more time to a 1-inch (3 cm) radius and draw another circle, depending on whether you prefer your center circle to be larger or smaller.

(continued)

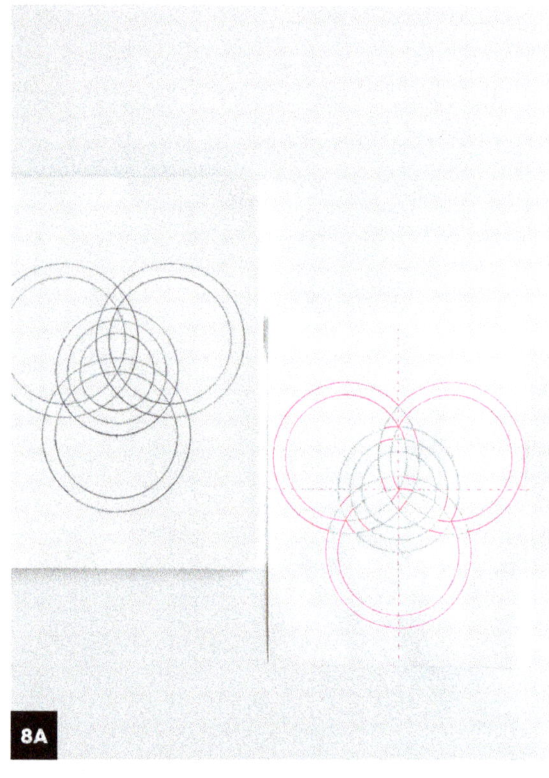
8A

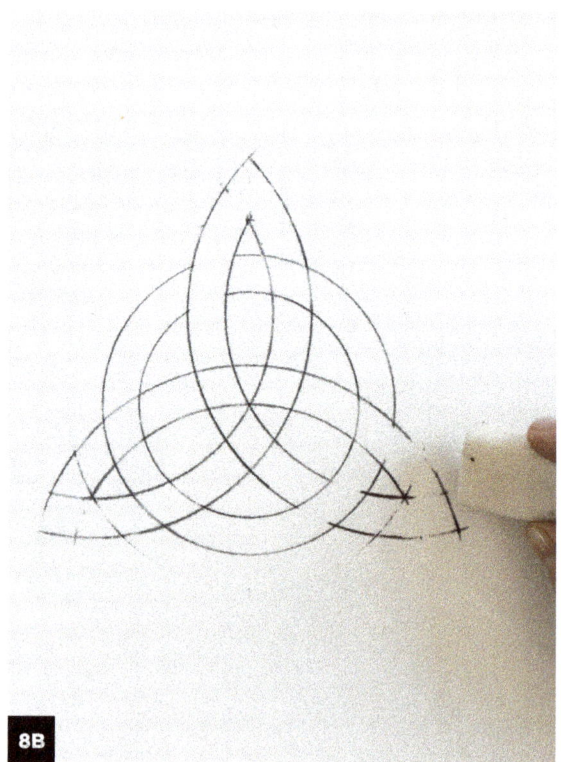
8B

8 Erase the lines indicated in pink.

9 Go in with your compass using a pen and trace the final symbol.

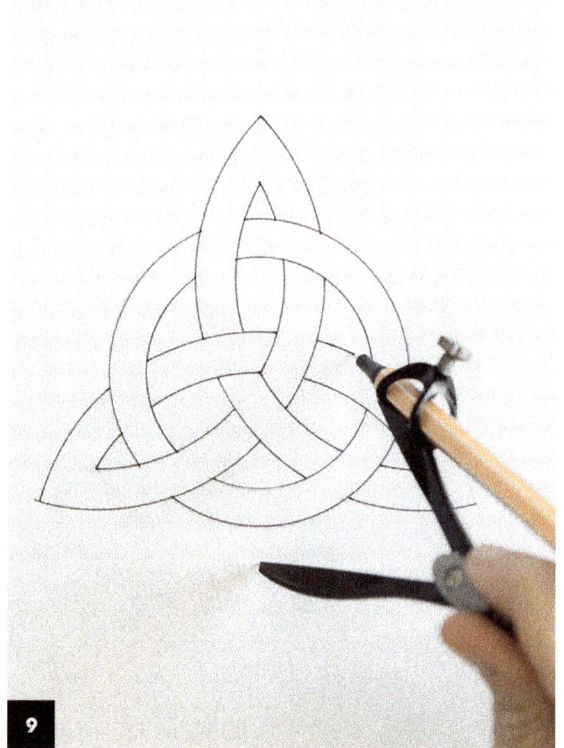
9

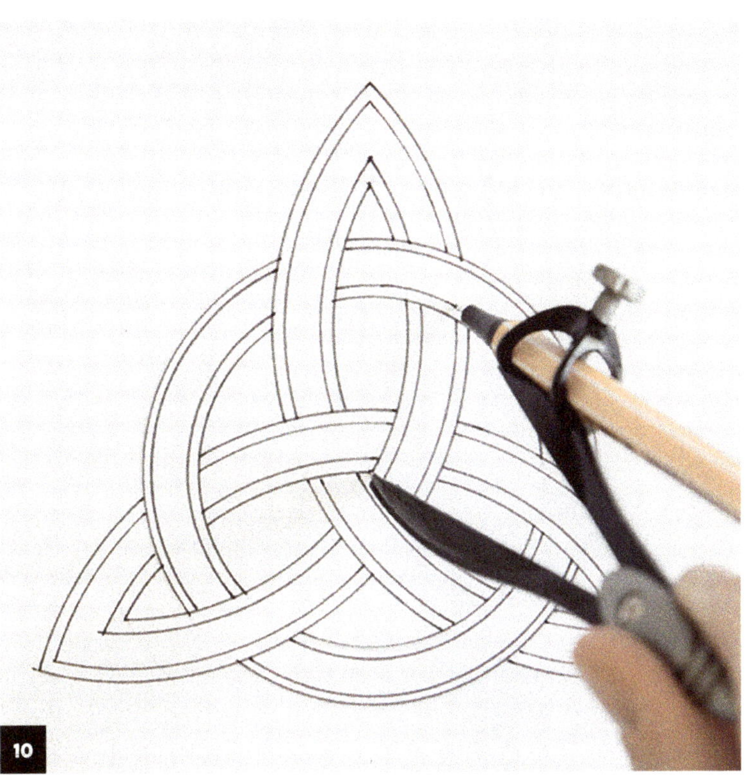

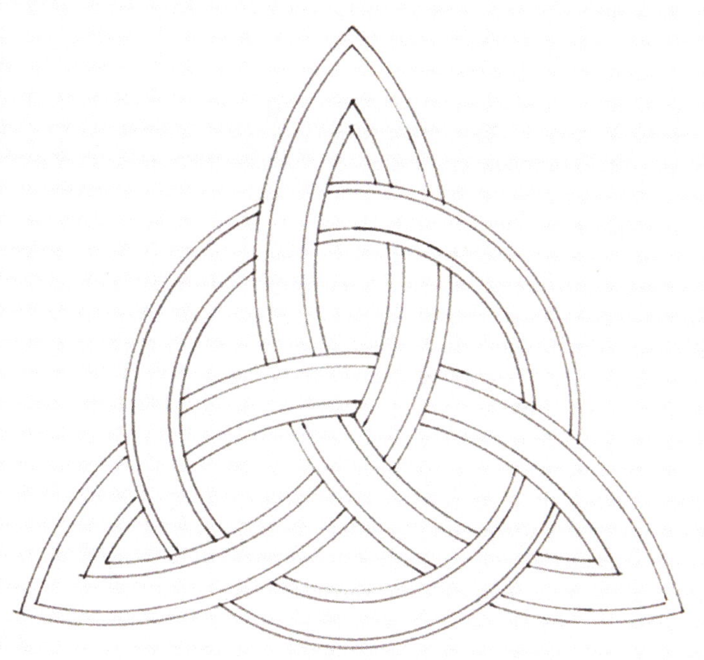

10 For an extra design element, trace thin rims around each circle.

11 The finished trinity knot.

ARTISTIC EXPLORATION: USING COLORED PENCILS AND BLENDING

A very relaxing and enjoyable way to add artistic value to our geometric shapes is with the beauty of color. I will demonstrate three simple ways to create gradient effects using colored pencils. I have found that drawing with colored pencils is extremely intuitive and comes naturally for most students. If you've never tried it, here are three easy, fuss-free ways to experiment with this technique.

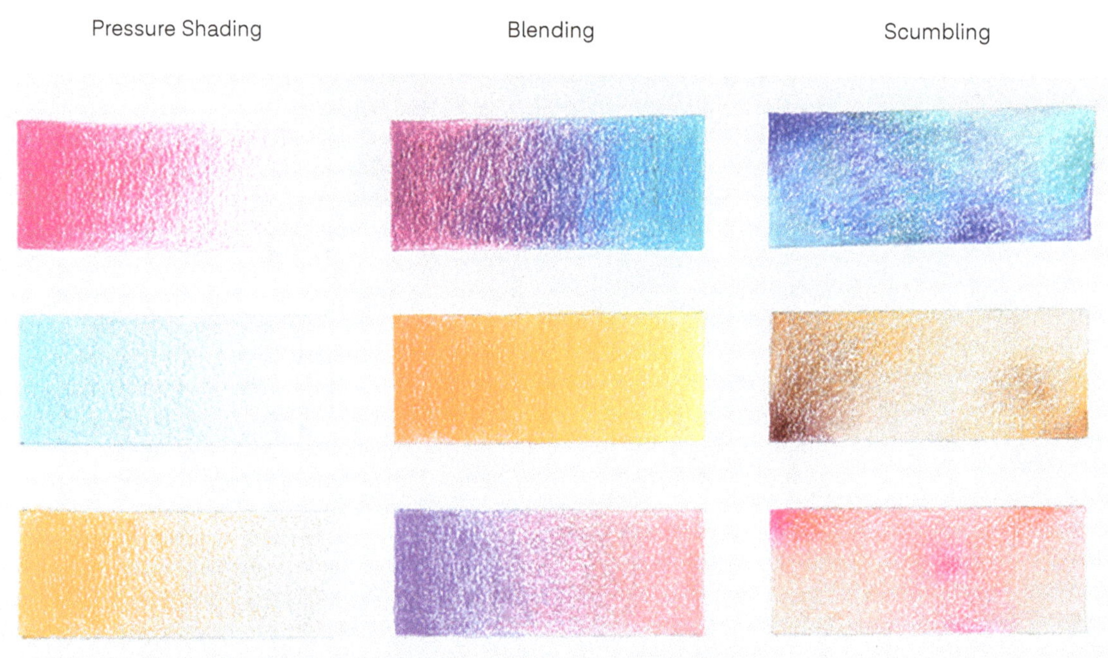

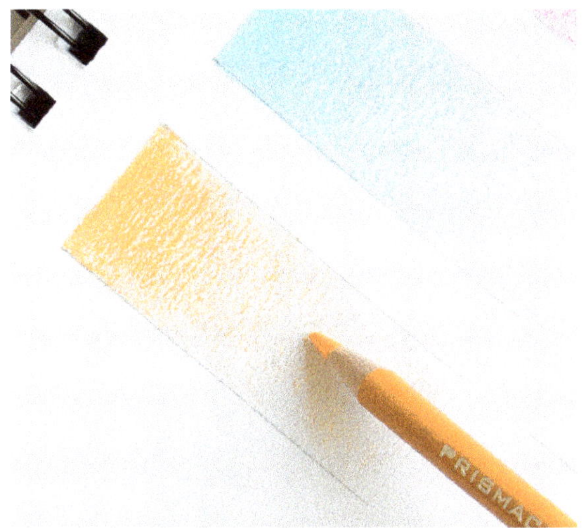

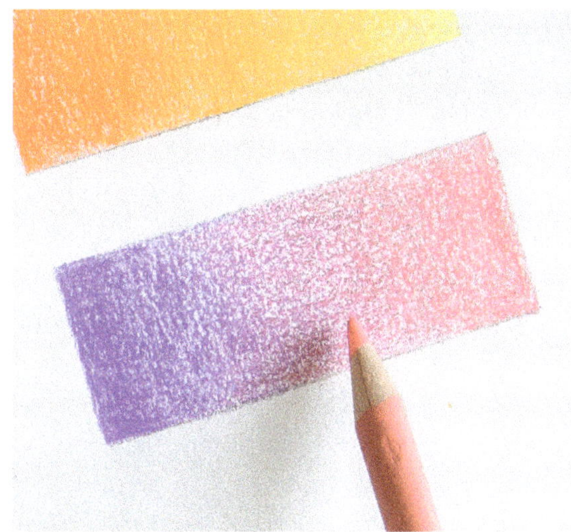

Pressure Shading

Choose one color and begin coloring! If you are drawing from left to right, begin with more force and gradually ease pressure as you continue to draw until your stroke disappears. You can go over the darker side again by carefully layering or simply adding more pressure. I like to color with shorter strokes, but I have found that some artists do better with longer strokes; as with all art, it is about getting to know yourself and your specific preferences.

Blending

To create a smooth color transition, use the same pressure-shading technique to start off. Then choose a second color to create a gradient. Ease pressure as you blend your second color into your first color. You can continue this method by blending a third color after that and so on.

TIPS

- Always begin with the darker shade and use your lighter shade for blending so you can overlay the original shade and it will look beautifully seamless.
- If you are new to color blending, use analogous color harmonies to make each transition easier. Examples:
  - » Violet → violet blue → deep blue → blue → turquoise → deep green → green → yellow green → yellow
  - » Magenta → red → orange red → orange → yellow orange → yellow → yellow green

Scumbling

This is a method where you draw in a circular motion. Also known as the "Brillo pad technique," it consists of tiny circles or squiggly motions. This is a lovely method that offers a lot of control and is great for shading. In this case, coloring geometry can be realistic if you are looking to create tridimensional interpretations or want an effect that is more abstract and free. I am inclined toward the latter, but it is totally up to you!

Beginning with the darker tones, color with this random squiggly motion and ease pressure as you color outward. Continue this motion around your selected area, finishing it off with your lighter tones for easy blending.

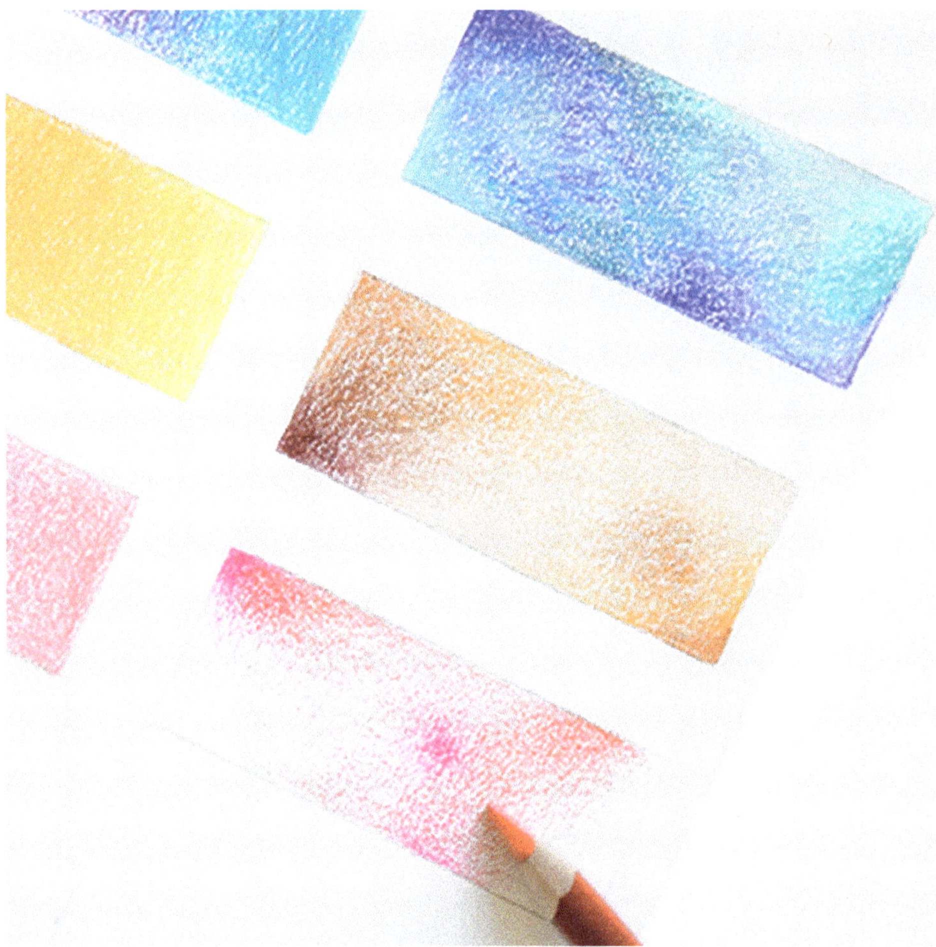

Before I begin this technique, I find it helpful to have a few harmonious colors picked out, usually in the same color scheme with dark and light options. In this case, I'm using a variety of pinks and creams.

COLORING YOUR TRINITY KNOT

1 Follow the drawing instructions beginning on page 31 and draw this shape on nice mixed media or drawing paper. I like a smoother surface when using colored pencils. For instructive purposes, I traced this first image with a black pen for higher contrast, but I would usually use a regular pencil when drawing.

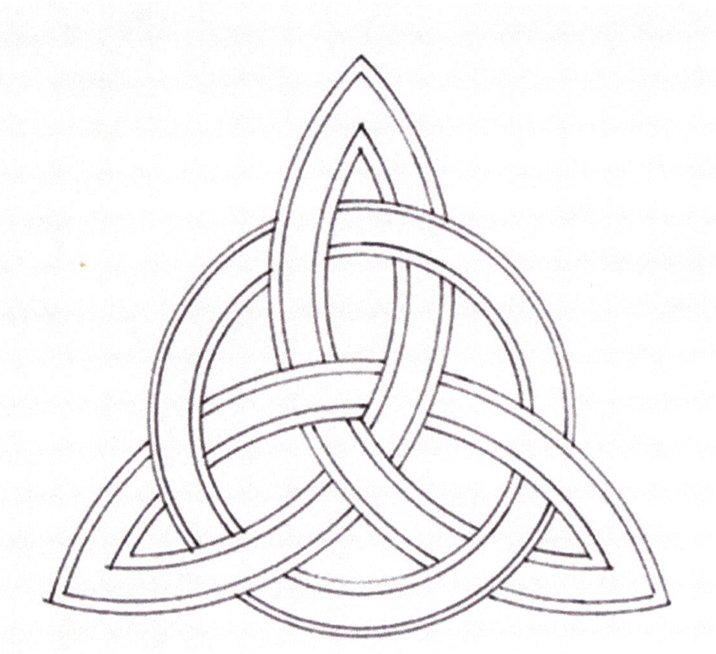

2 Select the colors you would like to use. As mentioned before, analogous color schemes are quite harmonious. My darkest value here is indigo blue. Use the blending technique (see page 37) and begin by adding a shadow behind each intersection. This will give the drawing a sense of depth.

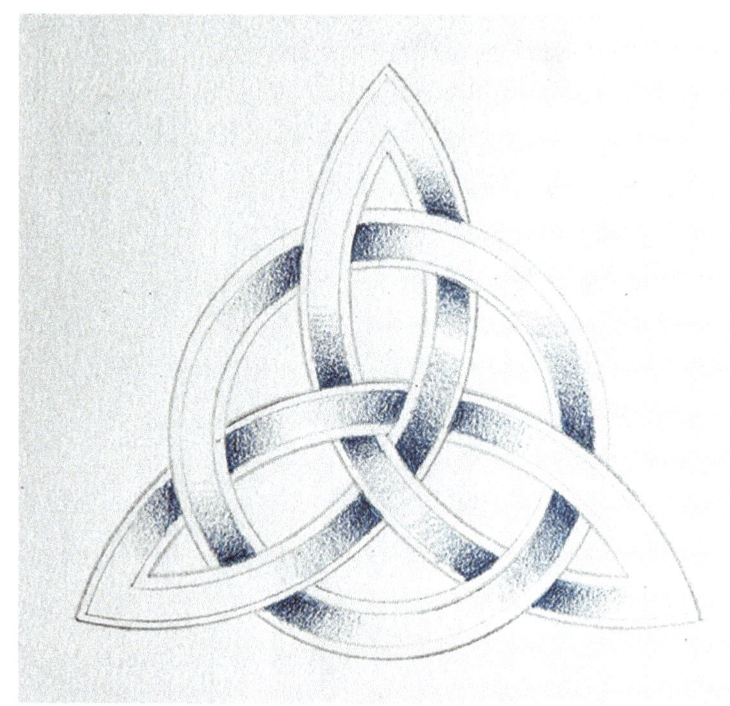

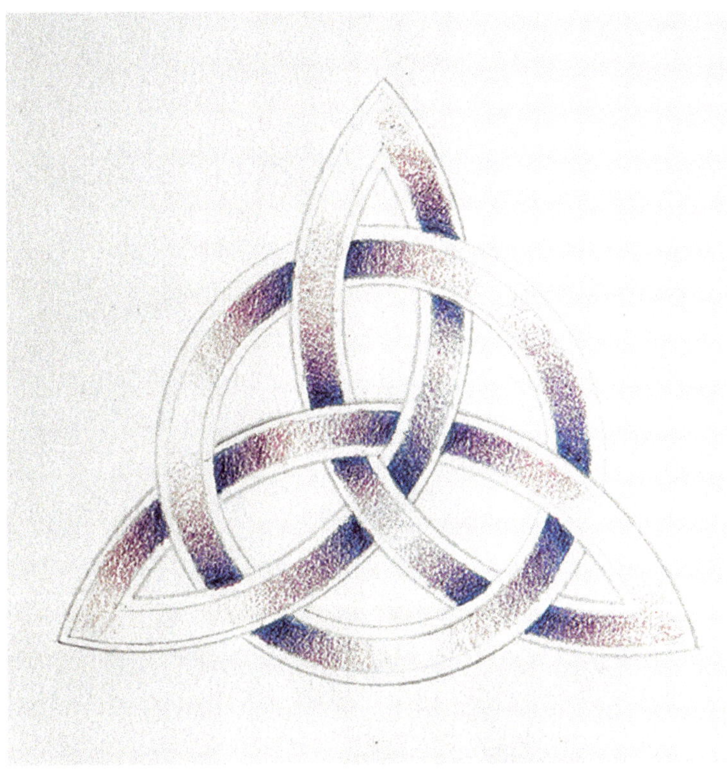

3 Continue blending in your next darkest color following the indigo areas.

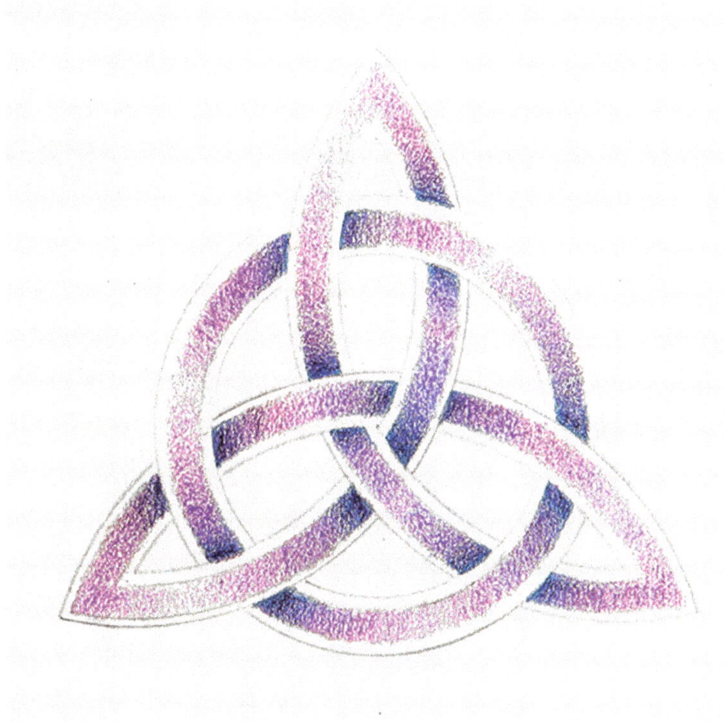

4 Keep going until you have filled the entire shape by blending colors. Leave the lightest tone as your last value and fill in the remaining areas to add some brightness.

(continued)

5 Have fun drawing the rims! I chose silver and gold pencils for this part, but you can also achieve great contrast by using ink, Micron pens, or gel pens.

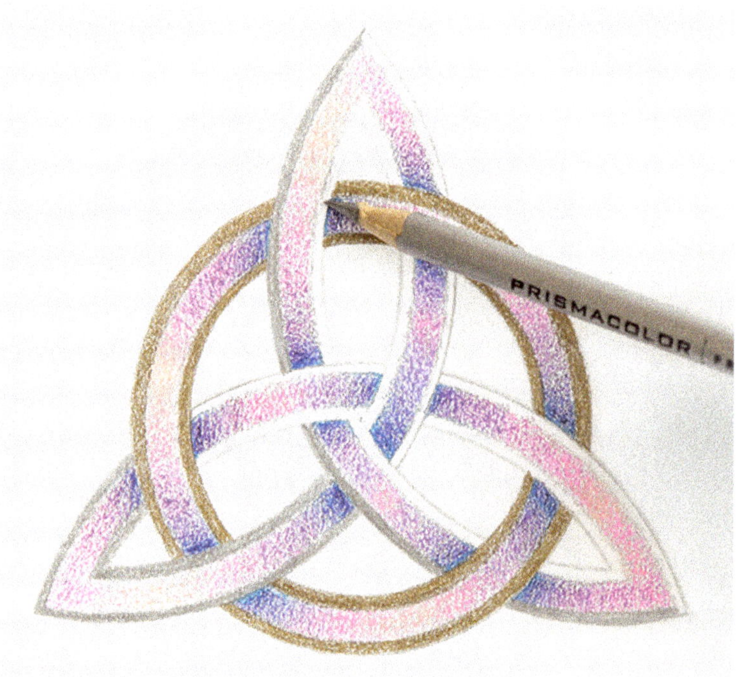

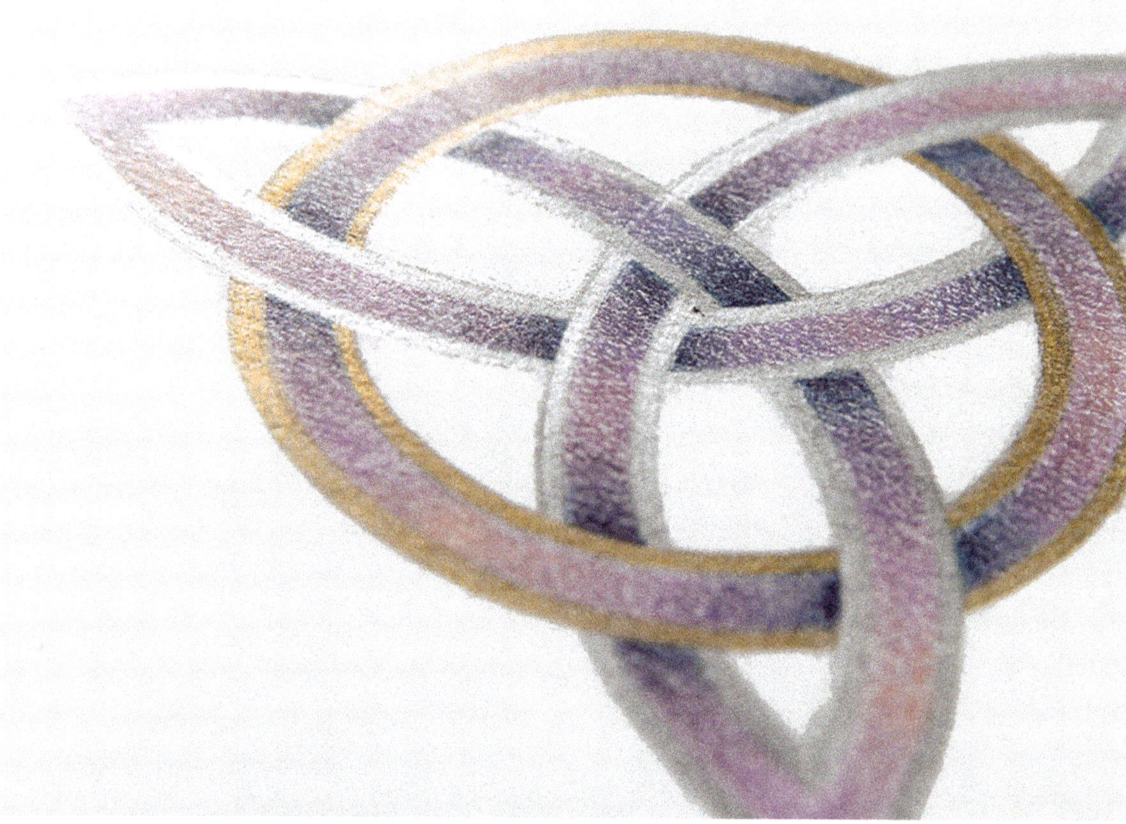

VARIATIONS

- Use the same trinity knot coloring method but draw on black paper for an incredible space-inspired interpretation (below left). For tips for drawing on black paper, see page 62.
- Using the simple coloring methods on pages 36–39, trace a vesica piscis and fill in different areas. For my creative interpretation (below right), I used a warm, earthy color palette and added a crescent moon as part of my composition. If you're curious about creating the perfect burst effect, see page 54 for instructions.

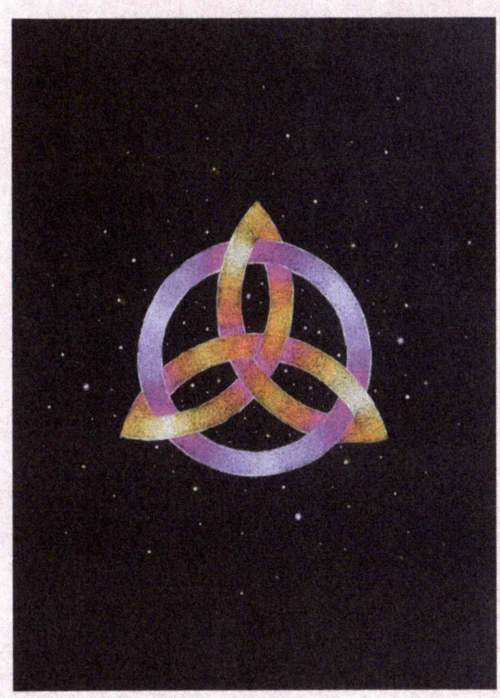

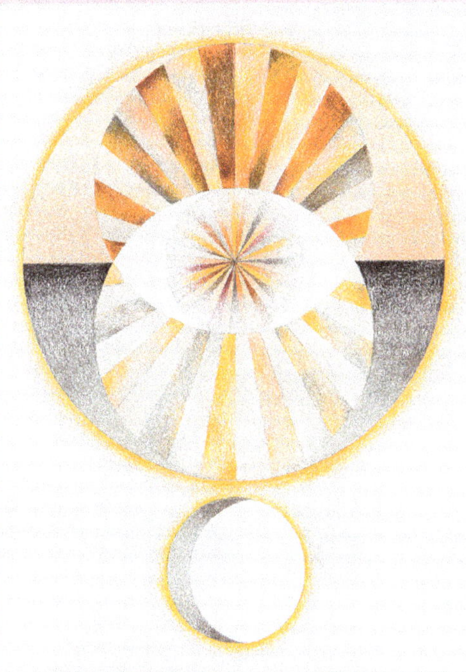

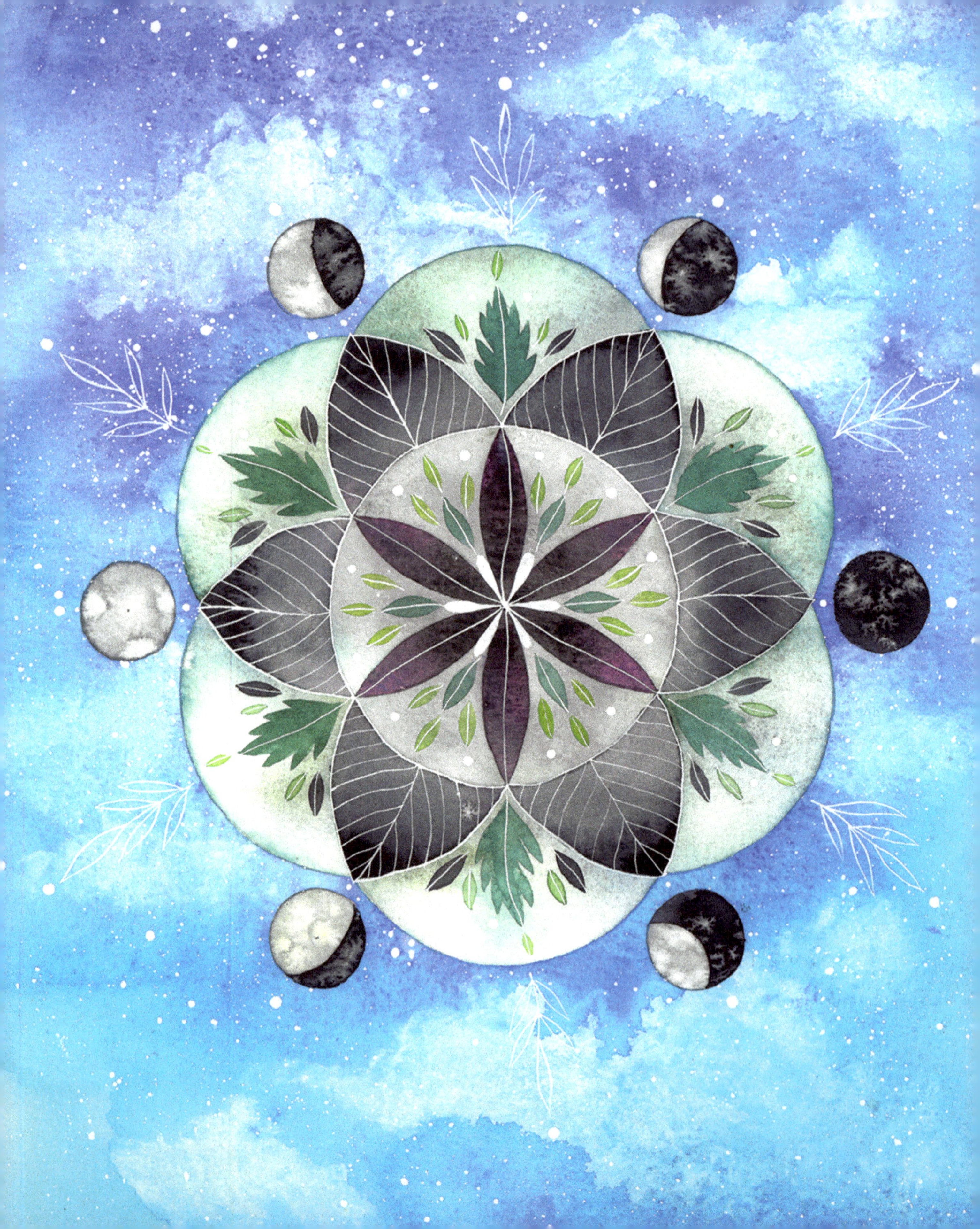

3

THE SEED OF LIFE

The seed of life represents the moment where our geometry grid is set in motion and our shapes begin to take on larger meaning.

BUILDING CIRCLES UPON CIRCLES

If we think of the circle as our source, the source continues to replicate itself flawlessly, connecting intersections while overlapping circles to create a blooming flower shape at the center. As you continue to explore more complex sacred geometry shapes, you will come to see that the seed of life is the basis for all other shapes. Once you get the hang of drawing these interconnected circles perfectly, all other shapes will be possible.

THE SEED OF LIFE: INTERPRETATIONS

Here are some symbolic meanings associated with the seed of life.

- Seven circles make up the seed of life, which are associated with:
  - Seven days of the week
  - Seven energetic points (chakras)
  - Seven colors of the rainbow
  - Biblical symbolism: seven deadly sins, seven days of creation, seven heavens
  - Seven continents
  - Seven seas
  - Seven pure notes
  - Seven metals of antiquity
  - Seven wonders of the ancient world

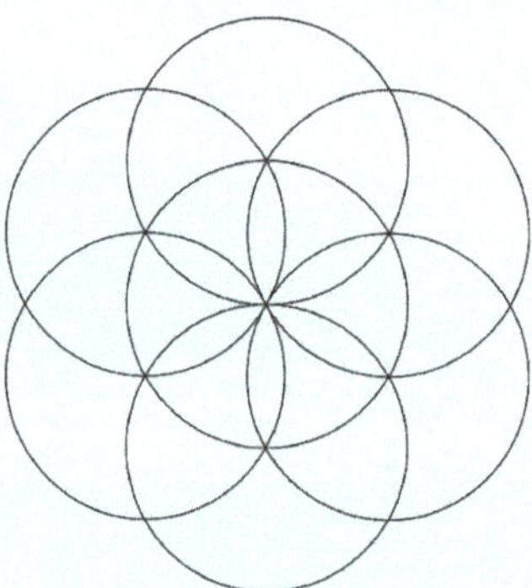

- Six petals are formed at the center, a representation of many forms found in nature, including flowers and snowflakes.
- A hexagon (hexagram star) is formed by connecting the six points of intersection.
- Essential building blocks of honeycombs are constructed through this perfect shape.
- Each intersection aligns perfectly with markings of a clock, representing perception and measurement of time.
- Precursor to the flower of life (see chapter 4).

Drawing Technique

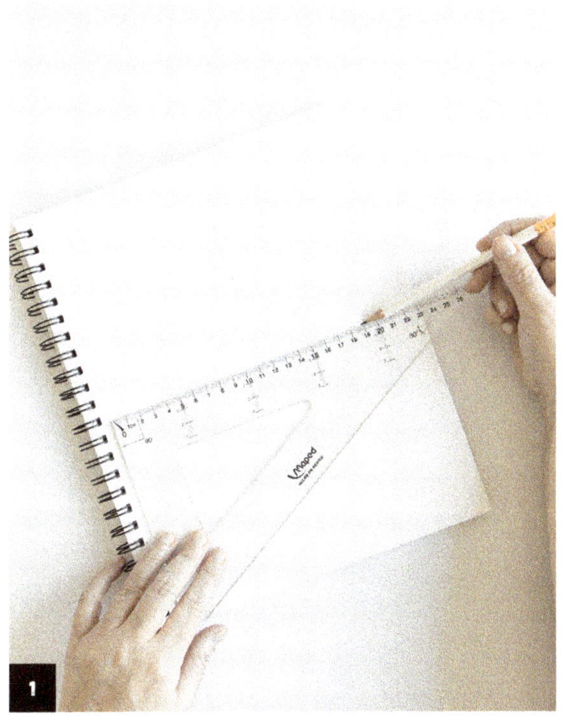

1

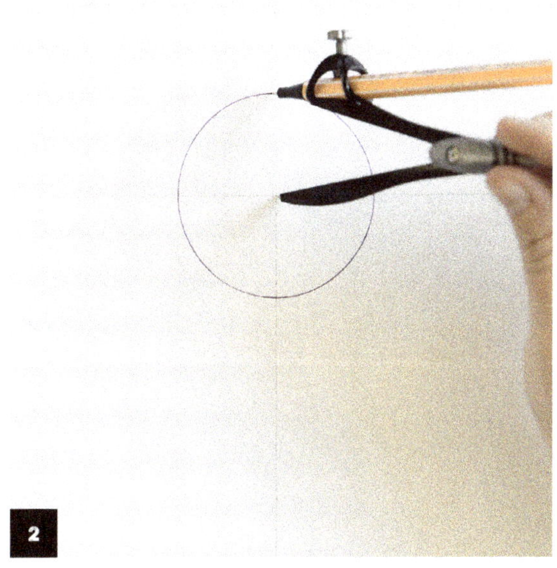

2

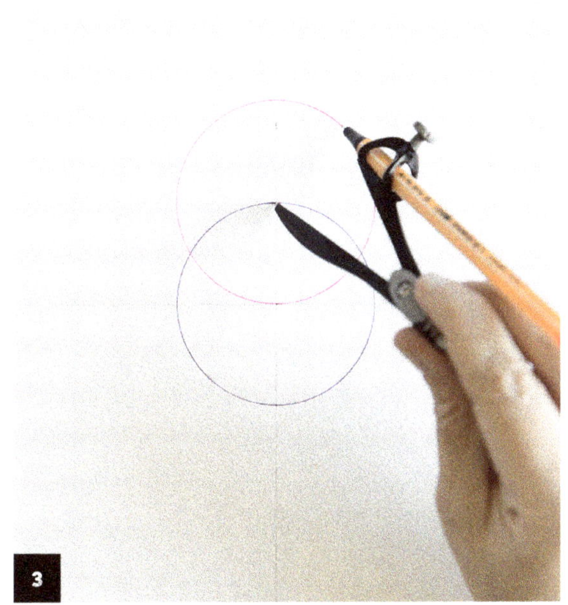

3

1 Begin by finding the center point of your paper. It's helpful to have a pencil line cross guide for drawing layout purposes.

2 Place the needle of your compass in the center and trace your first circle.

3 Without changing the distance on your compass's aperture, place your needle on any point of the circumference and draw another circle. In this case, we will be using the vertical guideline as a reference for an orderly drawing.

(continued)

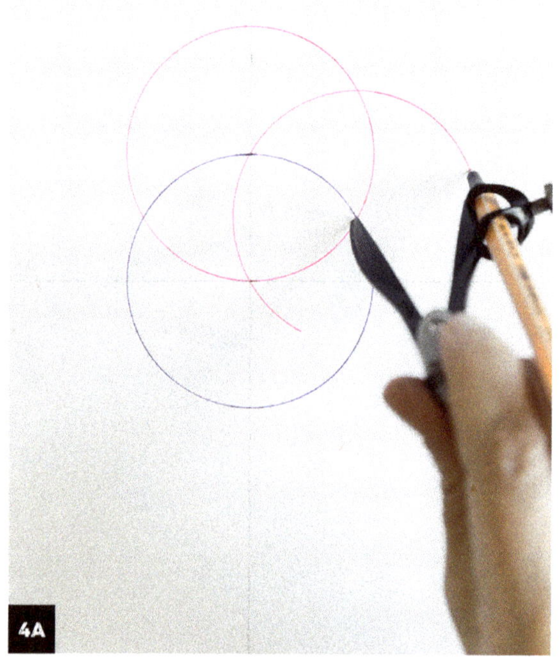

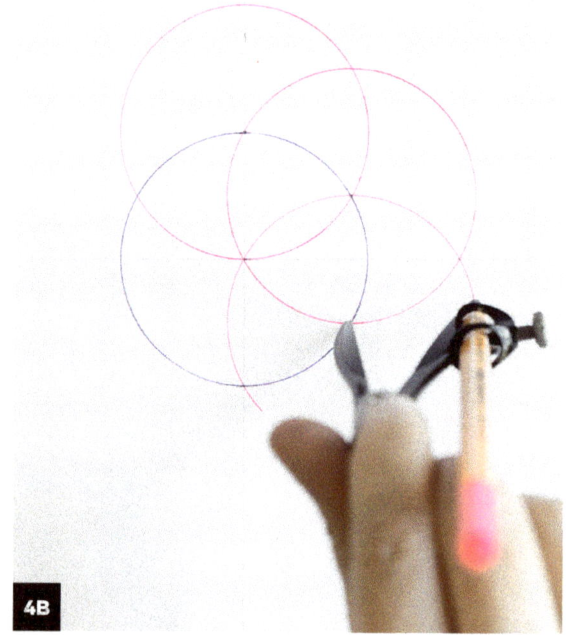

4 Draw a new circle around each intersection point created by your original circle and your most recent circle. For instructional purposes, I made the original circle violet and the surrounding circles pink.

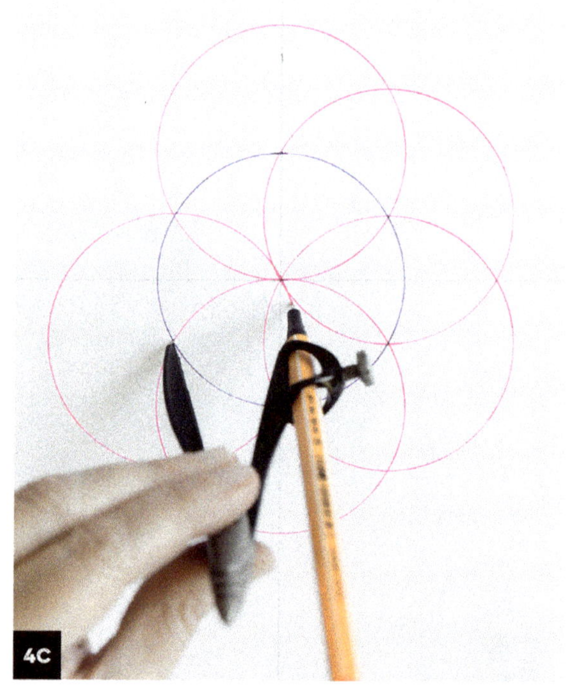

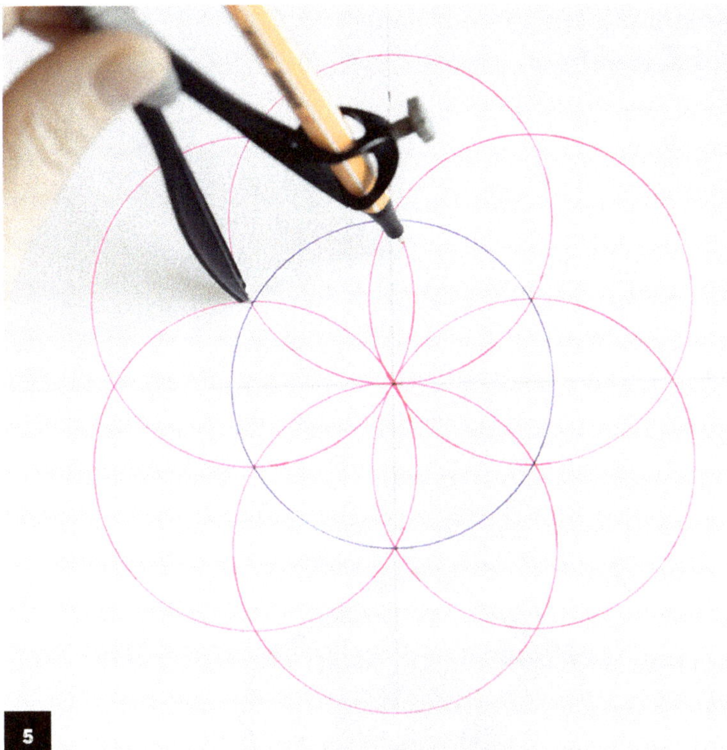

5

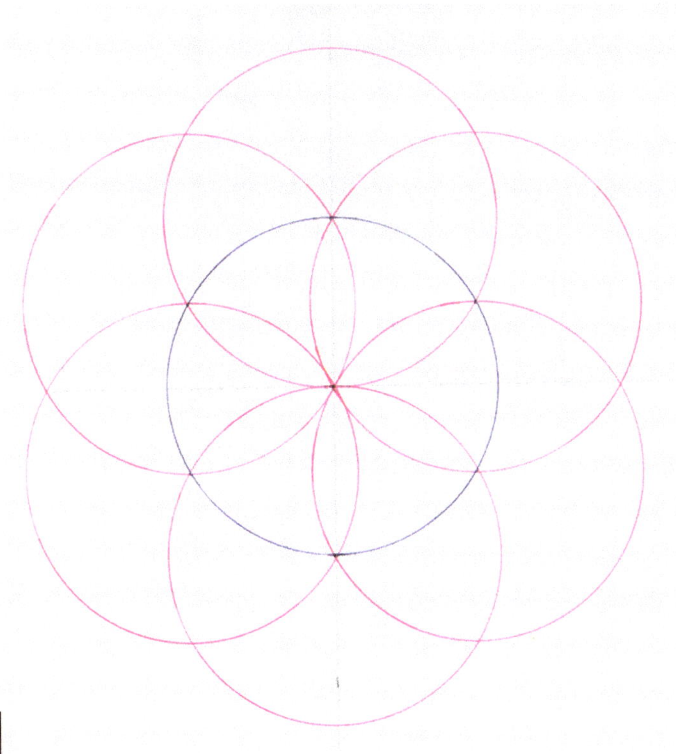

6

5 Keep tracing new circles around your original circle until the cycle is complete. Make sure to be very precise while tracing your circles, as even ¼ inch (1 mm) can throw the entire grid off. The deeper you go, the more apparent this will become.

6 The finished seed of life.

ARTISTIC EXPLORATION: SHAPES AND PATTERNS

Once you've got the hang of drawing a seed of life, it's time to explore! Your creative mission is to discover symbols, shapes, and patterns within this simple shape. Connect intersections, add organic drawings, shade different areas, or adjust your compass size to create inner or outer rims of circles. The possibilities are endless. The more you work with this shape, the more you will discover. Here are a few examples. Trace a few simple seeds of life and see what you can find for yourself!

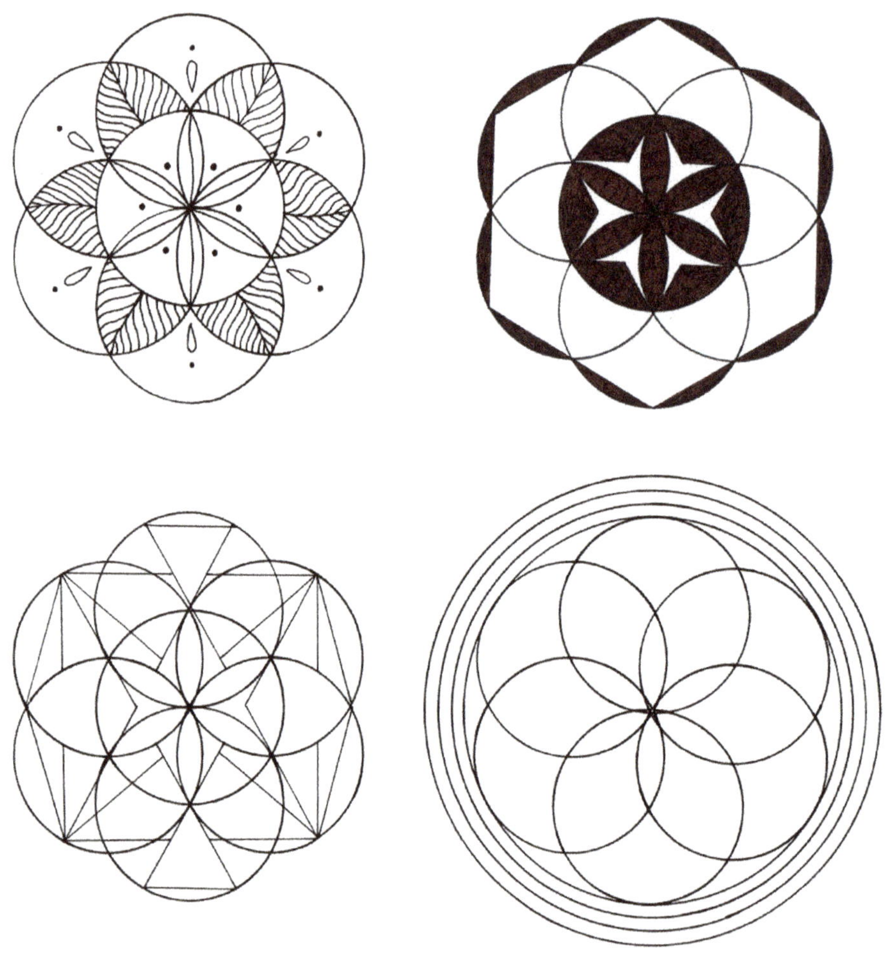

FINDING THE YIN-YANG SYMBOL

Yin and yang is a traditional Chinese symbol that represents duality. Opposite forces are interconnected in the natural world to create balance by complementing each other.

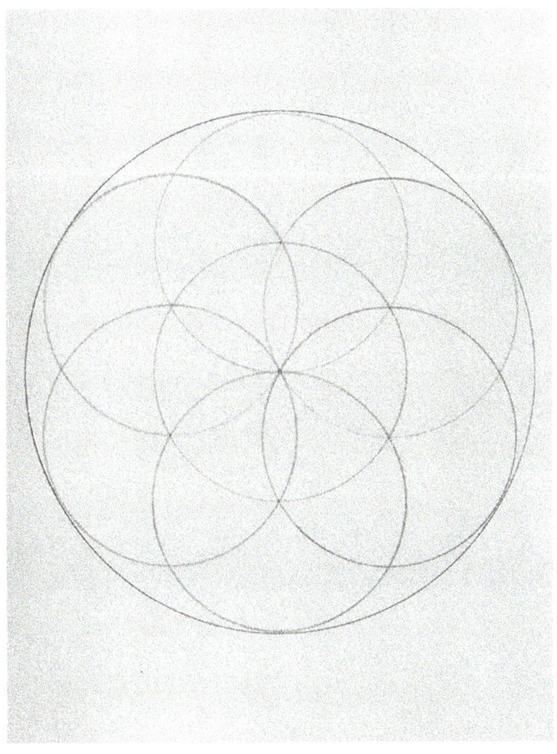

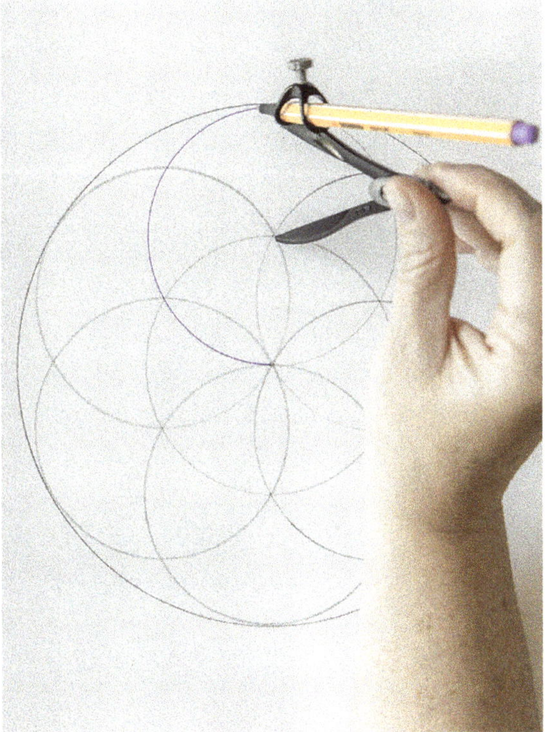

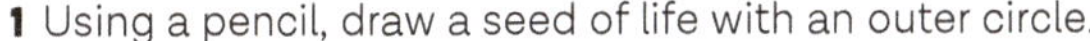

1 Using a pencil, draw a seed of life with an outer circle.

2 With your compass aperture open at the same distance as the original circle, use a darker color or pen to trace a half circle using the top circle as your guide. It helps to find the exact point where your needle was placed originally.

(continued)

3 Do the same on the bottom circle, tracing the opposing side of the half circle.

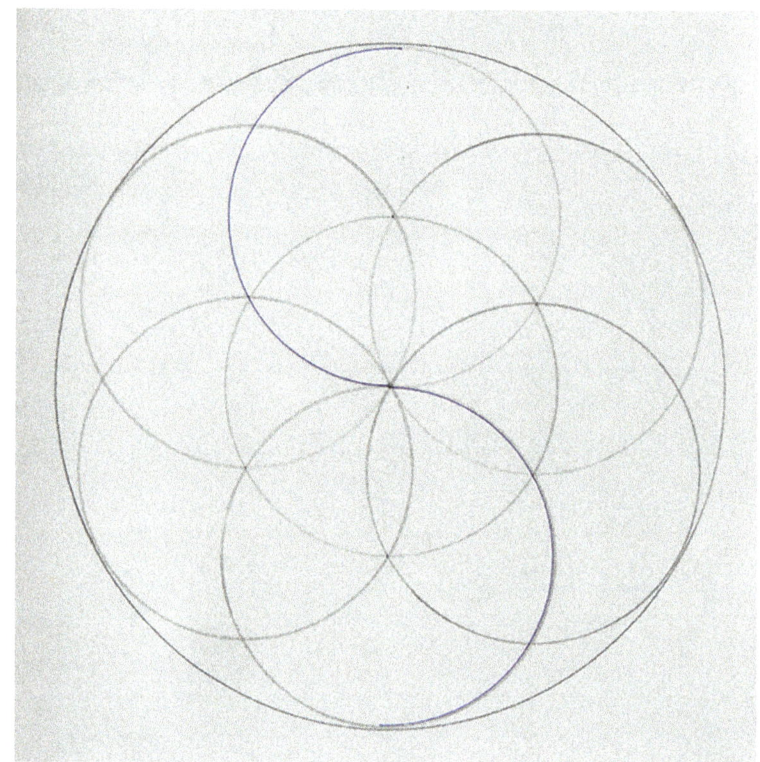

4 Place your compass needle at the center of your seed of life and open it to the distance of the total circumference.

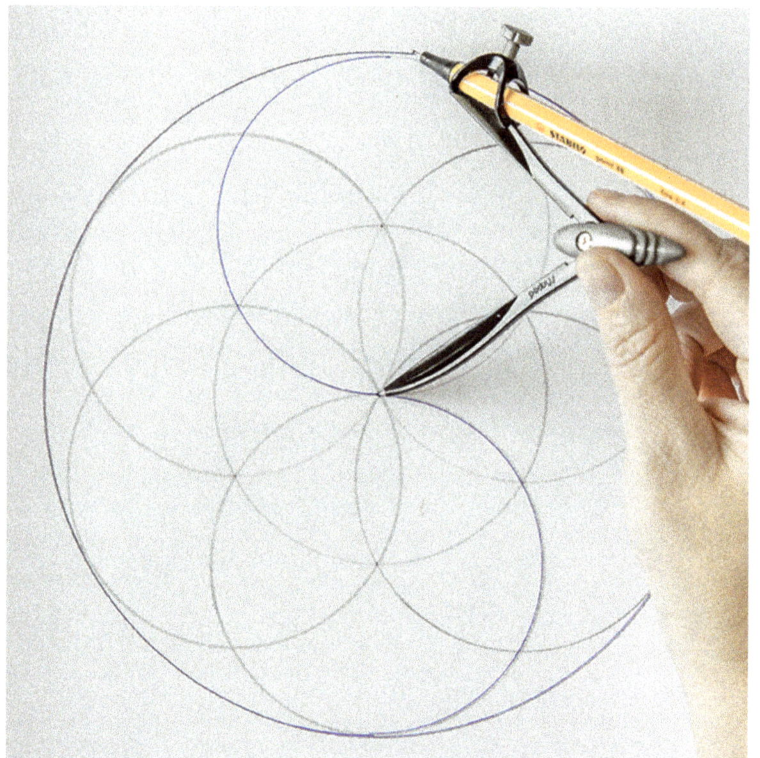

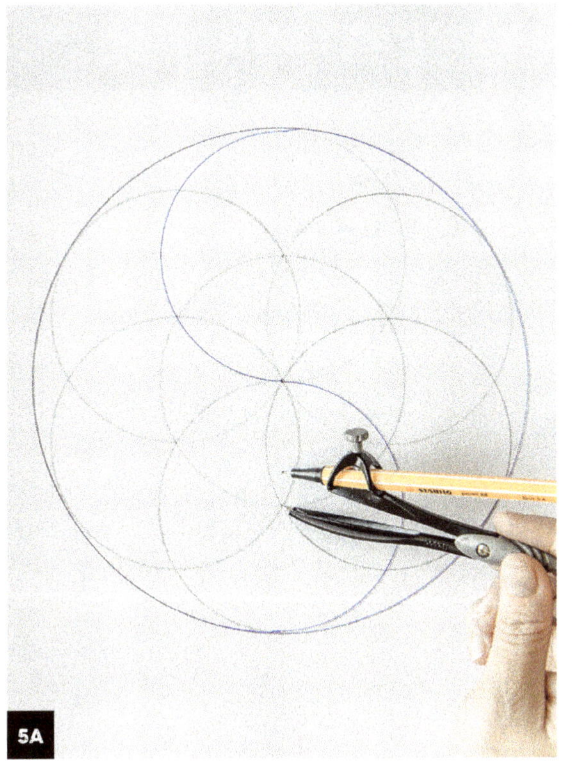
5A

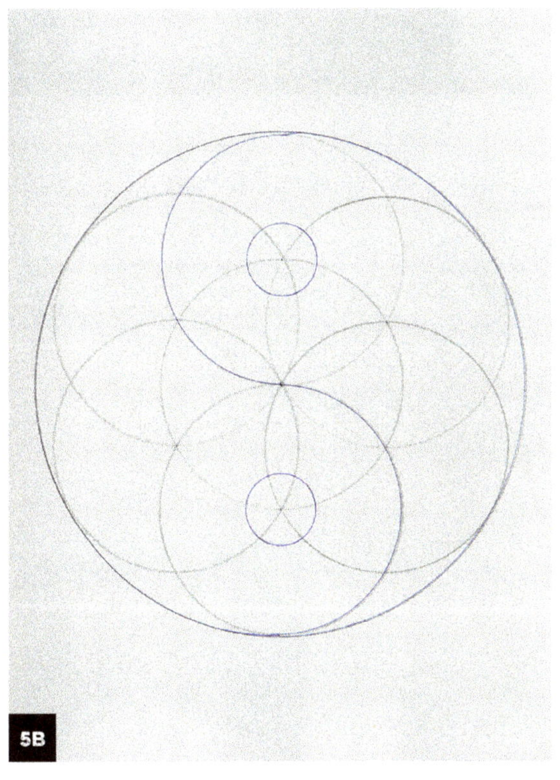
5B

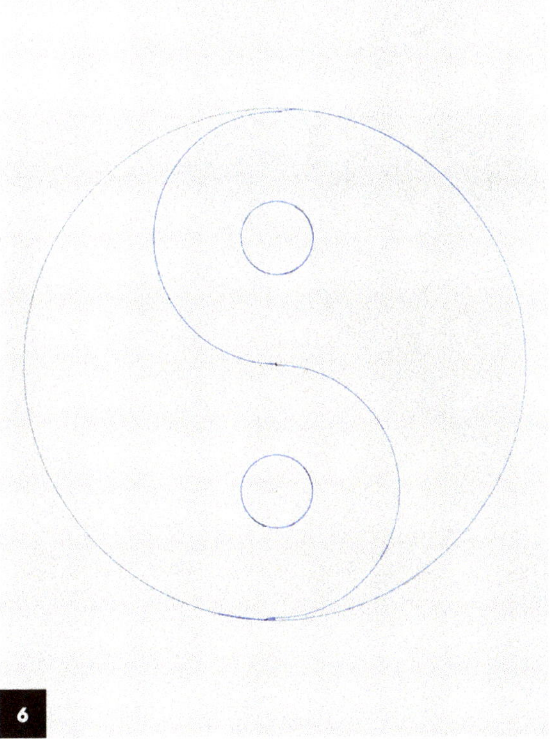
6

5 Adjust the compass to a smaller size and trace the corresponding circles.

6 Erase the pencil markings and you have a perfect yin-yang shape!

DRAWING A BURST PATTERN

When I first found that the yin-yang symbol was embedded in the seed of life, my mind was blown, and I immediately painted a burst of creative energy around the symbol. I painted each section using watercolor paints with sprinkles of salt for a mystical effect. To create a perfectly geometric burst around your yin-yang symbol, follow these steps.

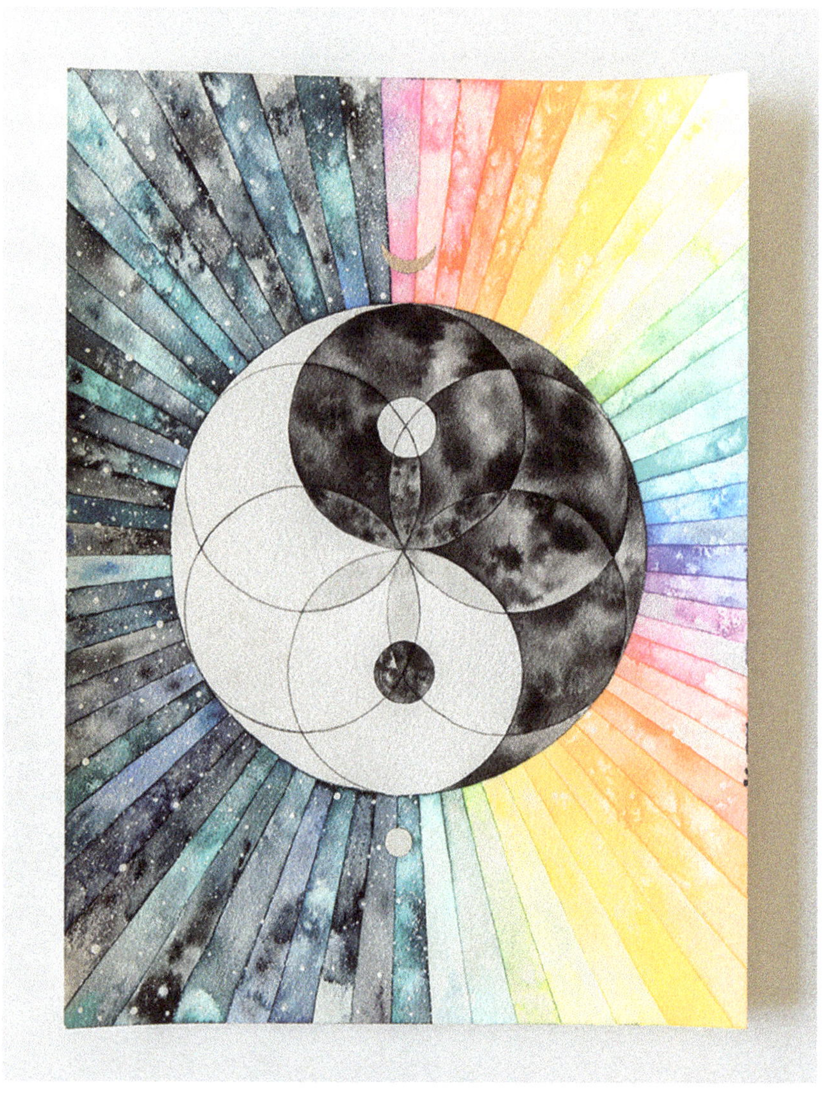

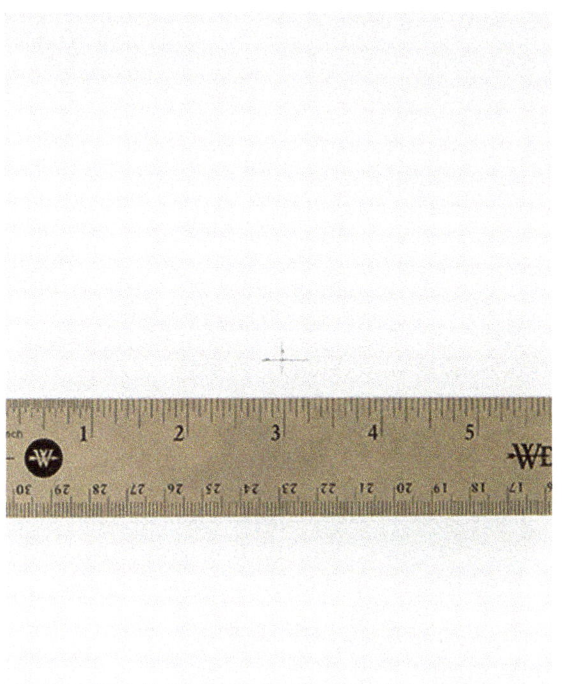

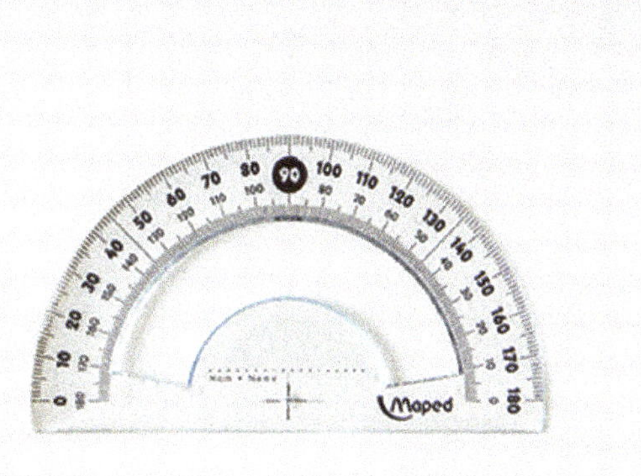

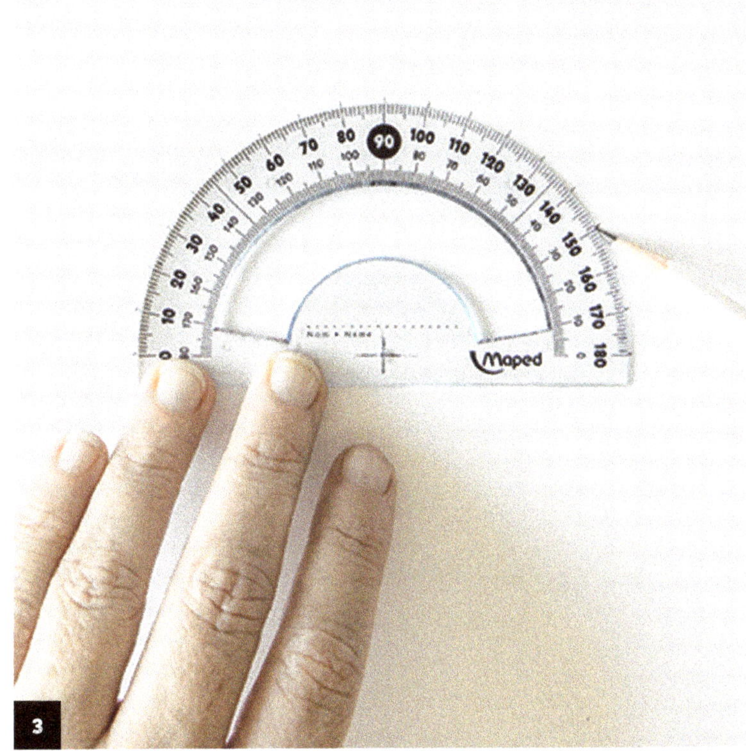

1 Find the center of your page and trace a cross using a straightedge or square rulers. Make sure this cross is exact and at 90-degree angles.

2 Place your protractor at the center of this cross.

3 Draw a point every 10 degrees.

(continued)

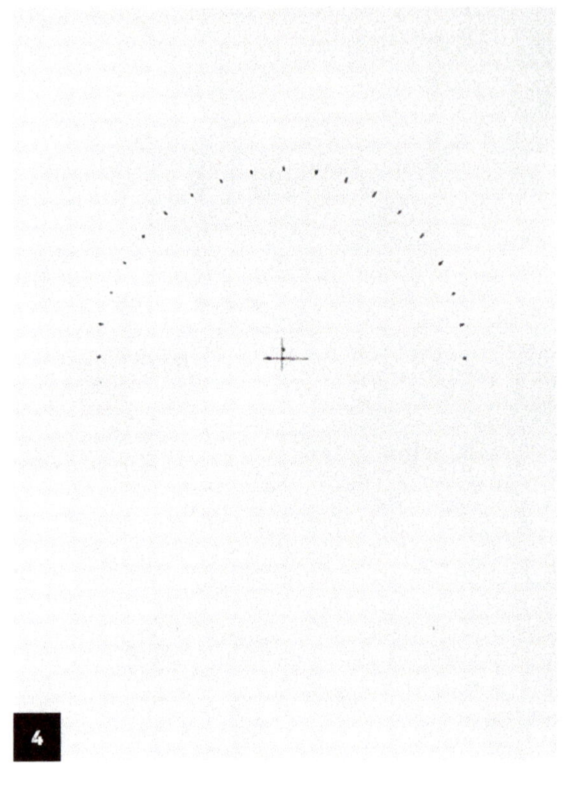

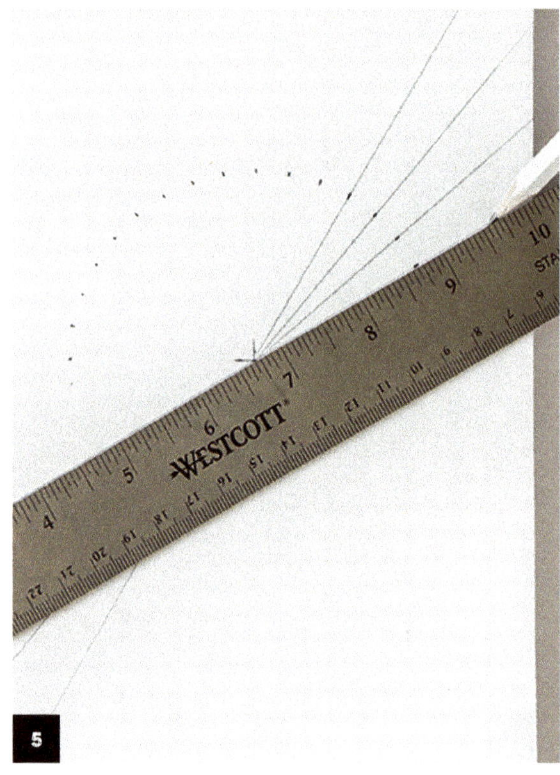

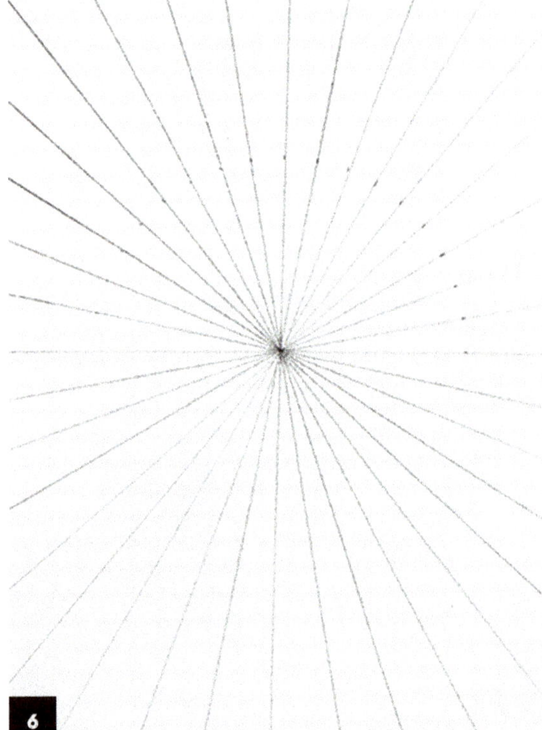

4 These points will be your guide for your perfect burst.

5 Using your ruler or straightedge, connect each point with the center. Trace all around to the other side of the page as well.

6 Now you have a perfect burst! You can play around with angles and integrate this pattern into artwork.

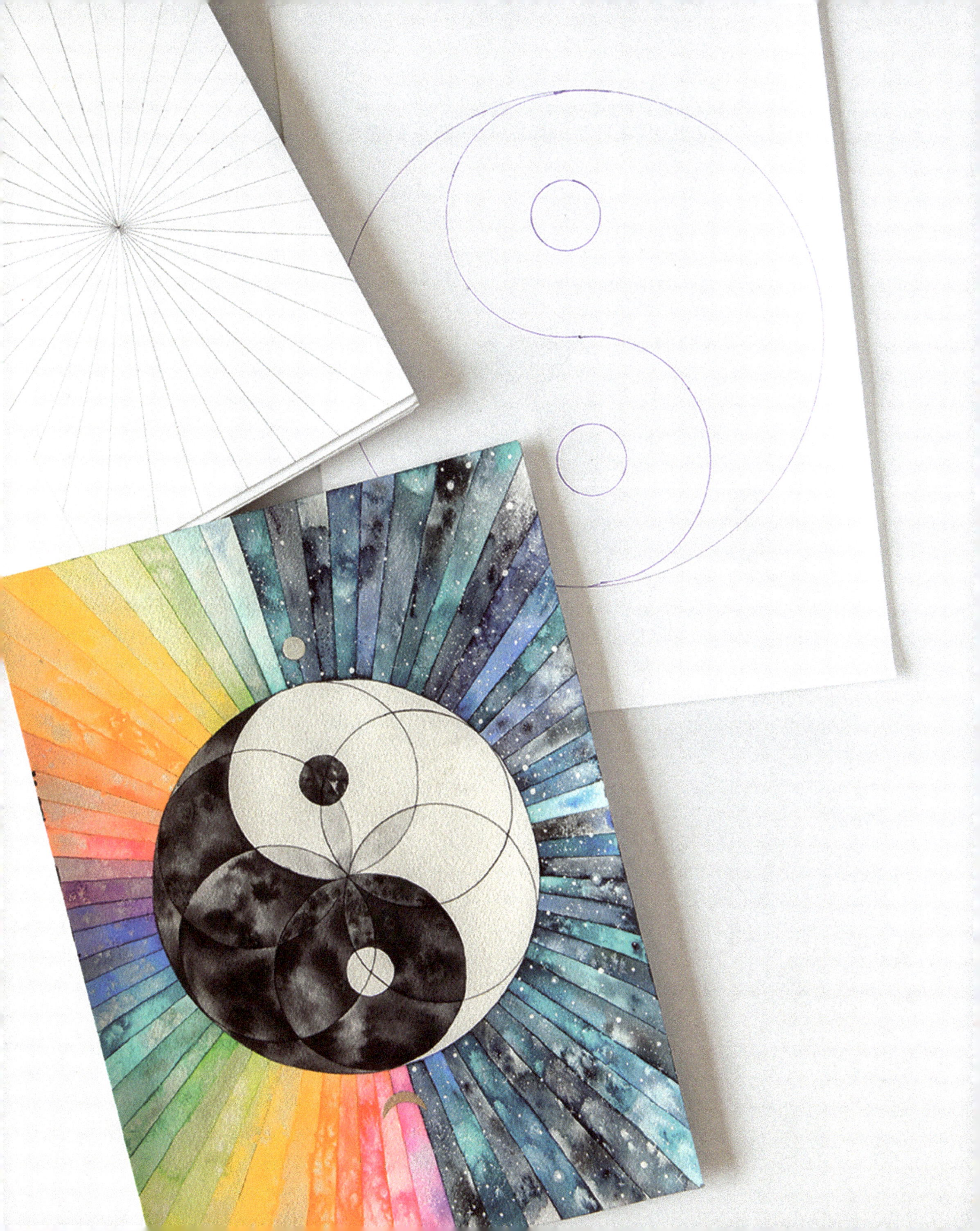

ARTISTIC EXPLORATION: MEDITATIVE ART WITH MOSAICS

This is a beautifully intricate technique to enhance your sacred geometry pieces—or any composition! Integrating mosaic formations into larger shapes will result in a mysterious, ancient aesthetic that integrates perfectly with this theme.

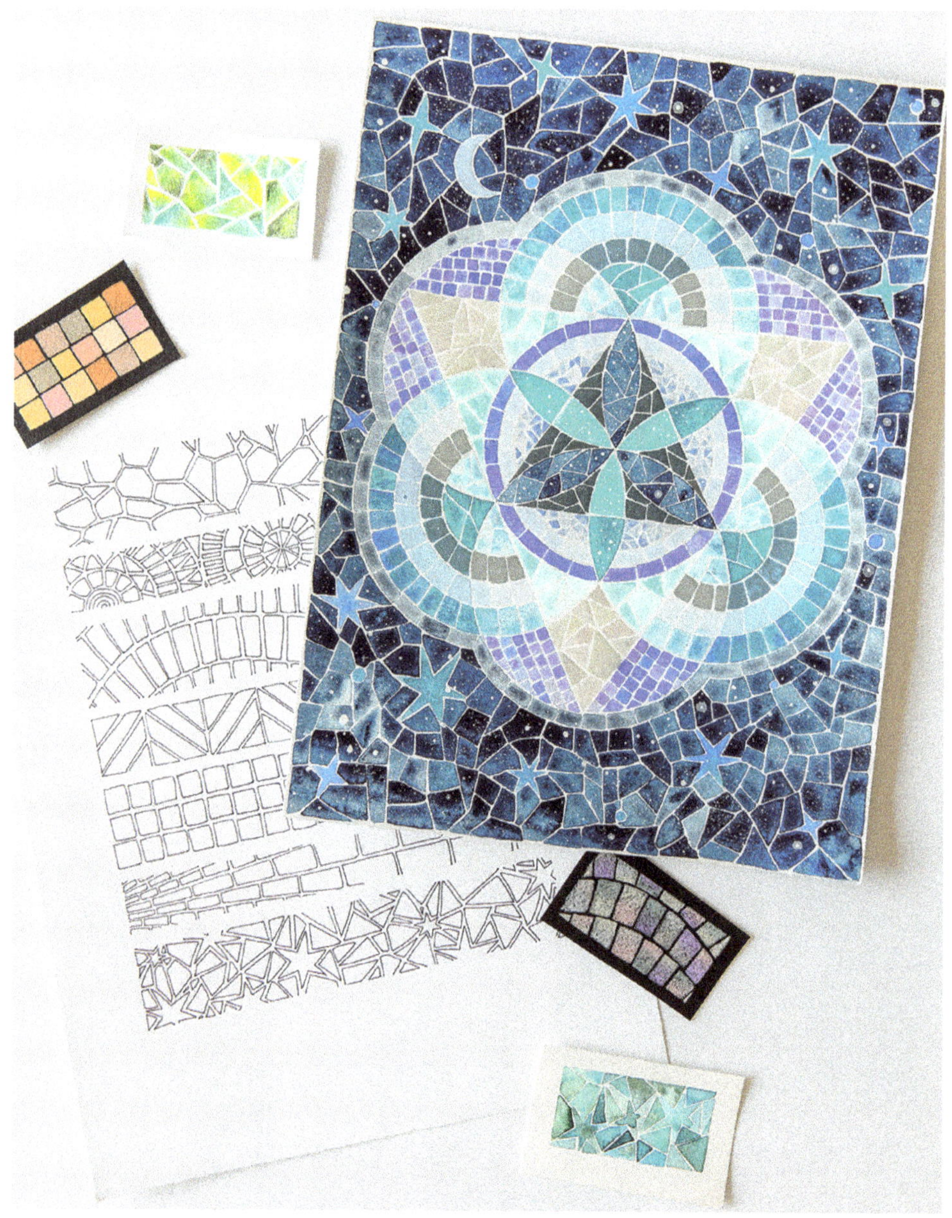

This is not a technique to be rushed through; it's a repetitive form of art making that will send you into a deep meditative state. Creating mosaic art has a calming effect and is extremely rewarding in the end. The trick is to get each mosaic shape as close to each other as possible. This may take some precision skills, so the more you practice, the more confident you will feel. Below are some patterns to explore.

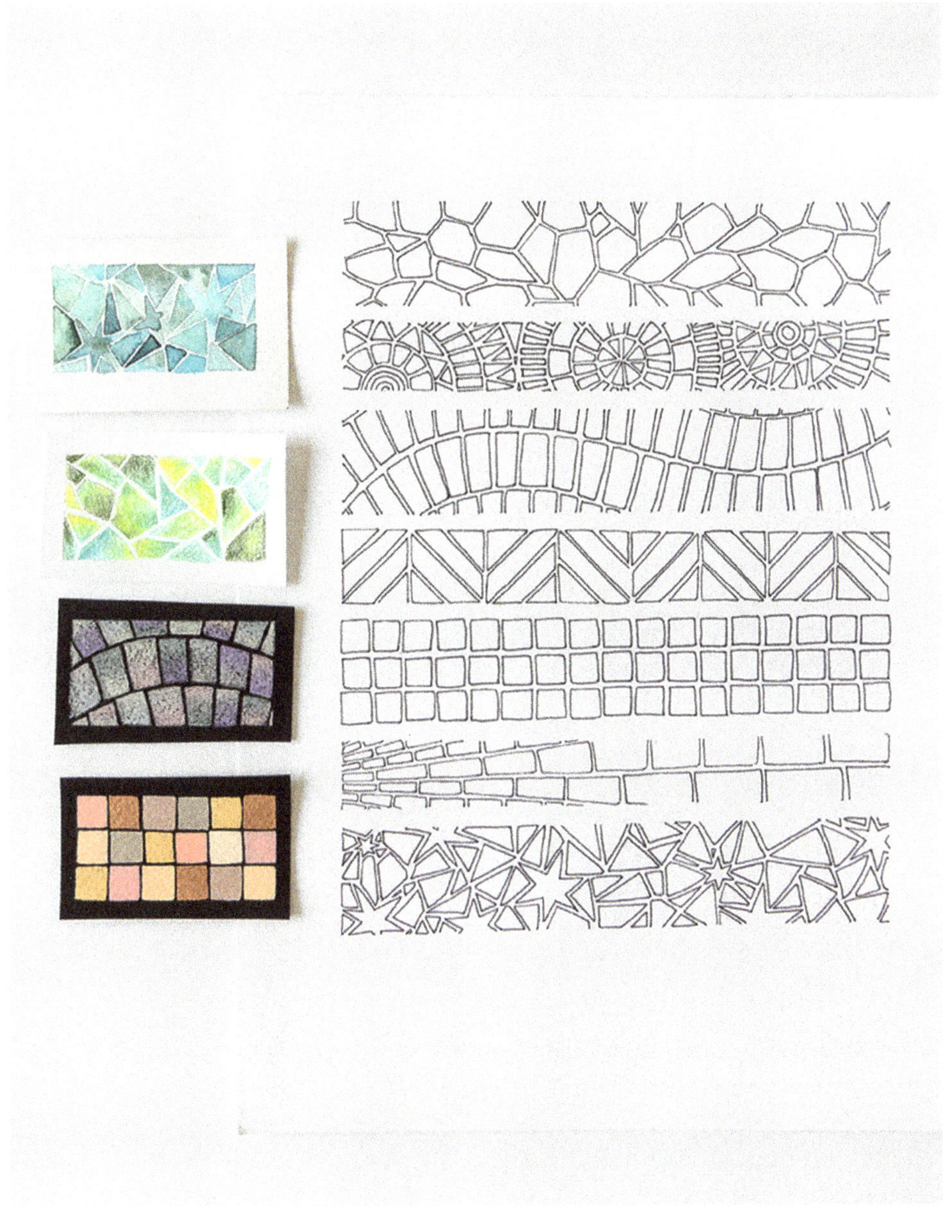

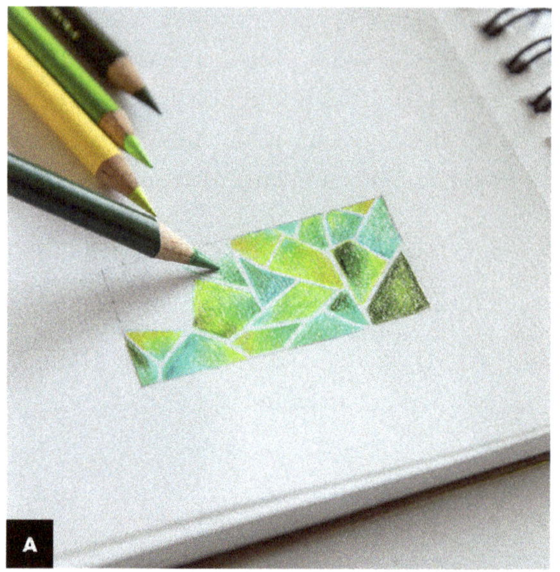

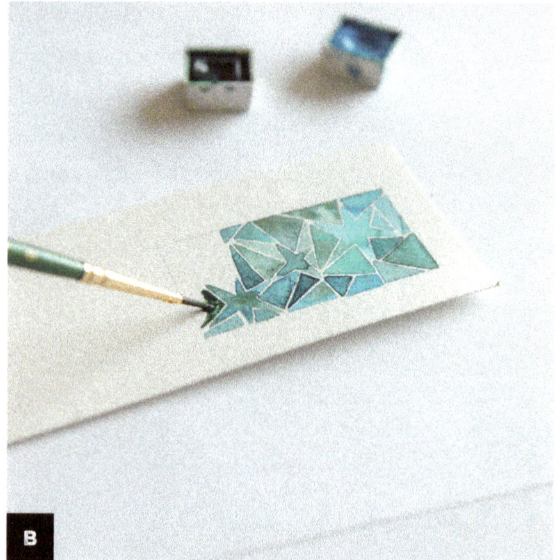

Here I used colored pencils **(A)** and watercolor **(B)**.

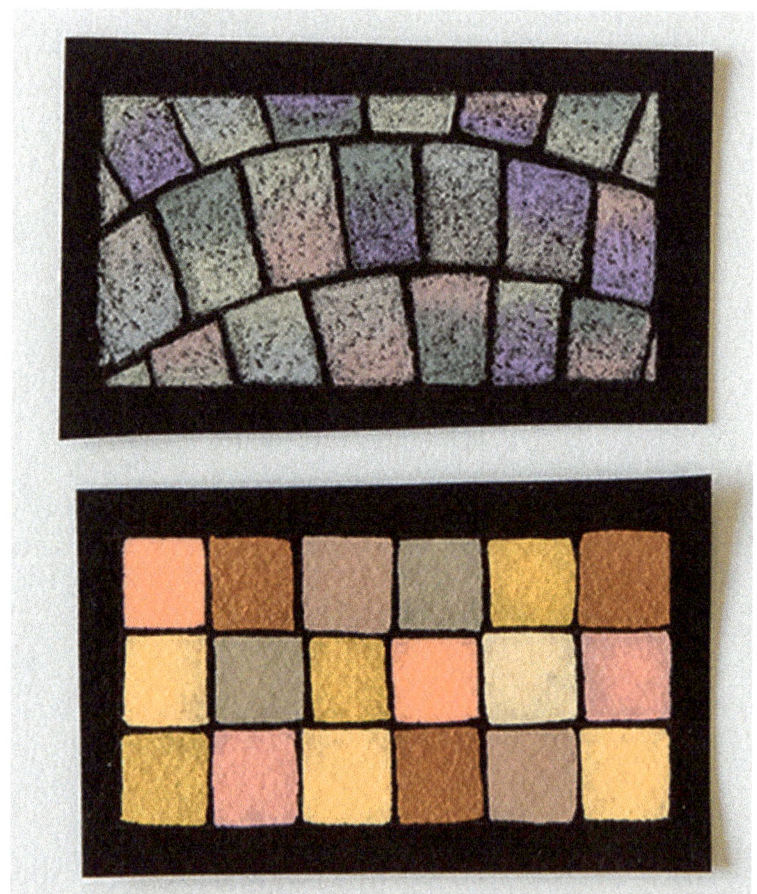

Try this technique on black paper using diverse mediums such as metallic paints or gouache.

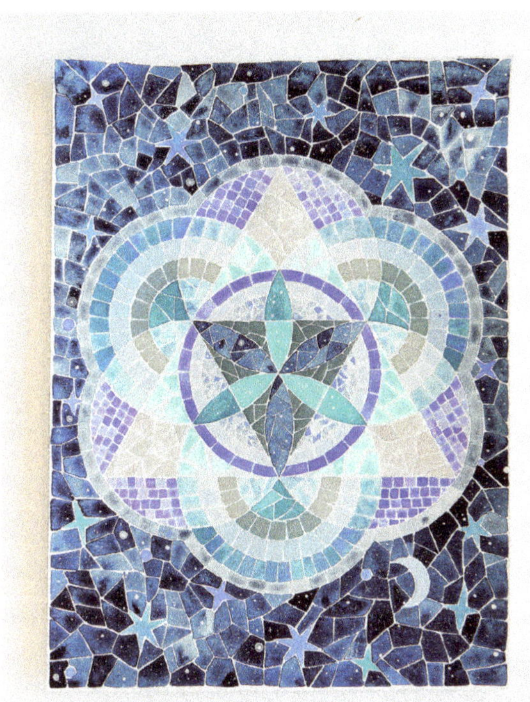

Mix and match different textures in your larger shape. The direction your mosaics are going in can also create an interesting flow to your final piece. For the best results, fill in your entire composition with mosaics that vary in size and style.

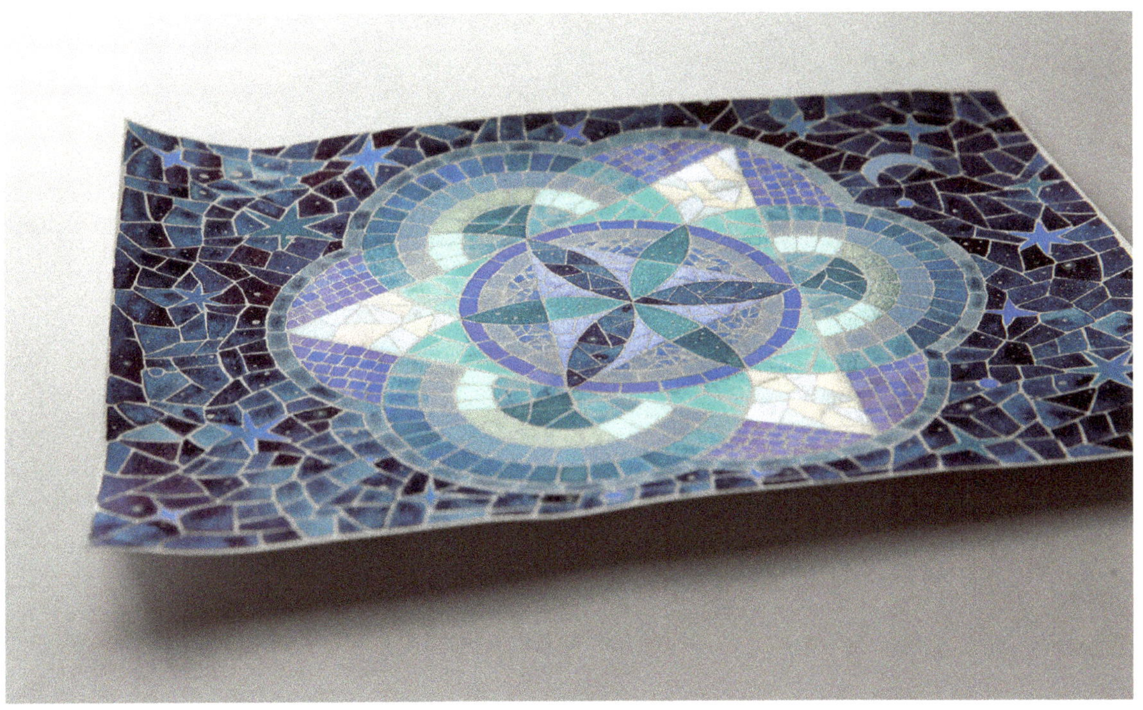

For this seed of life, I used a variety of blue watercolor paints and a touch of iridescent watercolors in selected areas.

DRAWING ON BLACK PAPER

Play with shapes, erase lines, add lines, connect intersections, or choose different areas to highlight. The amazing thing about sacred geometry is discerning new possibilities every time you draw, even with the most basic of shapes like the vesica piscis or the seed of life; each drawing can look completely different.

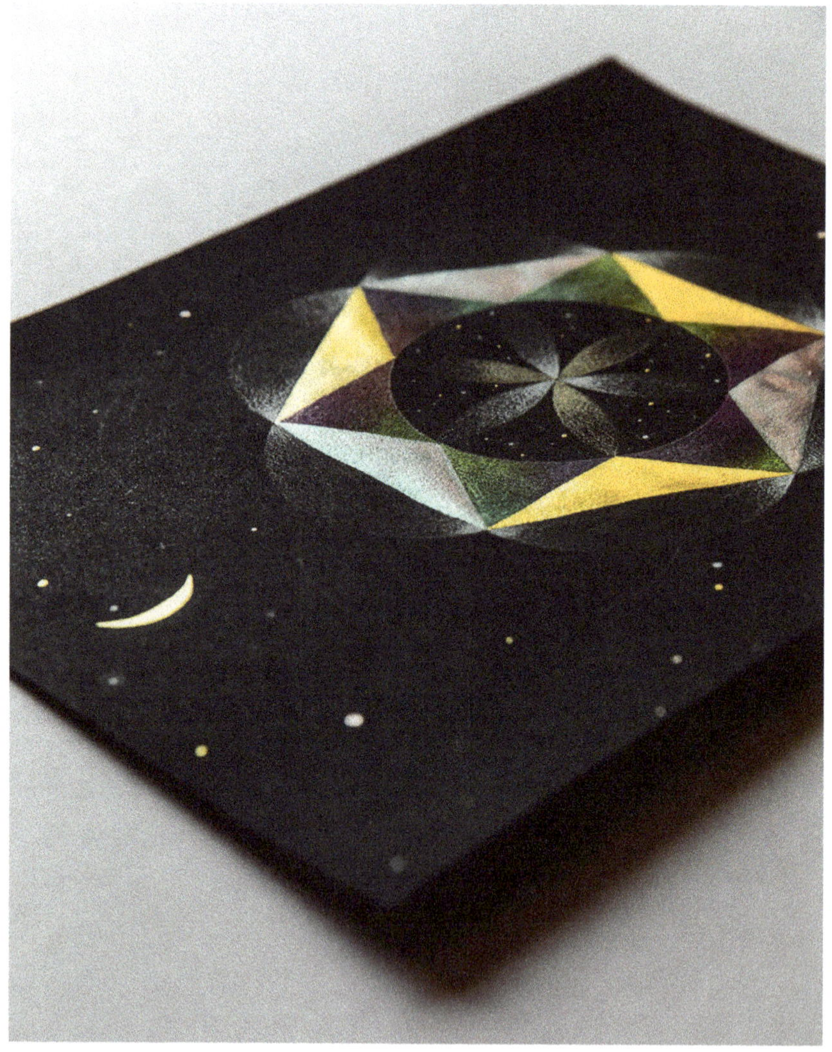

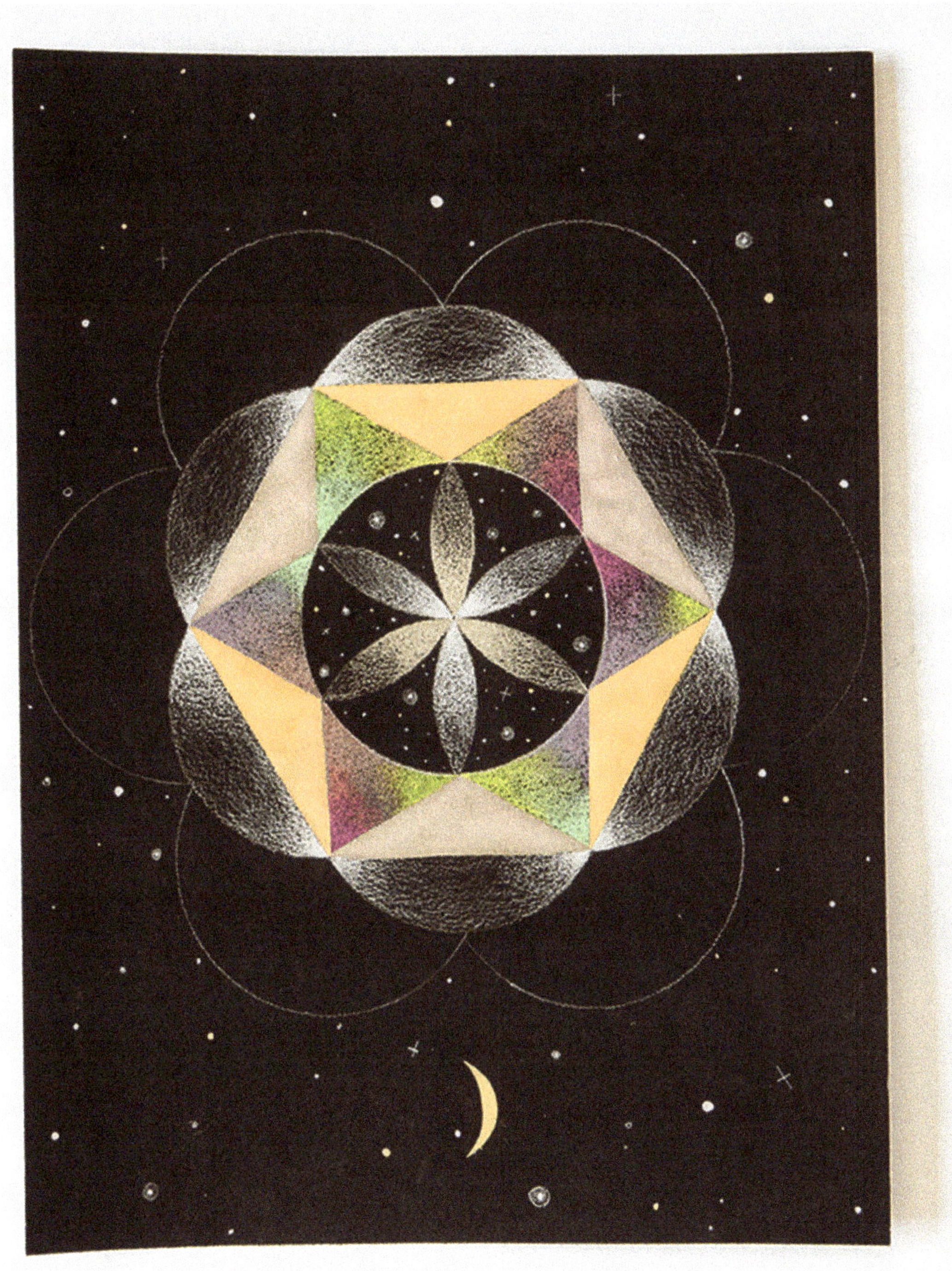

I enjoy experimenting with black paper, colored pencils, and touches of metallic paint. In this example, I am using Dessin Noir XL Extra Black paper by Canson, which is quite affordable and an interesting way to play with shape discovery. Keep in mind this paper will not handle wet mediums like watercolor and is best suited for drawing.

COLLAGE MOONS AND MIXED MEDIA

In this vesica piscis artwork, we'll use colored pencils and a bit of mixed media. As you can see, your shapes can look completely different every time, it all depends on the areas that are highlighted, the medium you choose, and your style.

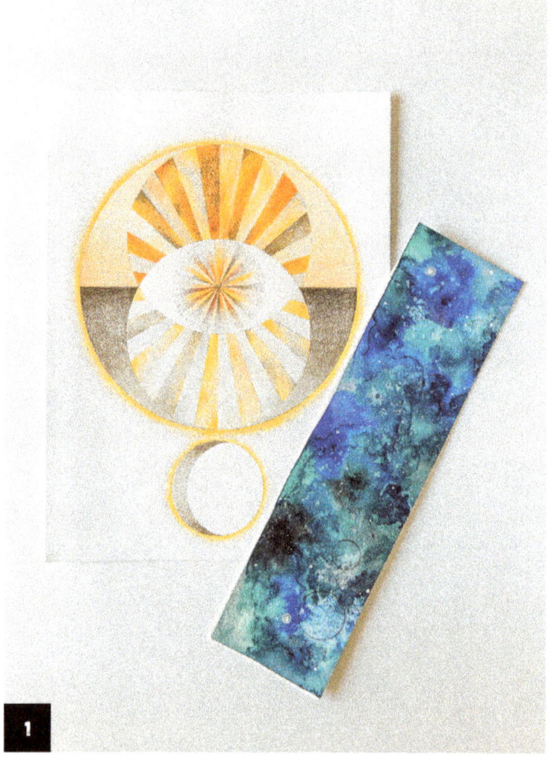

1

1 To demonstrate this example, I have a vesica piscis drawing and a strip of watercolor galaxy painting I had left over from a previous project. This is a great way to upcycle paint scraps!

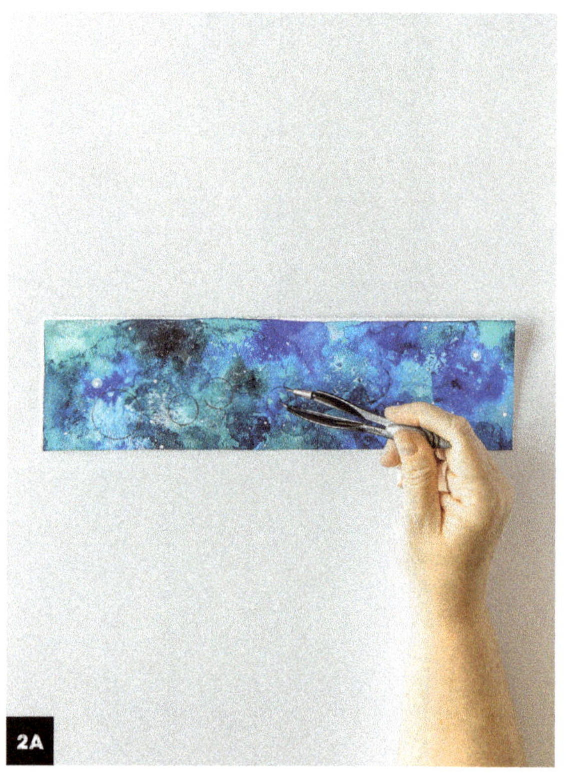

2A

2 Cut out circles to create mystical moons.

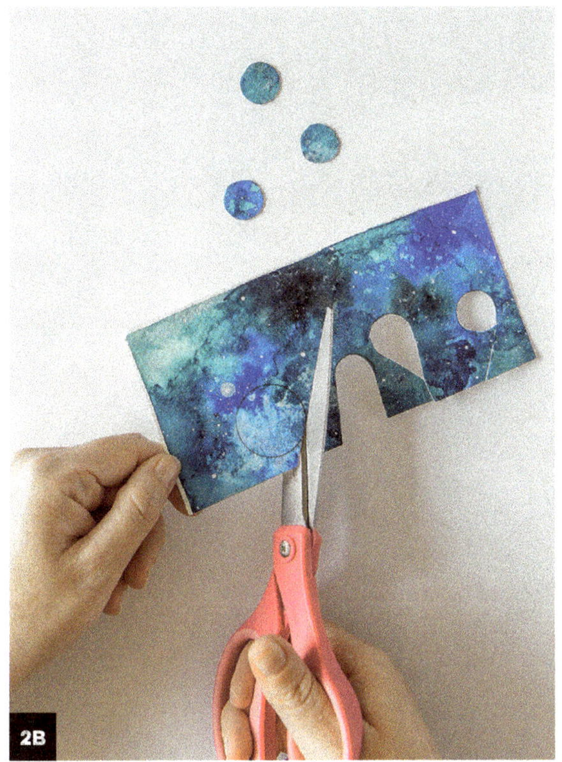
2B

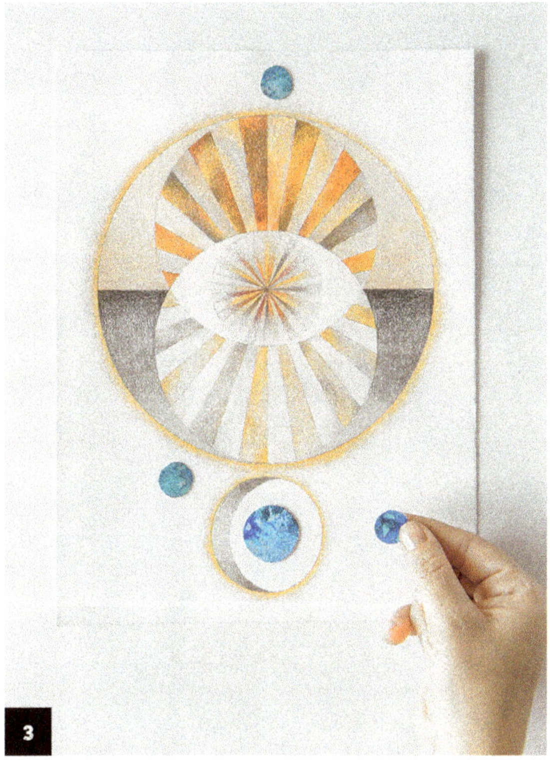
3

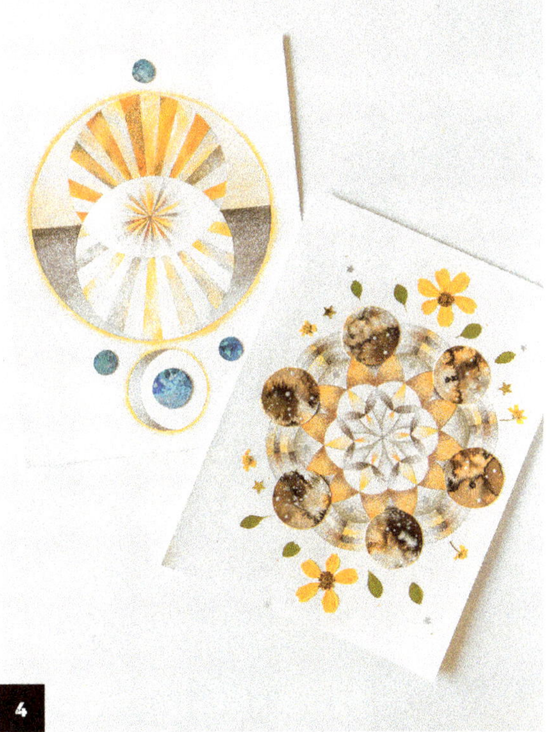
4

3 Using a light adhesive, paste your circles over or around your drawing.

4 I used a similar method in this seed of life as well. Feel free to add pressed flowers of your choice or any additional elements!

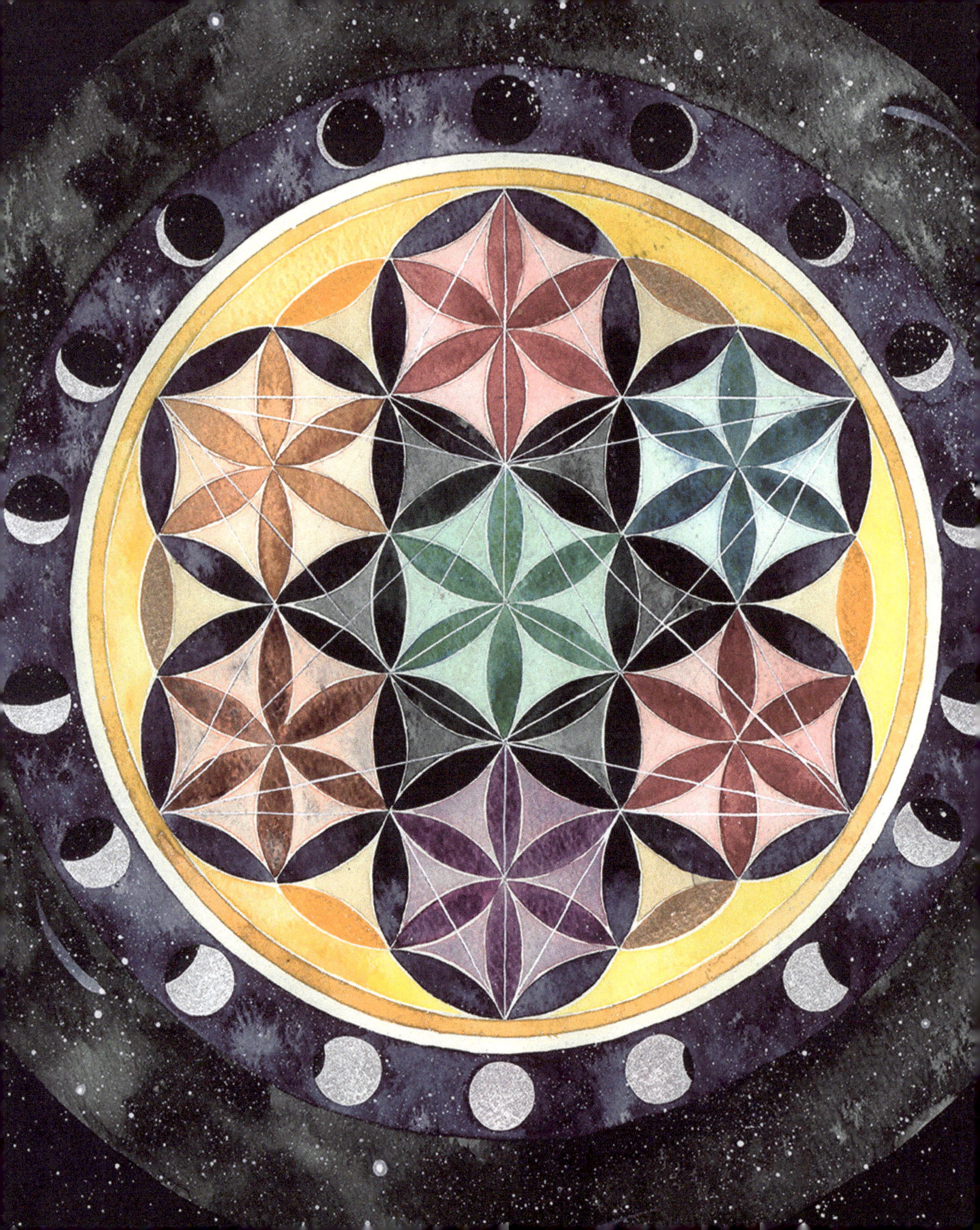

4

THE FLOWER OF LIFE

The flower of life is the most recognizable of all sacred geometry shapes. It's possible you've seen this formation in yoga studios, at holistic centers, or as a wellness brand logo. And if you hadn't noticed this before, you will now!

THE FLOWER OF LIFE IN MANY CULTURES

The flower of life has been around for much longer than our current era. In fact, it is estimated that this shape dates back to thousands of years BCE. It has been an important symbol in multiple cultures around the globe for millennia. Interpretations and fragments of this symbol show up in ancient sites and documentation, including the Osirion temple in ancient Egypt, the Cosmati Pavement in Westminster Abbey, Forbidden City temples in China, Hebrew inscriptions in Israel, and various temples in India, to name a few. You might also recognize it because Leonardo Da Vinci studied the flower of life and its mathematical properties extensively in his *Codex Atlanticus*.

THE FLOWER OF LIFE: INTERPRETATIONS

Here are some symbolic meanings associated with the flower of life.

- Symbolizes the unity of everything: We are all interconnected.
- Believed to represent the cycle of creation.
- The overlapping circles represent how we all come from the same source.
- Contains a total of nineteen complete intersecting circles and is traditionally shown contained in two larger circles to protect the knowledge that is beyond this pattern; as the shape expands, secrets are uncovered.
- Building block of the fruit of life, tree of life, egg of life, Metatron's cube, and the Platonic solids.
- Contains the basic shape of DNA strands.

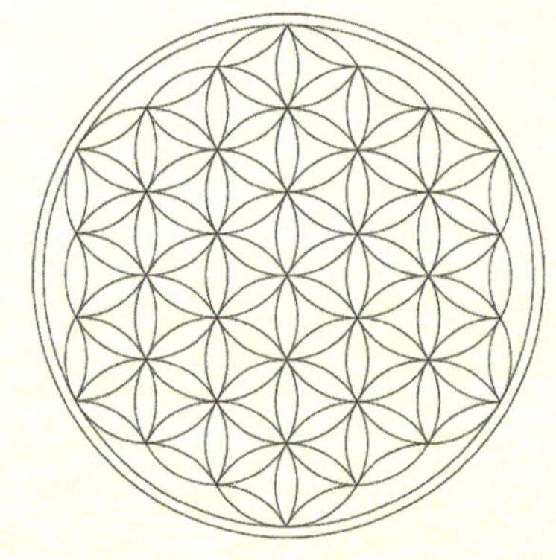

Drawing Technique

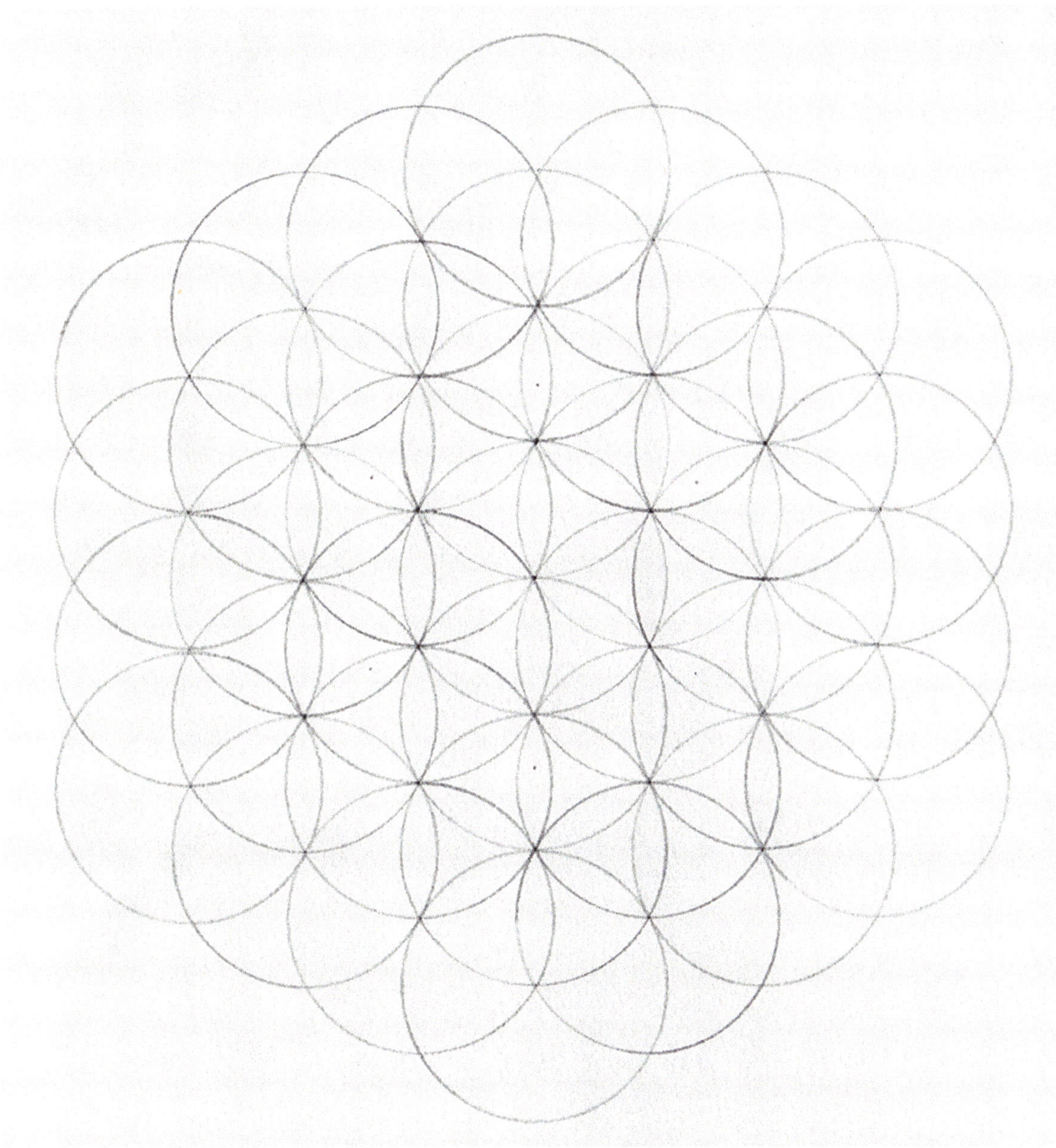

1 I have traced a pencil grid first for instructional purposes and will continue to draw intersecting circles using different colors for each round so it is easier to follow. This is not necessary in your personal process, but it's helpful to avoid confusion, and you might find it helpful for your first tries.

(continued)

2 Also for instructional purposes, I am tracing a larger circle with the needle in the center circle. The circumference will be set to another full circle around the original one.

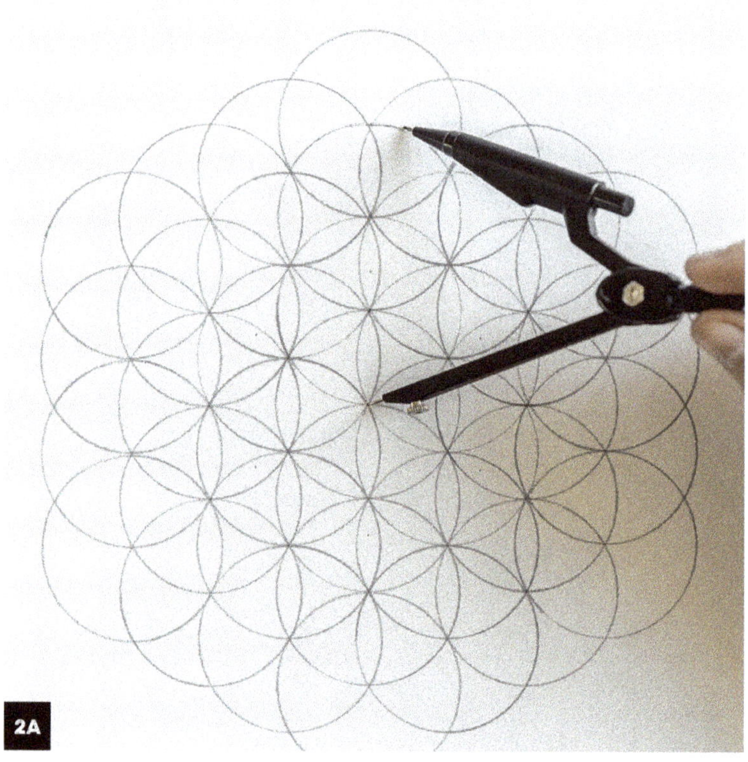

2A

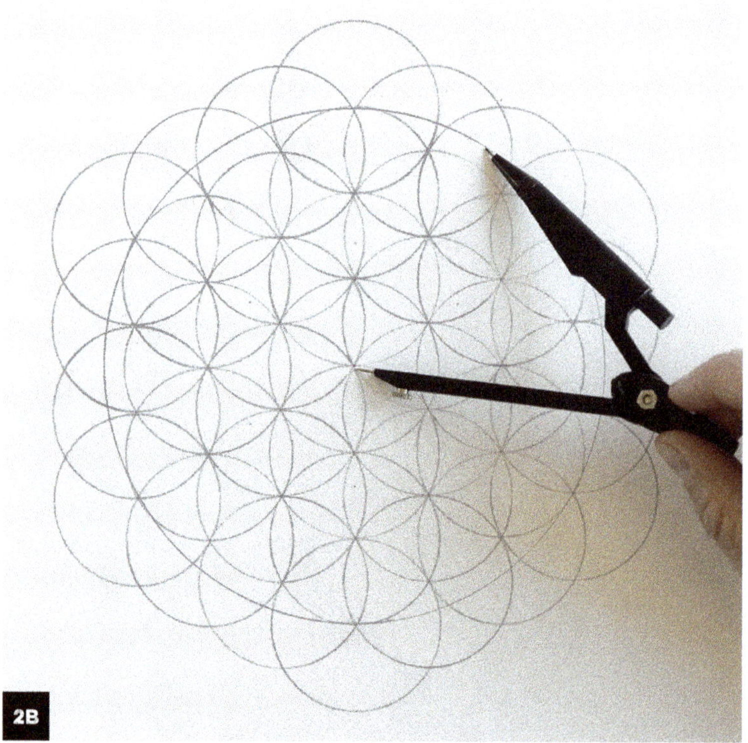

2B

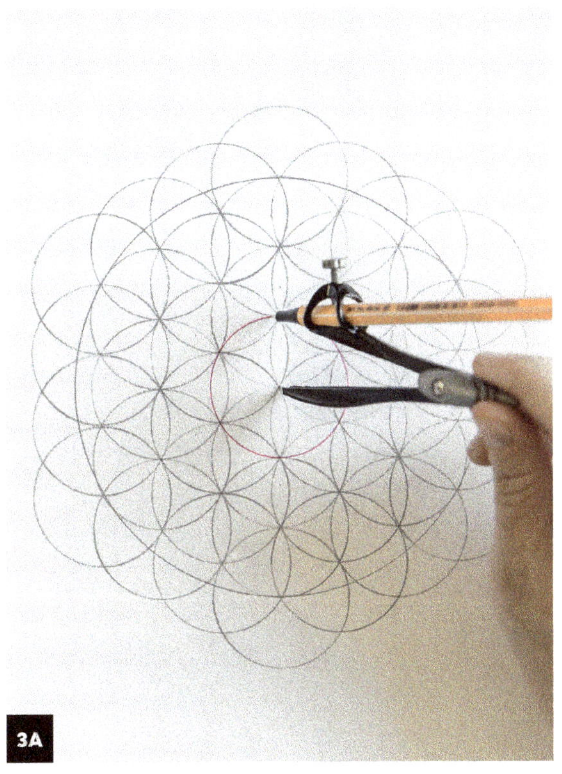

3A

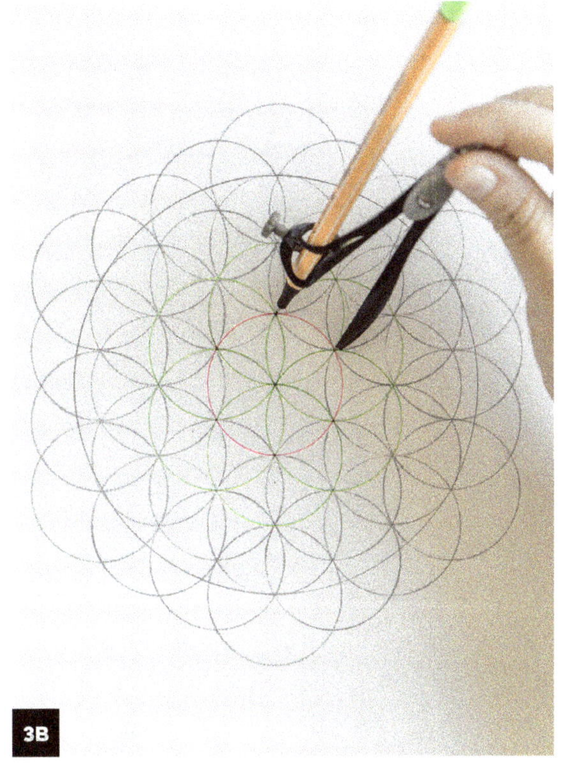

3B

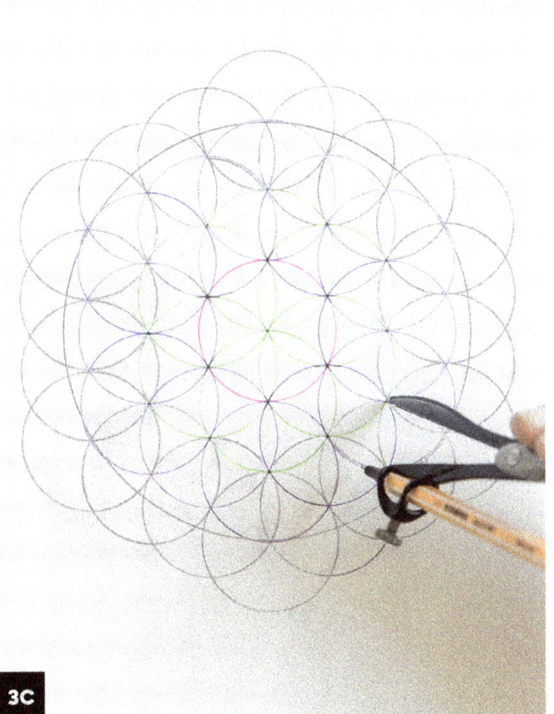

3C

3 To create a flower of life, start out by drawing a seed of life (see chapter 3). The concept is similar to the seed of life, and you will continue to draw circles around intersections. Notice how pink is the center circle, green is the first round, and now we continue with violet circles for a third round at each intersection of the green circles.

(continued)

4 Complete the inner petals of each violet circle by placing your needle at the intersections of each violet circle, but do not complete the circle. These end at the boundaries of each violet circle. For reference, I am using orange ink for these half-circles.

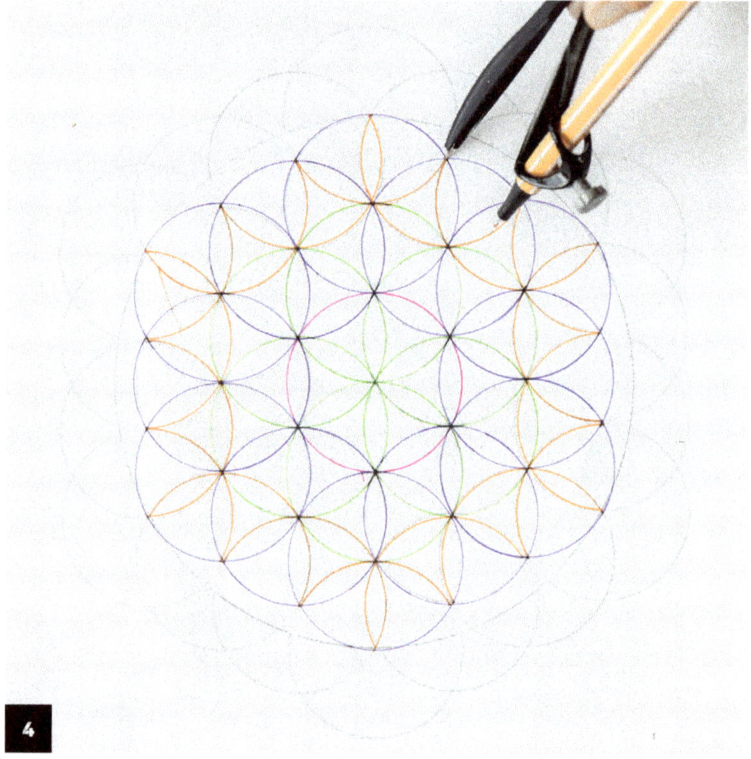

5 As mentioned above, the flower of life is traditionally represented with two large circles around the full shape. This is said to protect the full knowledge of upcoming shapes to be unlocked in this grid. Open your compass to the large circle boundary, then open it a bit larger for the second circle.

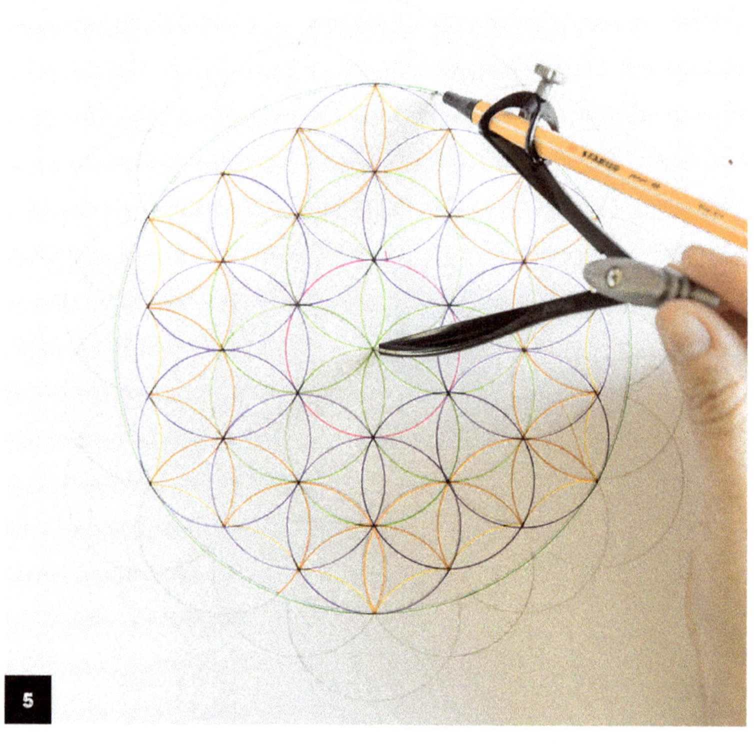

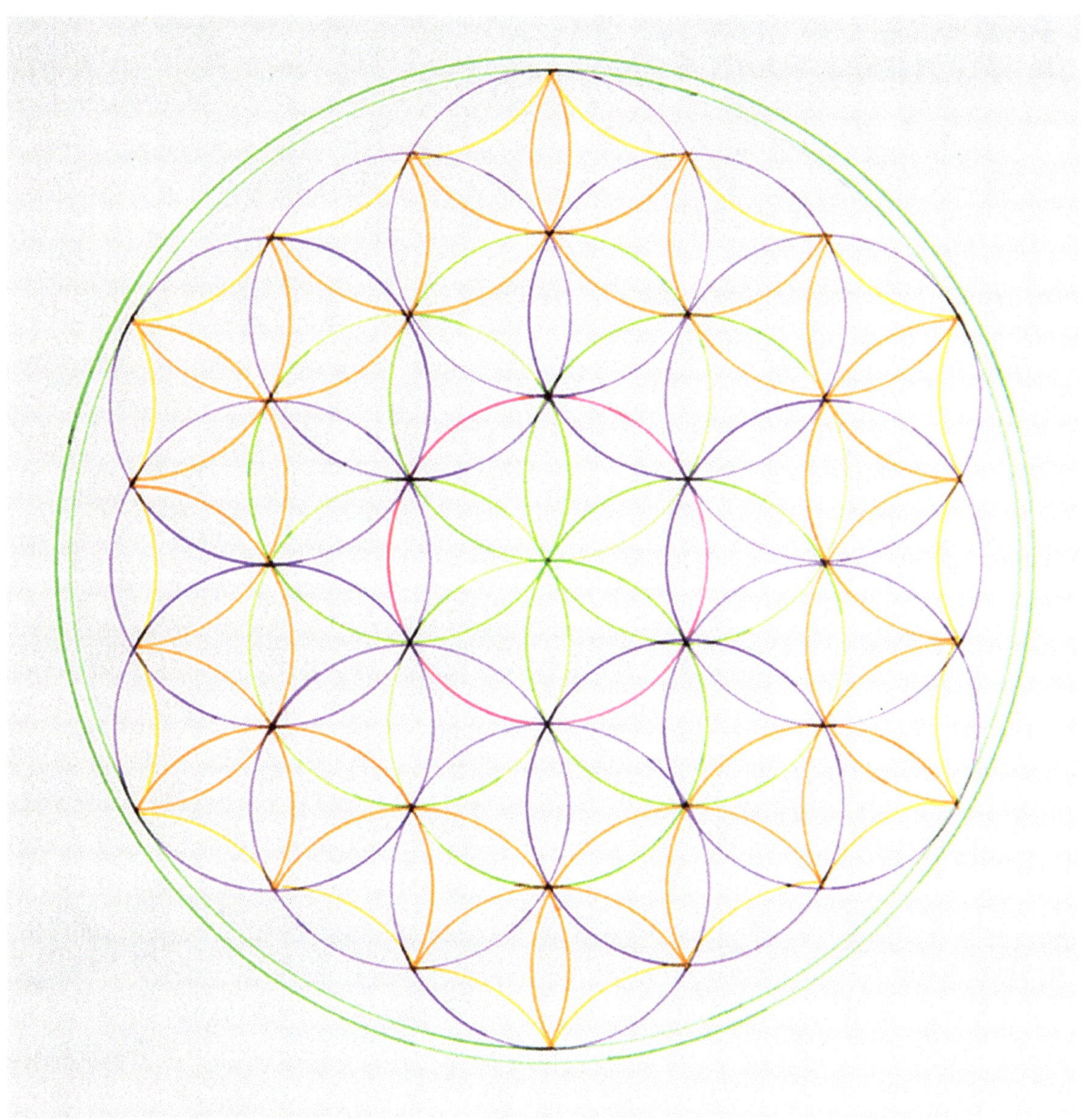

6 Erase any pencil guidelines, and you have just created a flower of life!

FLOWER OF LIFE EXPANDED PATTERN

It is said that once the protective outer circles of the traditional flower of life are dissolved, all kinds of secret formations begin to emerge. This includes the fruit of life, tree of life, egg of life, Metatron's cube, and the Platonic solids, which we touch on in upcoming chapters. There is also much to explore once we expand this formation into an infinite pattern. This grid can go on for as long as your drawing surface will allow.

Drawing Technique

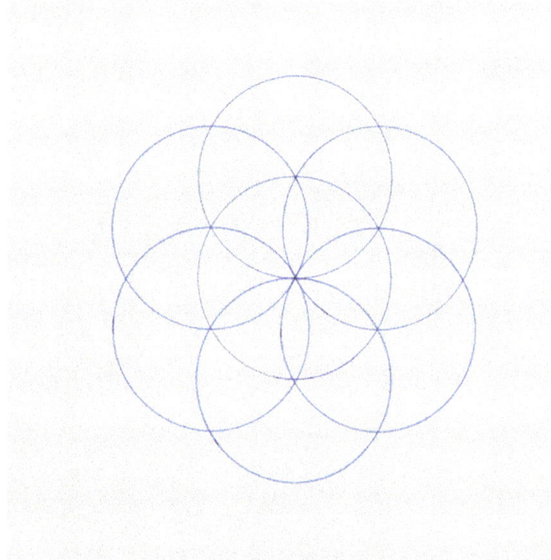

1 It's easiest to demonstrate this grid by starting with a simple seed of life shape, or you can begin with a full formation of the flower of life (omitting the outer circles) and continue from there.

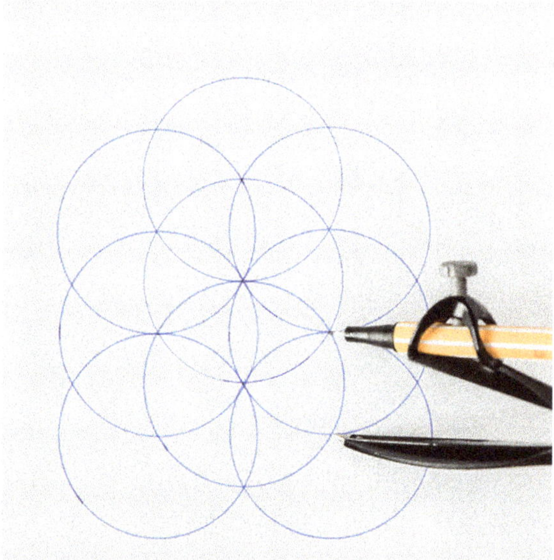

2 Without changing the aperture of your compass, place your needle on the outer intersections of your circle formations. I placed two new circles underneath my original seed of life.

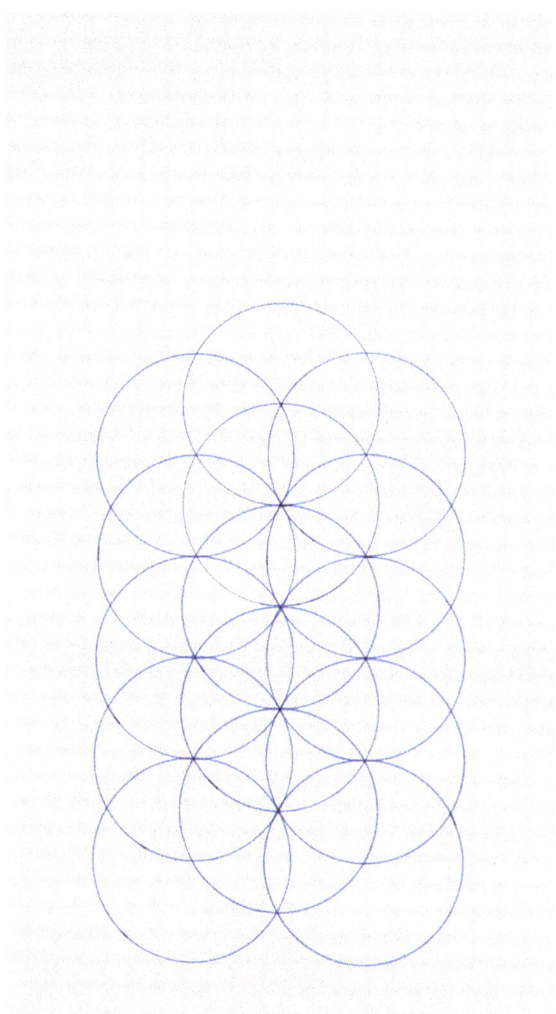

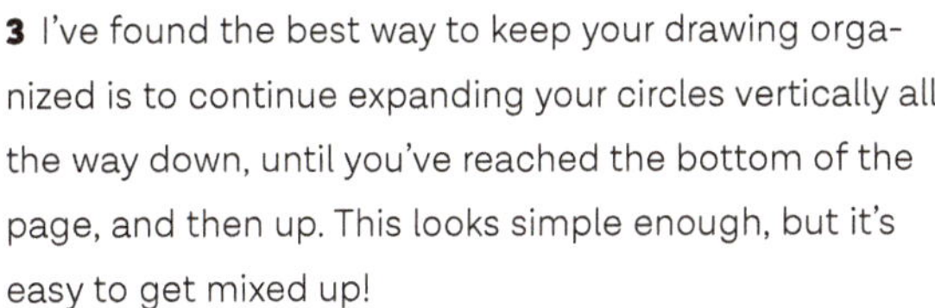

3 I've found the best way to keep your drawing organized is to continue expanding your circles vertically all the way down, until you've reached the bottom of the page, and then up. This looks simple enough, but it's easy to get mixed up!

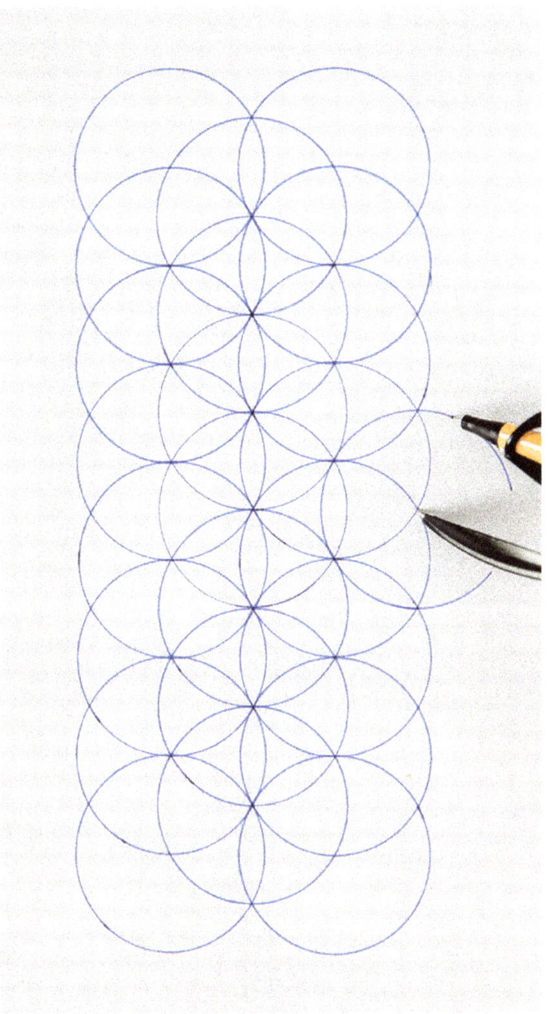

4 Once your first vertical column of circles is complete, continue to trace circles on each side, always using intersections as your center point.

(continued)

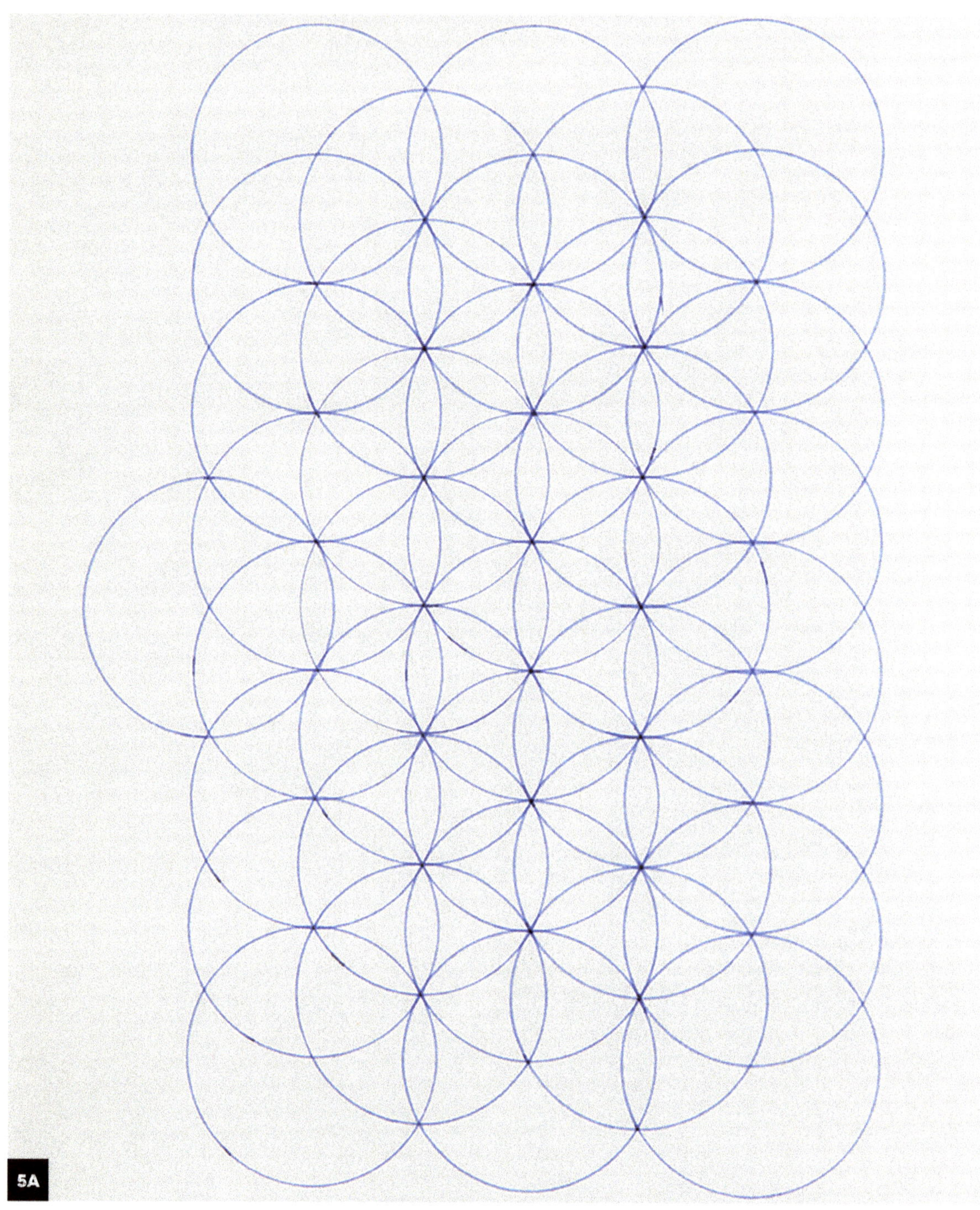

5 Fill the pattern until the circles are close enough to the edge on each side. You can play around with the grid as you please: Smaller circles will make a tighter pattern. Erasing or highlighting certain areas can also be interesting, and you can even begin to connect intersections to see what kinds of geometric formations pop up.

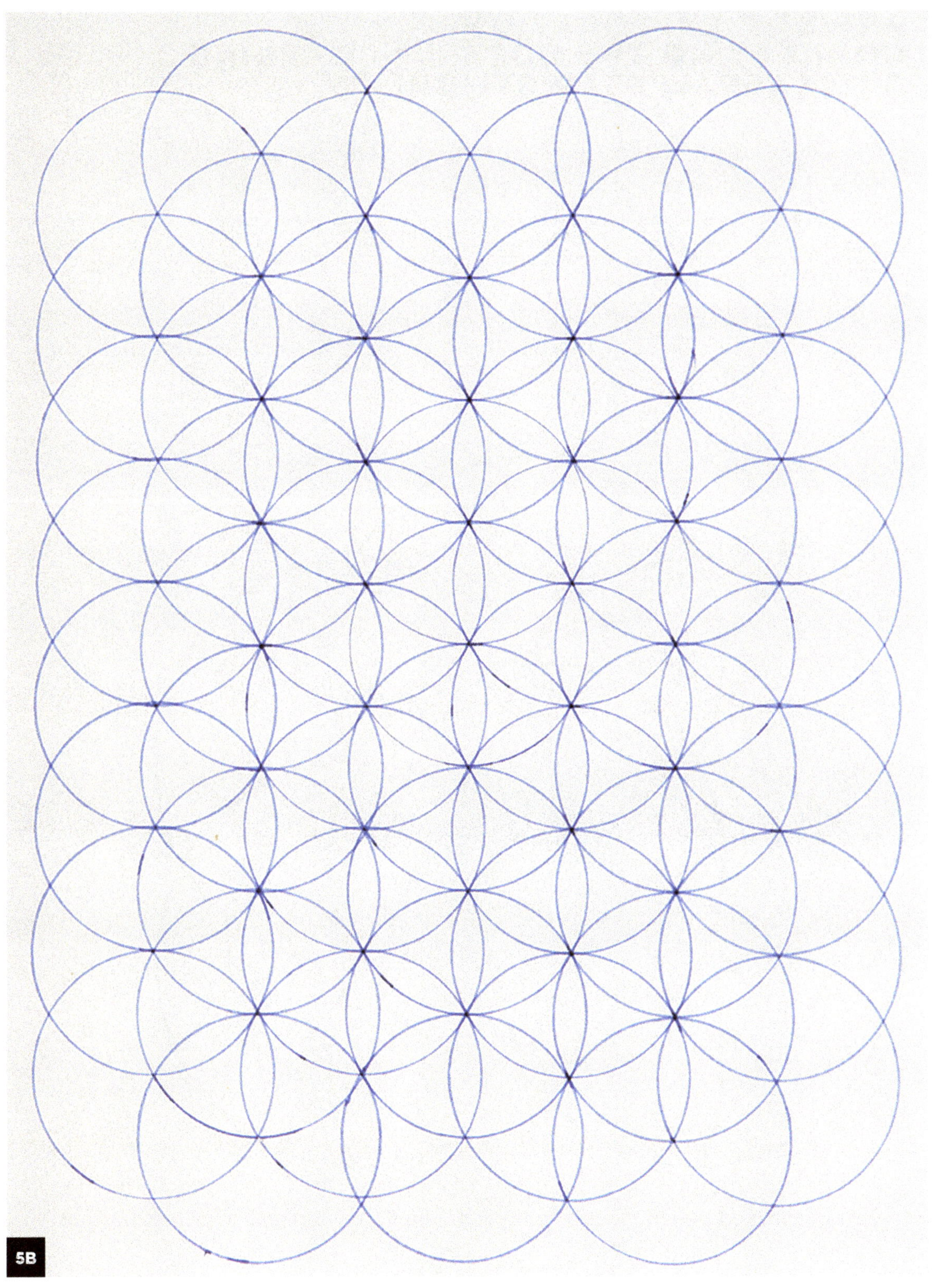
5B

ARTISTIC EXPLORATION: CONNECTING THE DOTS, UNCOVERING A HEXAGRAM STAR SYMBOL

Just as you explored shapes within your simple vesica piscis and seed of life, you can continue on with patterns in the flower of life to create exquisite works of art. Observe how the hexagon can be found in the center if you repeat this on a grid or on its own.

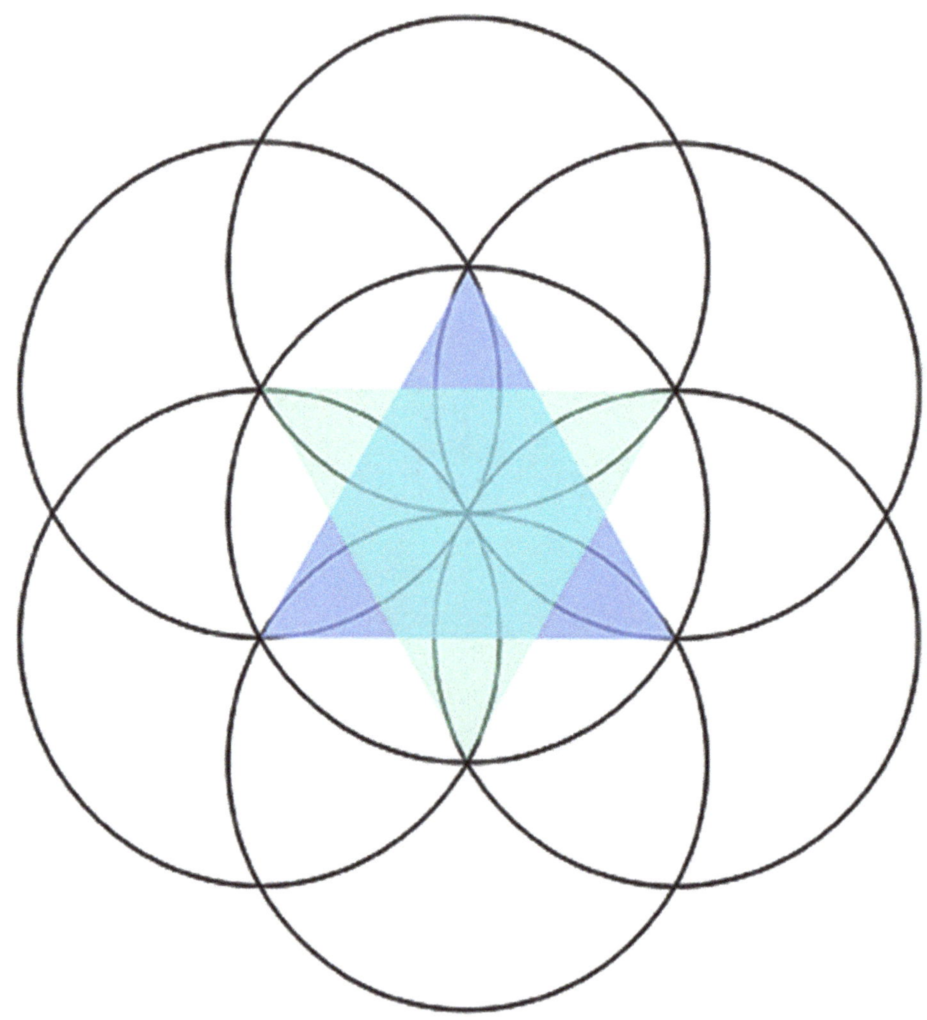

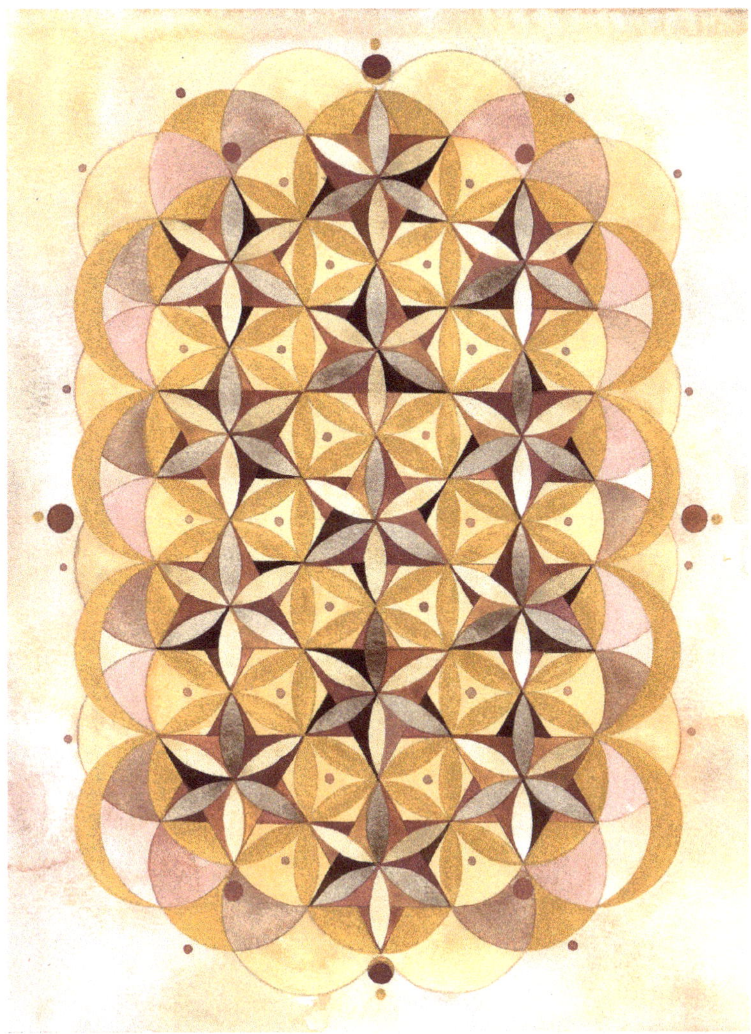

Here is an example of a simple grid where I connected intersections using a straightedge to highlight hexagrams within each individual formation.

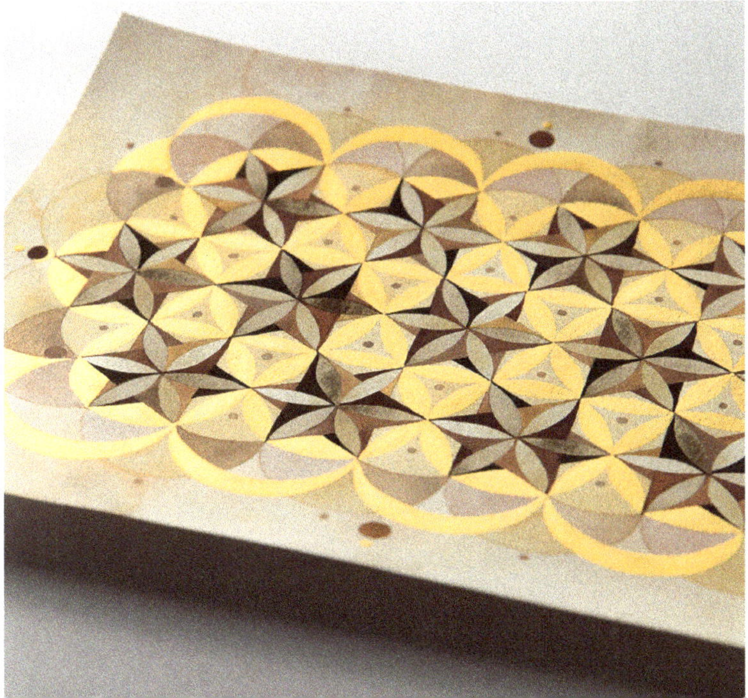

I decided to use watercolor as my medium with an earthy color palette and finished it off with gold paint for details.

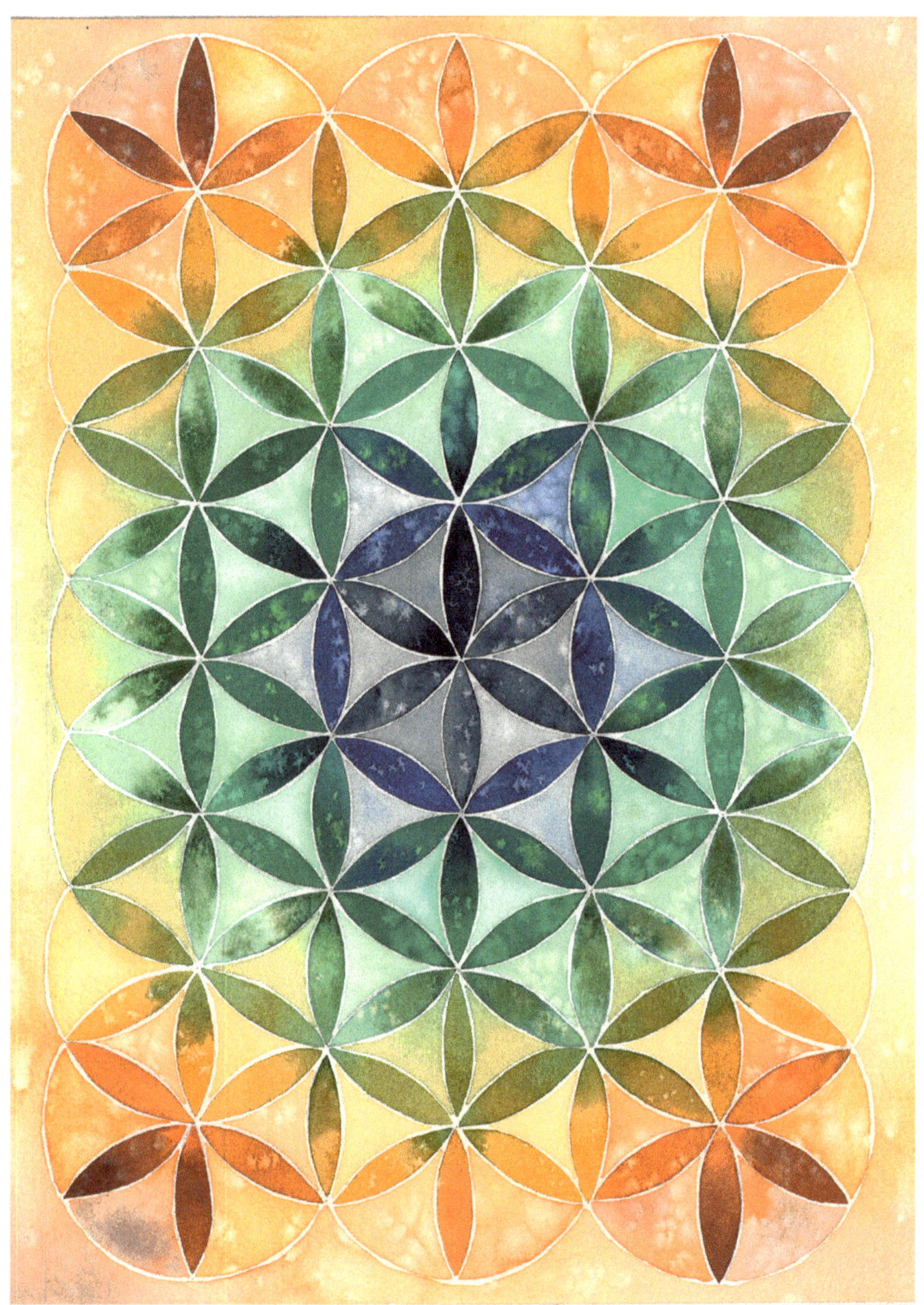

In this example, I used watercolor in a radial colorful scheme with a dash of salt to create an interesting reaction to the paint.

RAINBOW WATERCOLOR FLOWER OF LIFE

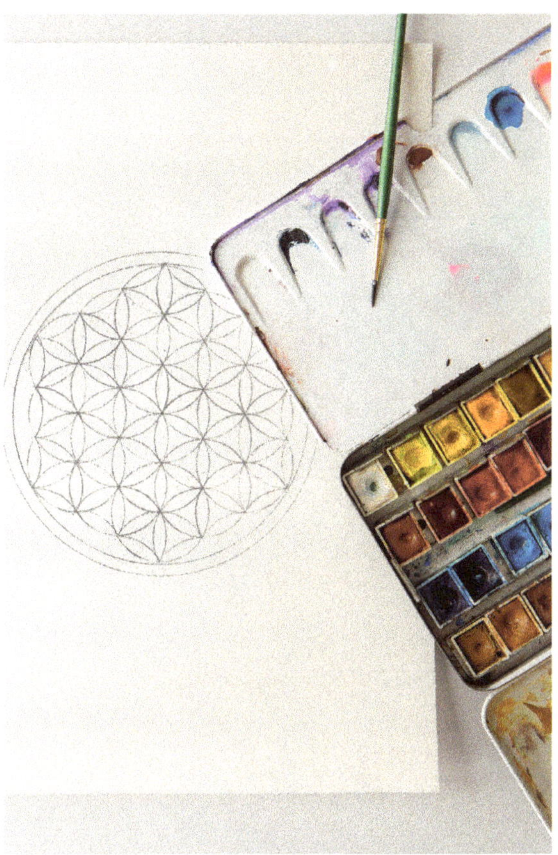

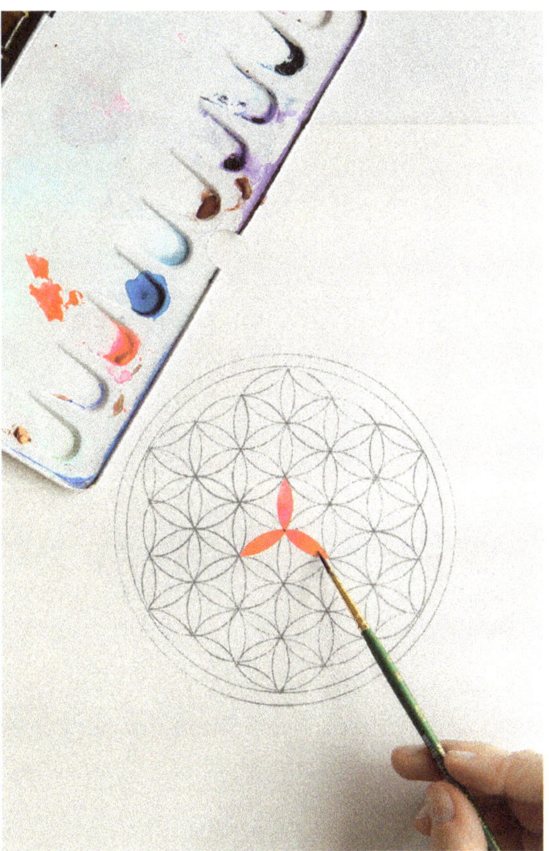

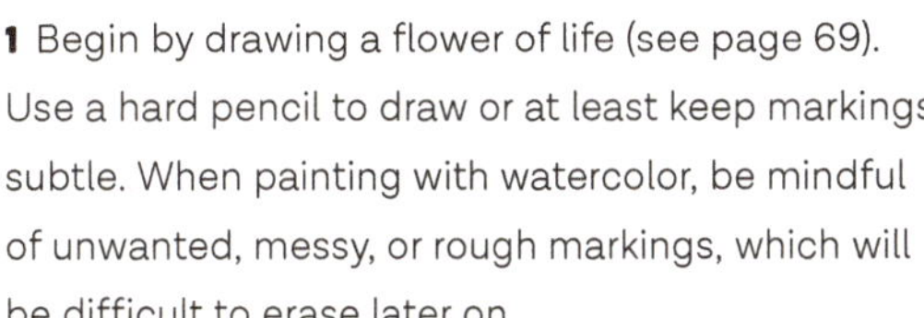

1 Begin by drawing a flower of life (see page 69). Use a hard pencil to draw or at least keep markings subtle. When painting with watercolor, be mindful of unwanted, messy, or rough markings, which will be difficult to erase later on.

2 Start painting the inner petals using magenta/red tones.

(continued)

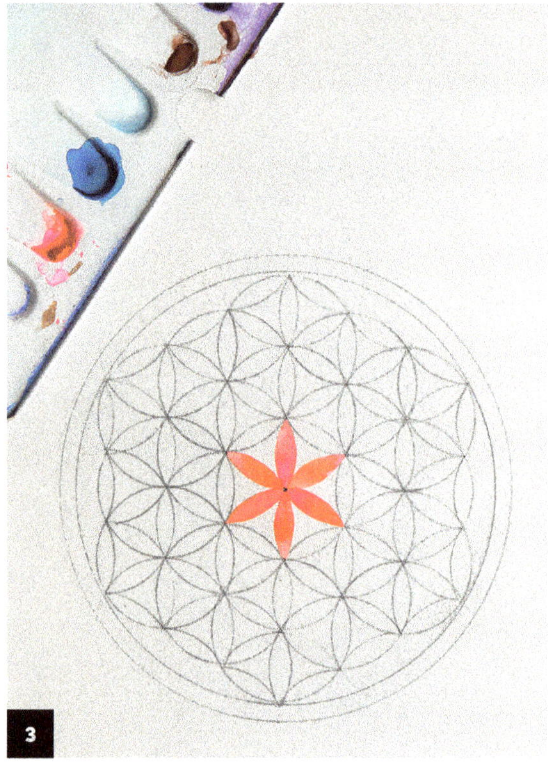
3

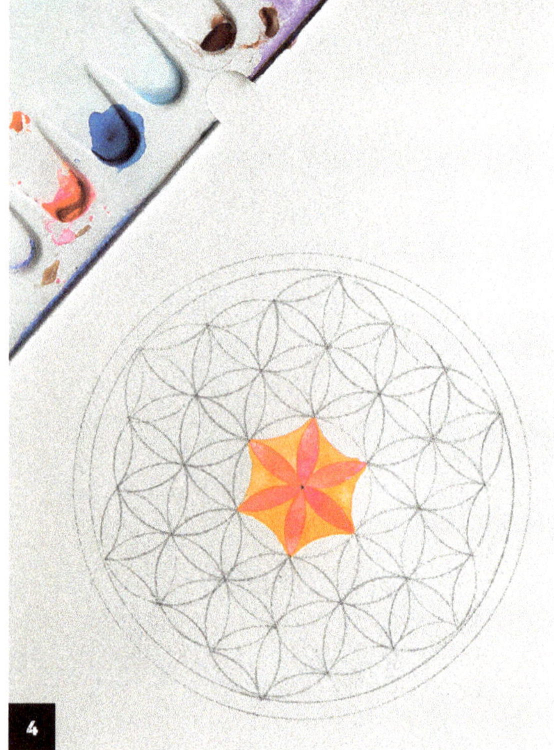
4

3 When using watercolor, it's always important to skip shapes that are too close together; allow just a bit of drying time to avoid areas bleeding into each other.

4 Continue painting your grid in the order of the rainbow: red → orange-red → orange → yellow → yellow-green → green → turquoise → blue → violet → red-violet.

5 Always let previous areas dry before painting the neighboring ones.

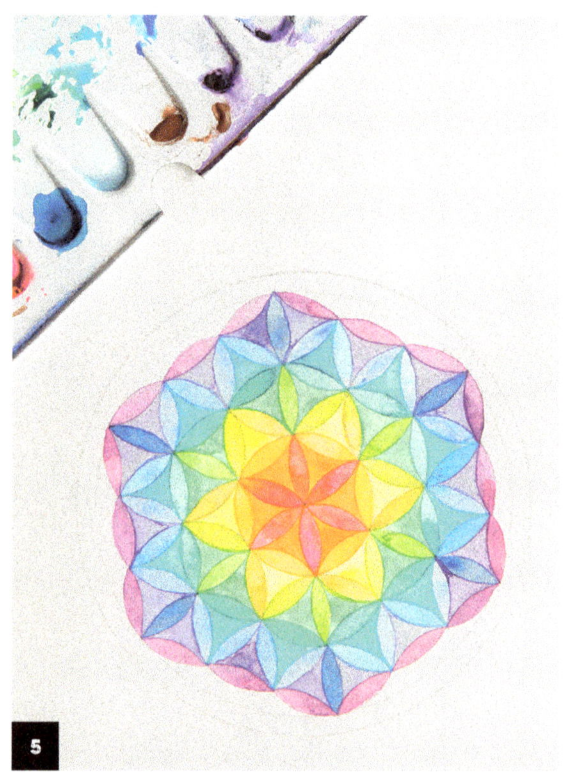
5

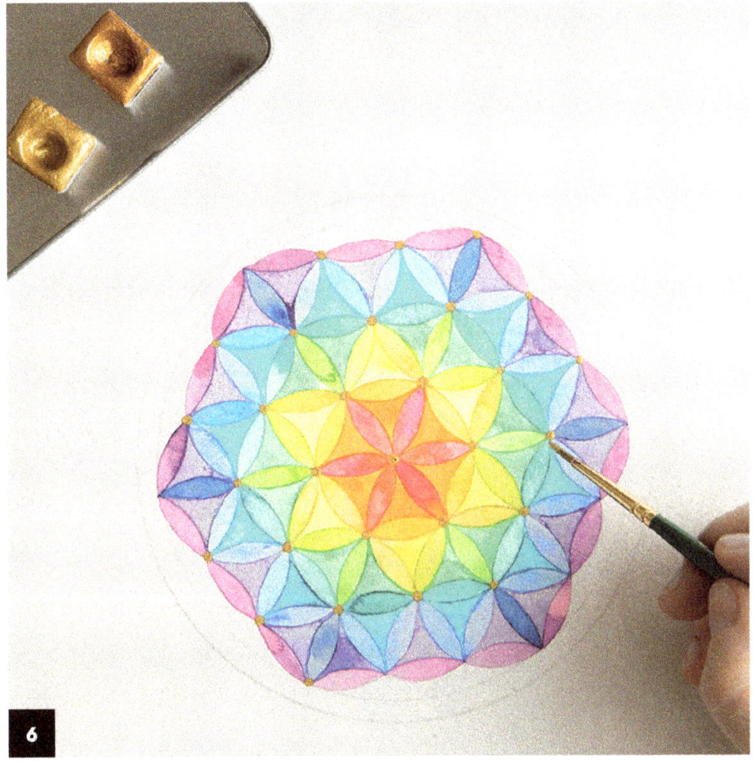

6 Once you have finished the watercolor painting, feel free to add interesting details. I'm using gold paint to add small dots at each intersection . . .

7 . . . and around the rim!

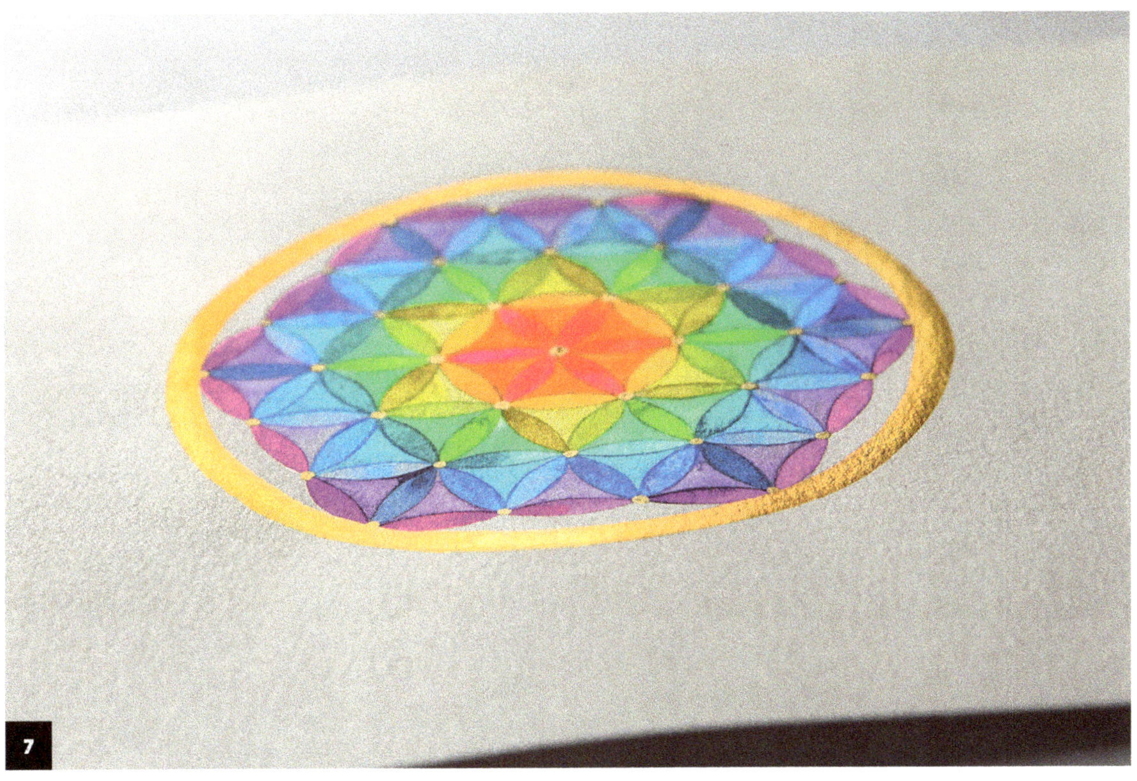

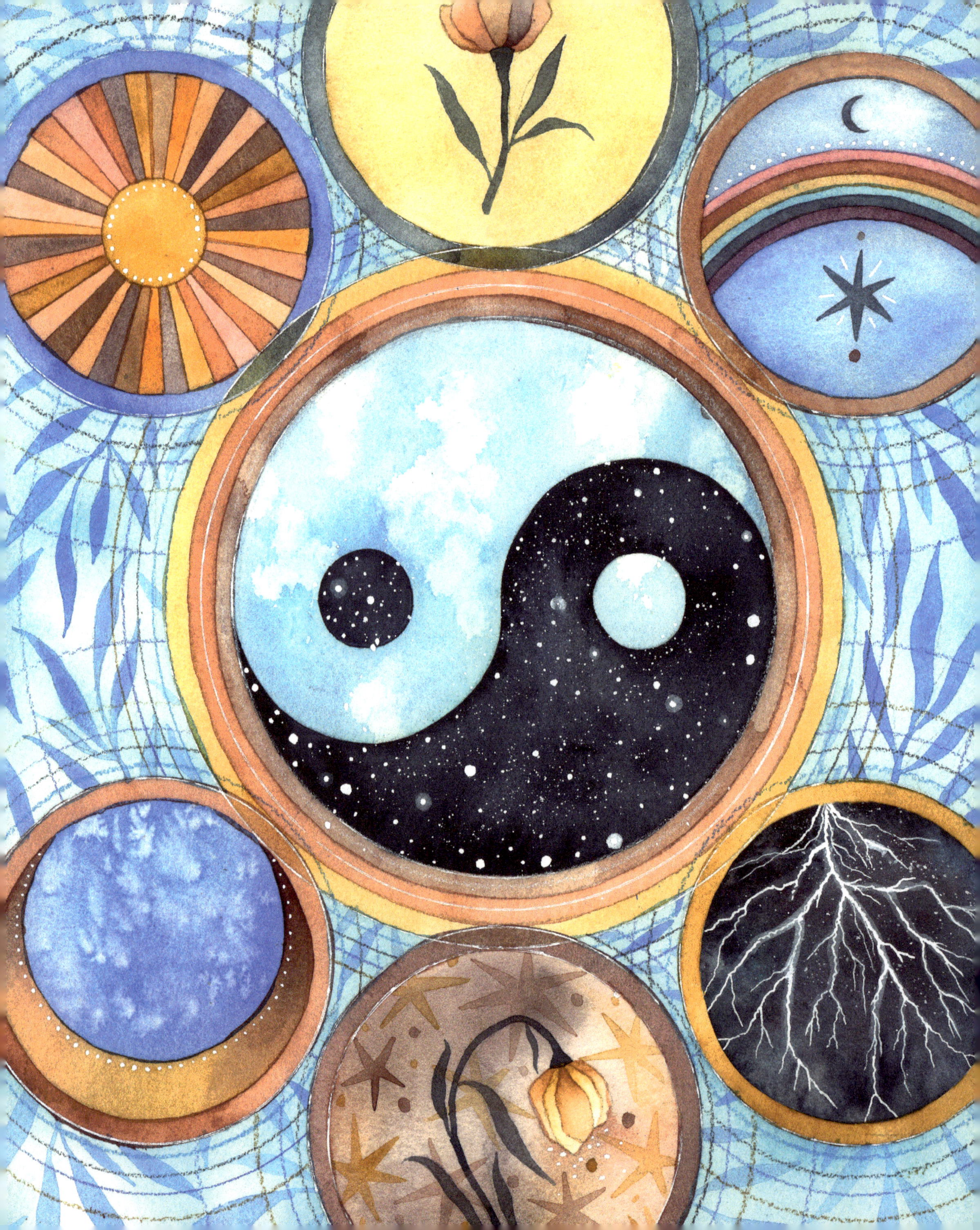

5

COMPLEX SHAPES BUILT FROM THE FLOWER OF LIFE

Once you have understood the basic structure of the flower of life, new forms will become apparent. Each of these shapes has meanings of its own and is also a building block for even more complex shapes to come. You will notice by now that sacred geometry is a growing system with a life of its own.

THE EGG OF LIFE

The egg of life emerges when you erase the lines intersecting the central circle.

THE EGG OF LIFE: INTERPRETATIONS

Here are some symbolic meanings associated with the egg of life.

- This shape is an intermediate point between the seed of life and the flower of life.
- Symbolizes creation.
- Can be drawn in three-dimensional form using spherical shading techniques.
- When represented in three dimensions, the shape actually contains eight spheres, as one is hidden behind the visible circles.
- Represents the eight-cell stage of human conception or the beginning stages of an embryo.

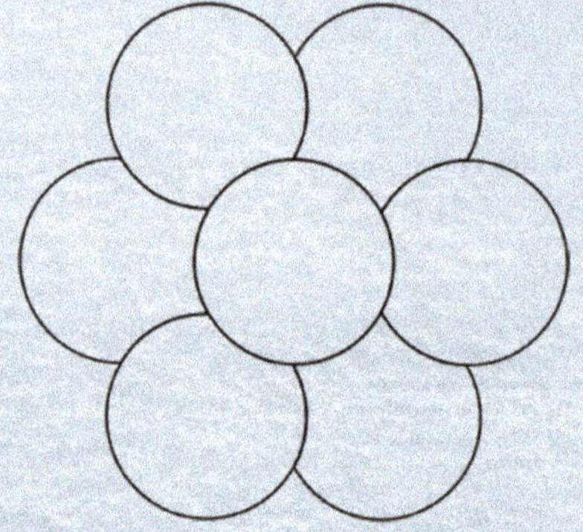

Drawing Technique

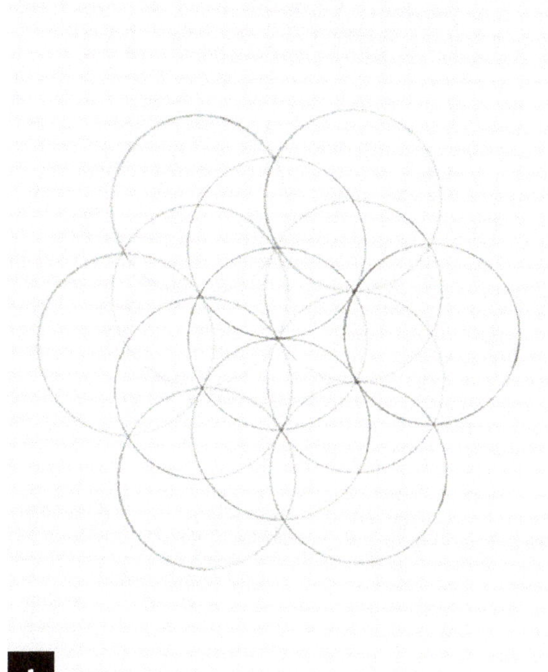

1

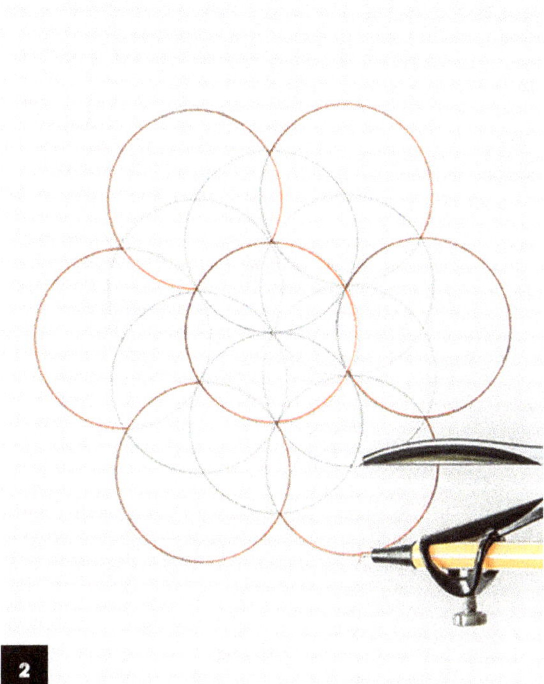

2

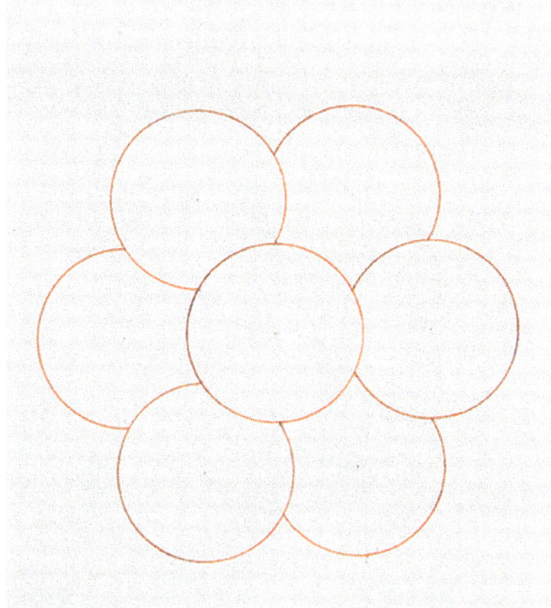

3

1 Start by tracing a seed of life with an extra round of circles to surround the shape. Use a pencil so you can erase specific lines later on. You will have thirteen intersecting circles at this point.

2 Trace the circles as demonstrated using a pen or darker color.

3 Erase the original pencil guides to uncover the egg of life.

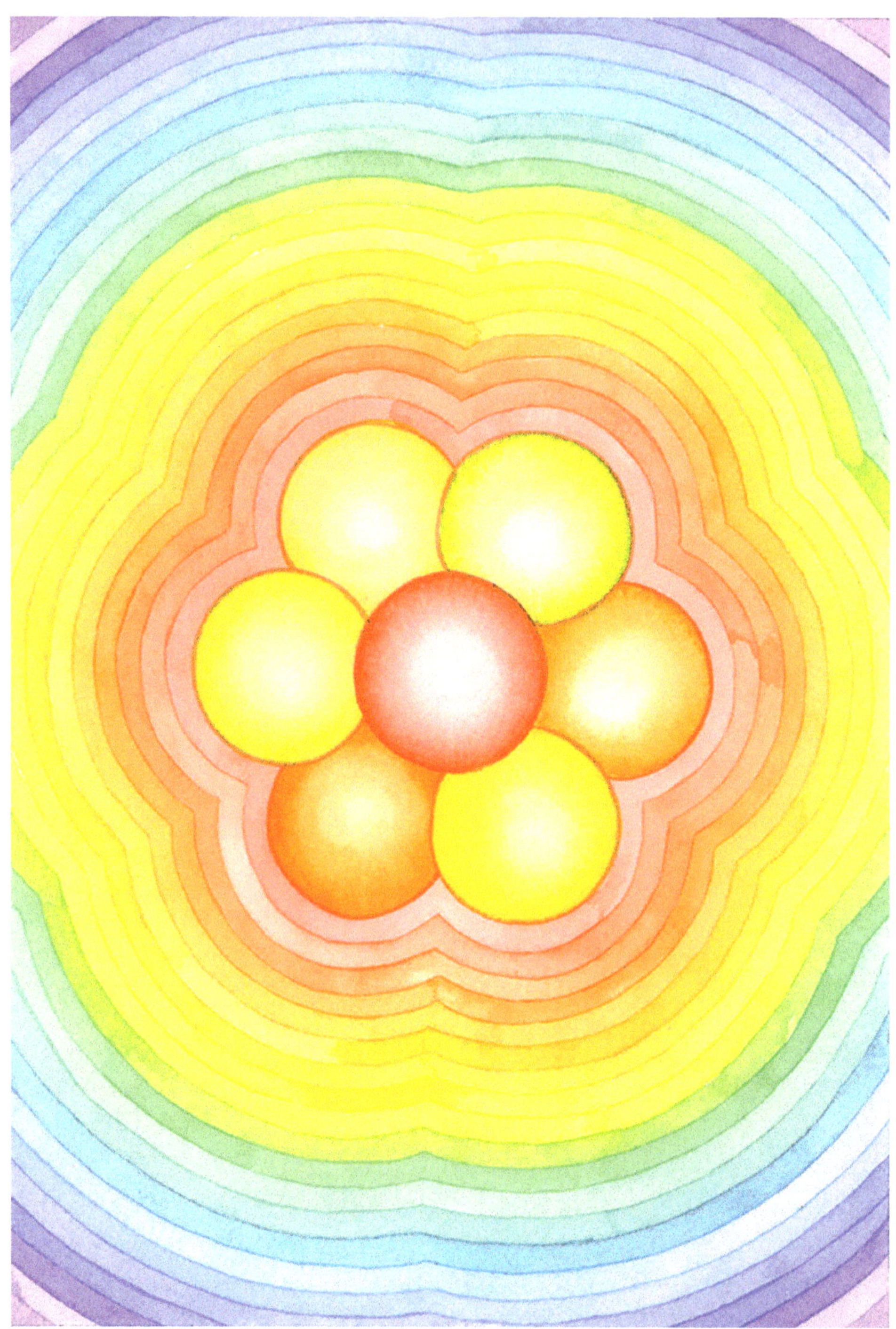

Traditionally, the egg of life is shaded in spherical form to enhance the three-dimensional shape. In this example, I am using a more realistic shading method by letting the watercolor blend into a lighter tone at the center of each circle.

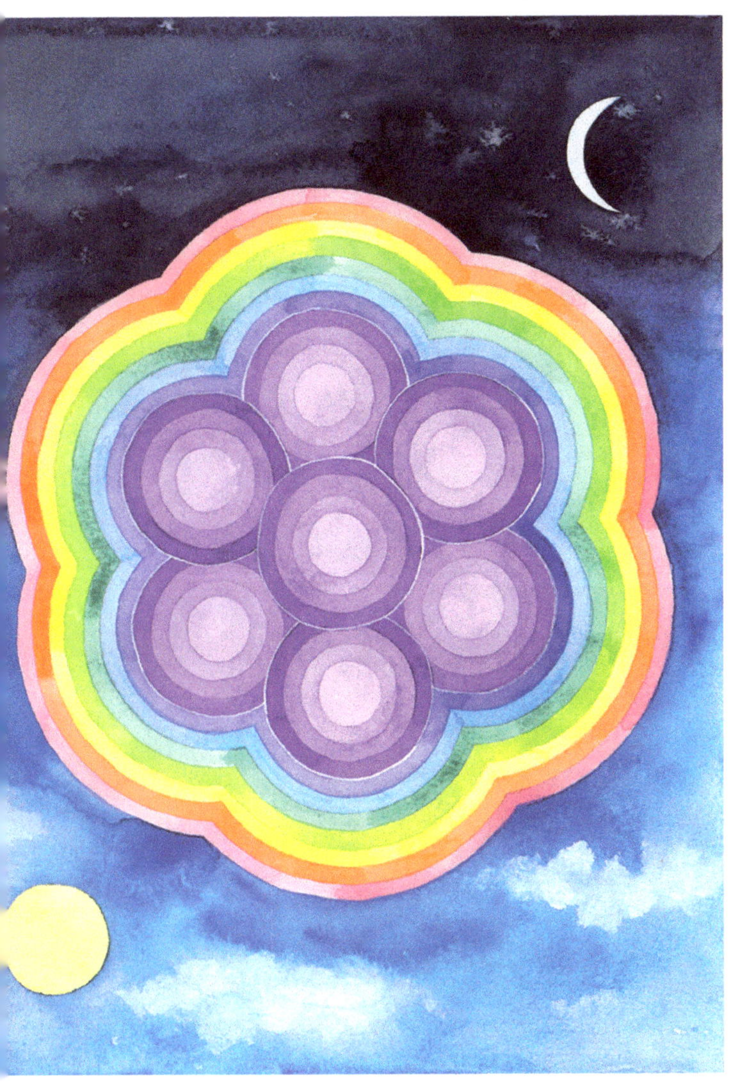

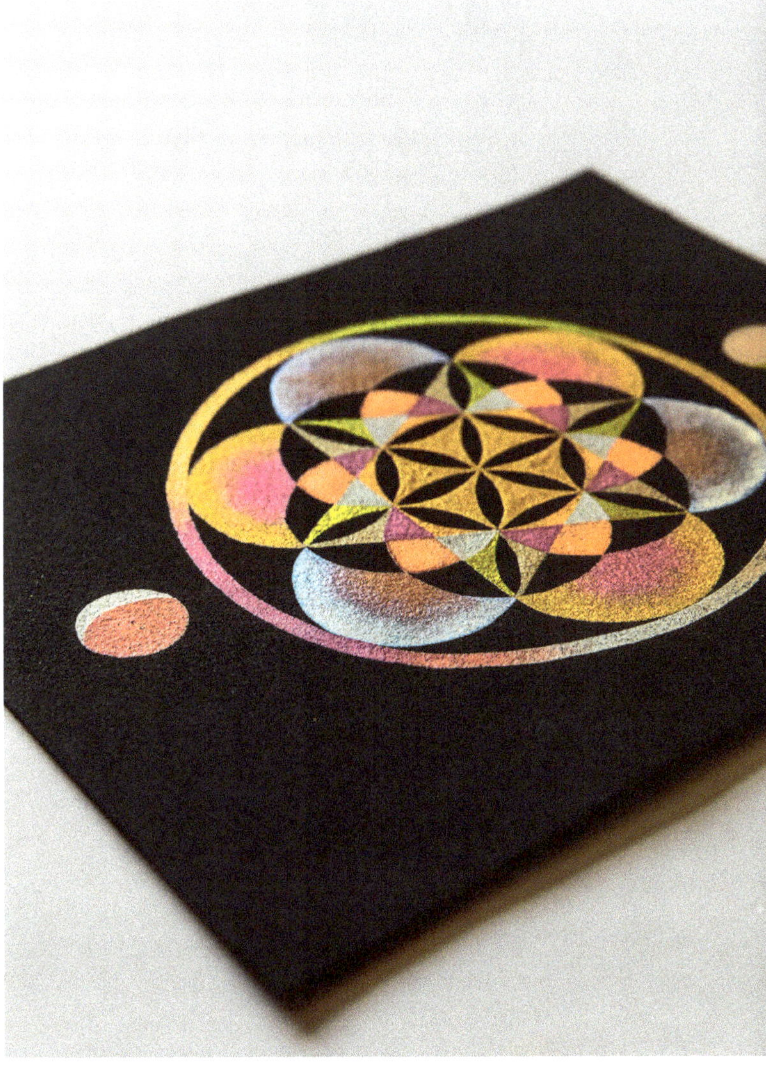

In this example, I am going for an illustrative style where I create the illusion of shading by painting darker rims toward the edge of each circumference. Feel free to explore this shape before erasing the lines to create the classic egg of life form, the halfway point between the seed of life and the flower of life. As with other shapes, connect lines and enhance selected areas. The possibilities are truly endless.

In this example, I am using metallic paint on black watercolor paper.

THE TREE OF LIFE

The tree of life connects circles on the perimeter along a central axis to create an elongated form. The tree of life is deeply symbolic, and studying its origins and interpretations can take many years.

THE TREE OF LIFE: INTERPRETATIONS

Here are some symbolic meanings associated with the tree of life.

- Considered a mystical diagram, most commonly known for its presence in Kabbalah.
- A hierarchical structure representing the forces in the universe and human behavior, considered to be a road map for our soul.
- Depending on the tradition, each line and connecting node represents different aspects of existence. The nodes are associated with a variety of symbols, including colors, numbers, deities, archetypes, values, and celestial bodies, while the lines represent paths. When divided into vertical sections, these nodes and paths form pillars; when divided horizontally, they represent levels associated with elements in nature.
- The tree of life shape is encoded in the flower of life.
- Considered to be a map of the universe and a sign of unity.

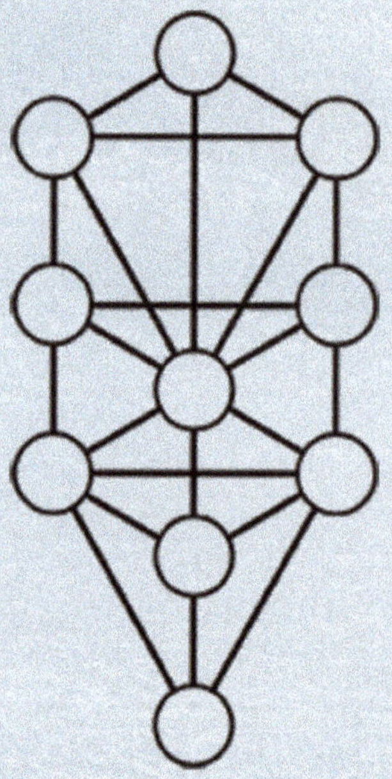

Drawing Technique

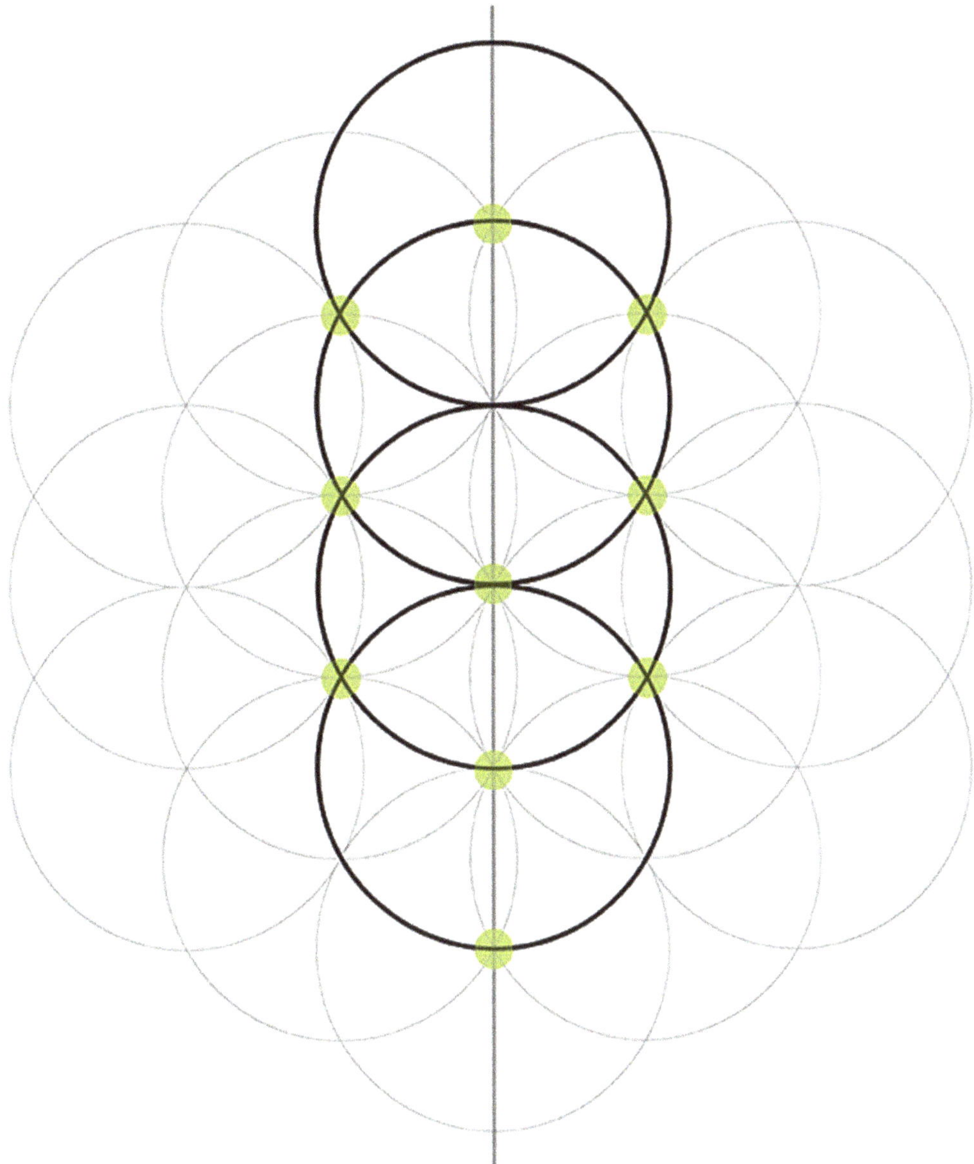

1 Once you have an understanding of how to draw the flower of life (see page 69), it's pretty straightforward to connect the dots encoded in this shape. In this image, you can observe the grid as a guide, or you can simply trace two overlapping vesica piscis formations with a vertical line as a center guide. Observe the green markings. These are your nodes that will connect the tree of life shape.

(continued)

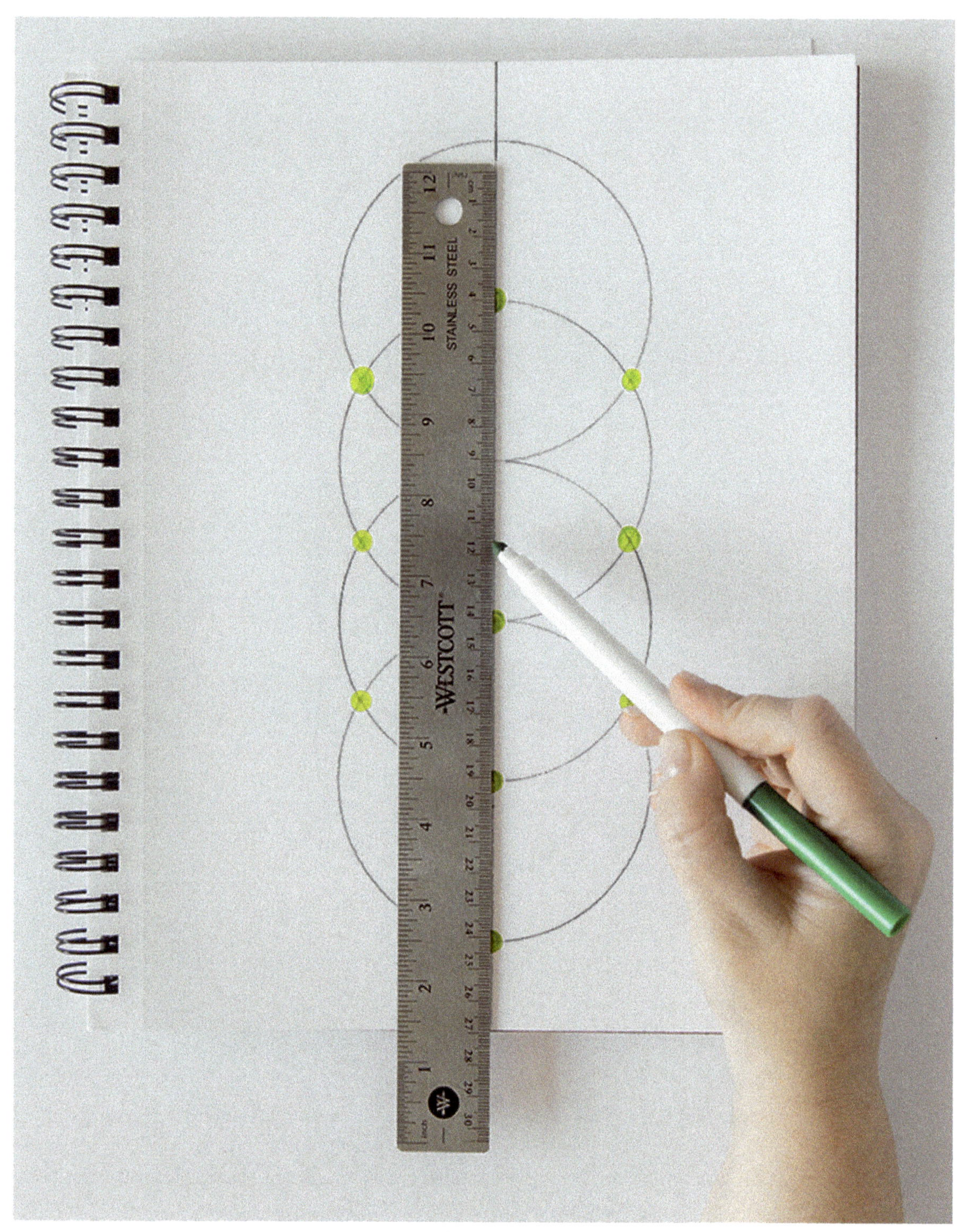

2 Using a straightedge, connect the nodes. These lines represent your "paths."

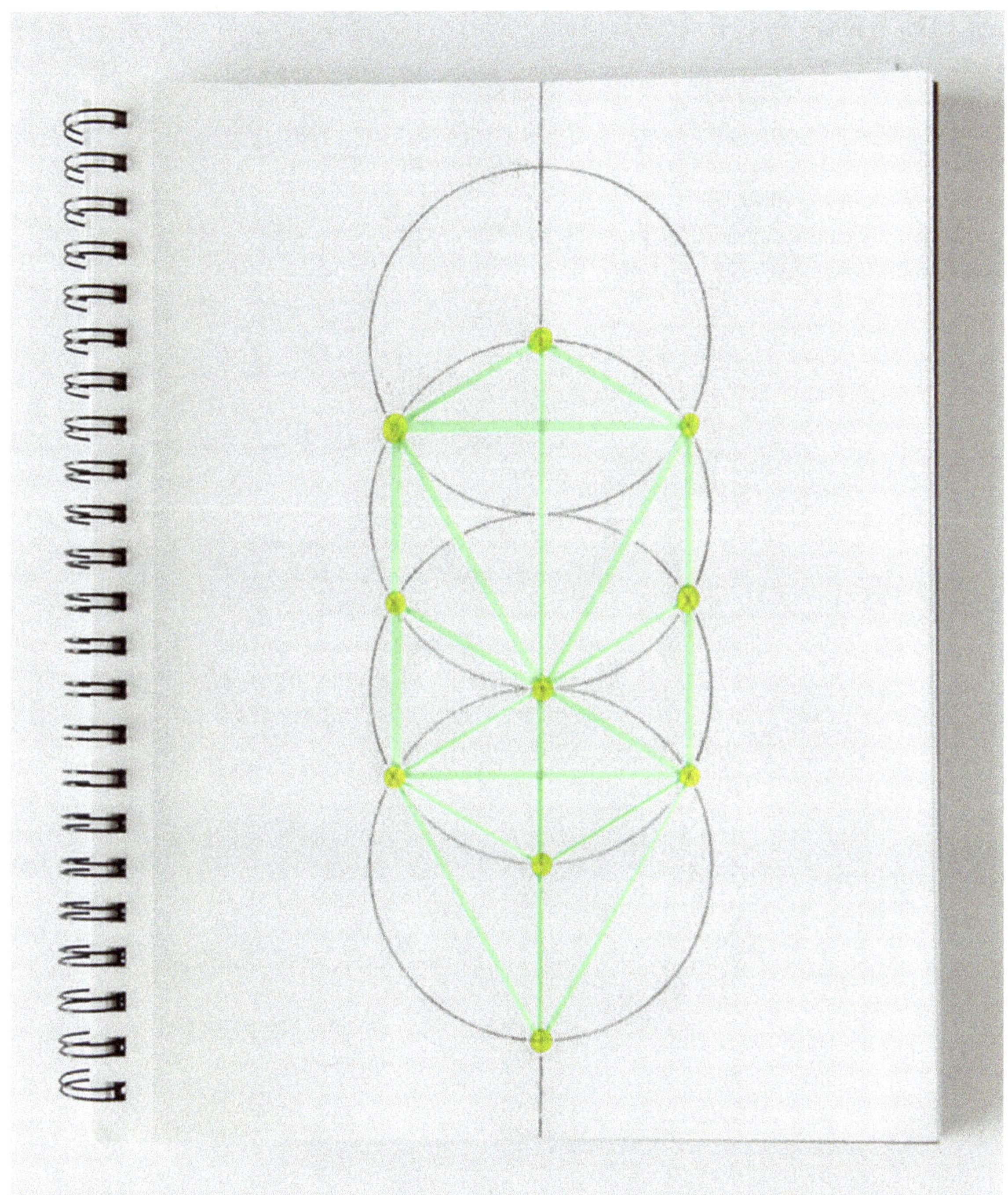

3 The connecting lines should look like this. This is the basic skeleton of a tree of life. Explore with color, width of lines, and node sizes to create a diagram of your own! See page 98, later in this chapter, for a tree of life painting project.

THE FRUIT OF LIFE

The fruit of life adds circles to the perimeter to create elongated arms, much like a six-pointed star or snowflake. In its final form, it consists of thirteen nonintersecting circles.

THE FRUIT OF LIFE: INTERPRETATIONS

Here are some symbolic meanings associated with the fruit of life.

- As in nature, the fruit is the outcome of the flower.
- The final shape is revealed when the flower of life pattern continues to grow once the bounding circles are removed.
- The fruit of life is the geometric foundation for Metatron's cube and therefore the Platonic solids.
- To uncover the fruit of life, sixty interlocking circles are drawn revolving around the central circle; for this reason, this shape has been associated with the measuring of time.

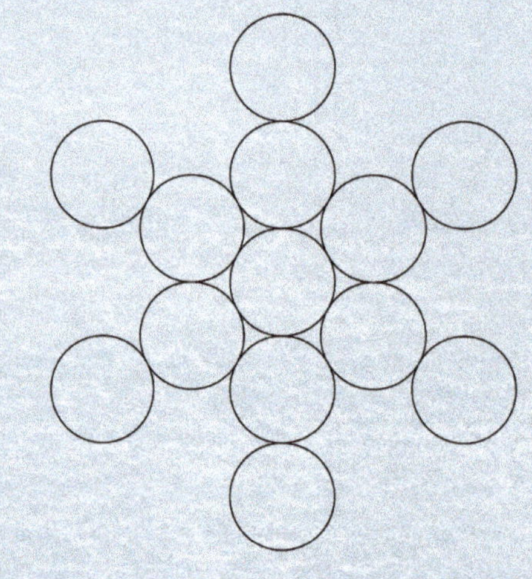

Drawing Technique

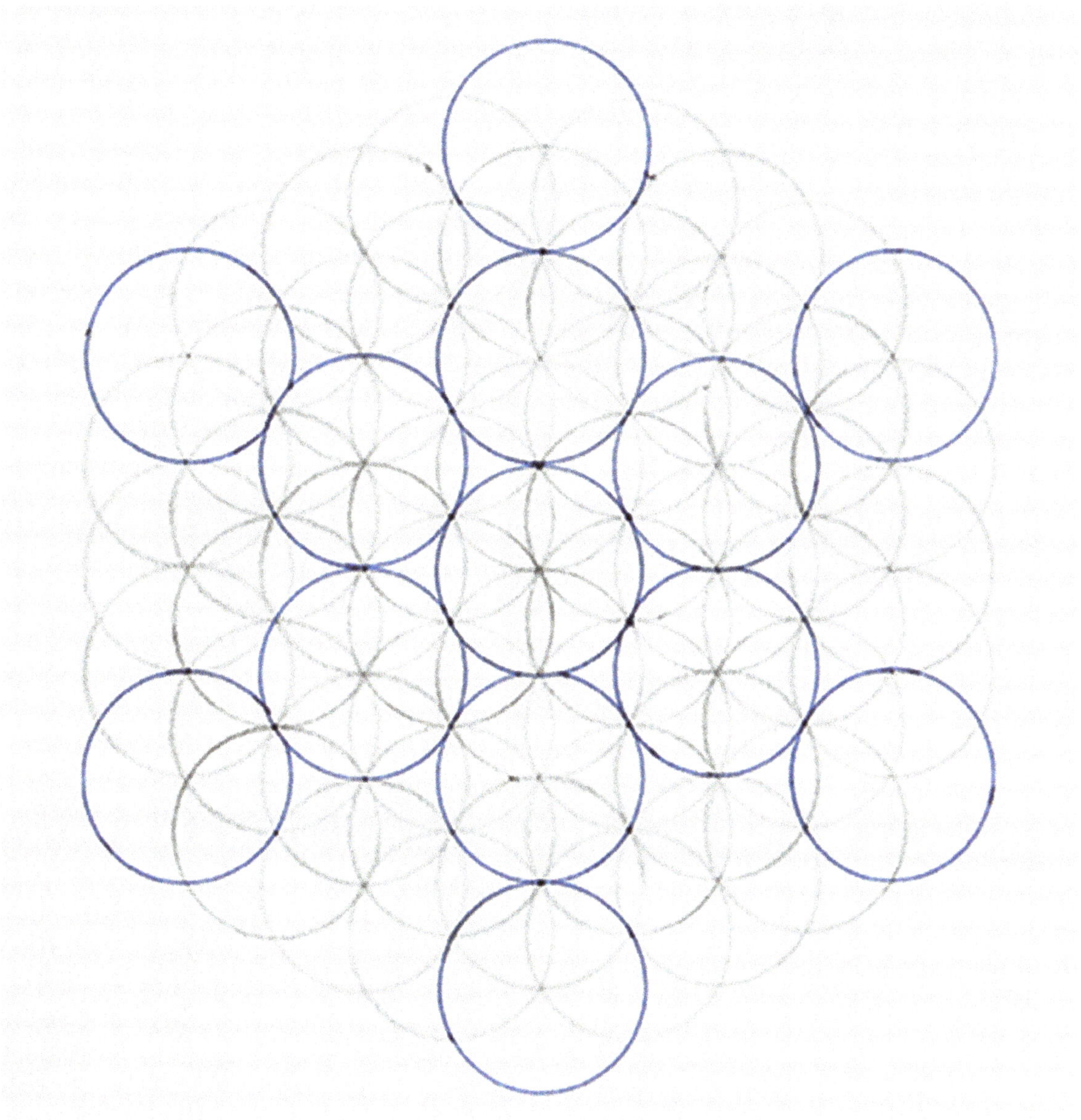

1 Begin with a grid that consists of sixty-one interlocking circles. This is the natural continuation of the flower of life, once the outer circles are removed. The grid will have an overall hexagonal form. This is considered to be an important moment of discovery, because once the boundaries are removed, geometric secrets are revealed. Select the thirteen nonintersecting circles as shown to trace over your grid.

(continued)

2 It's helpful to use a pencil for your grid and a pen for your final shape so you can easily erase the original interlocking circles and only your final shape will remain.

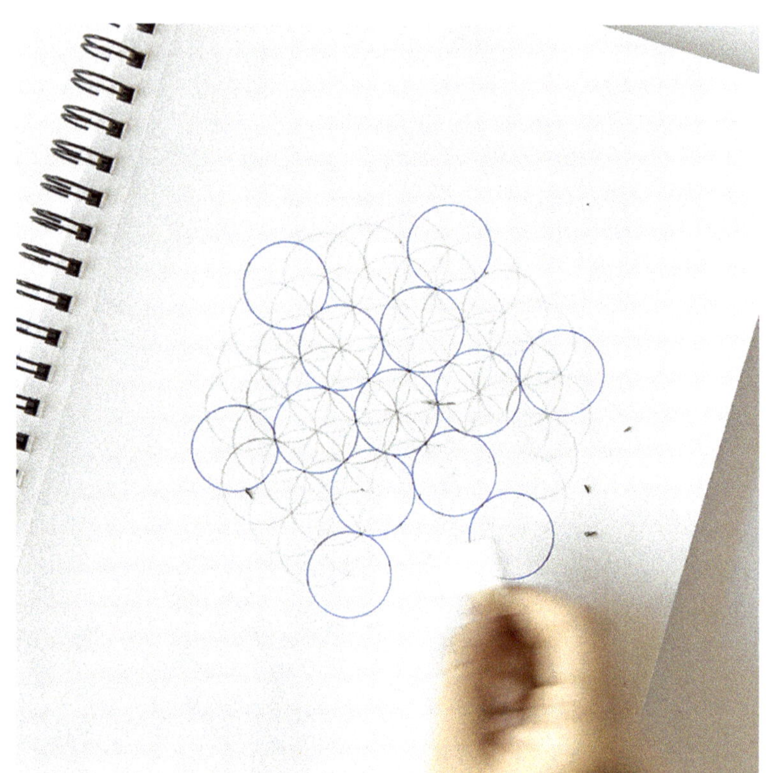

3 This is the fruit of life!

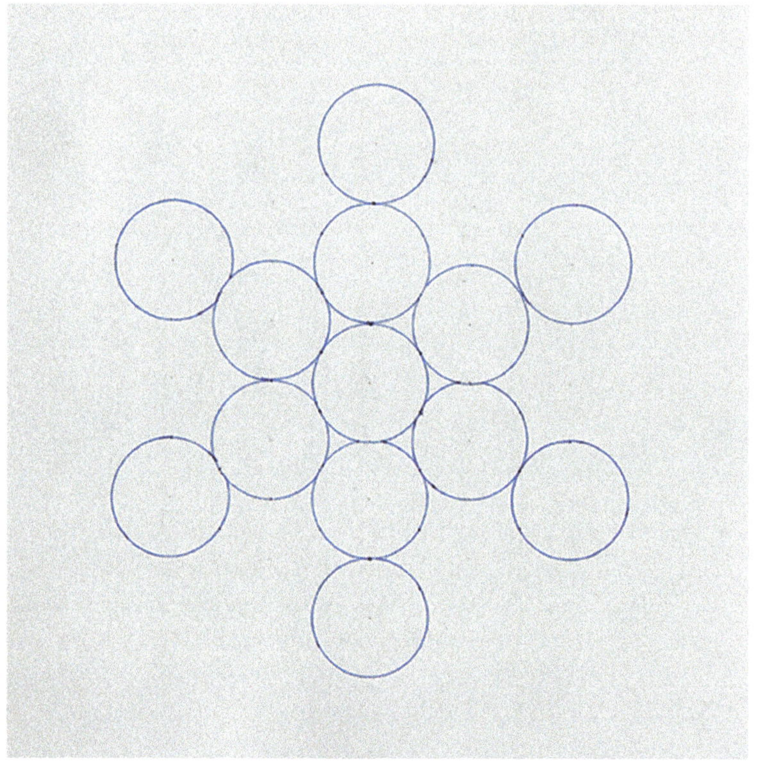

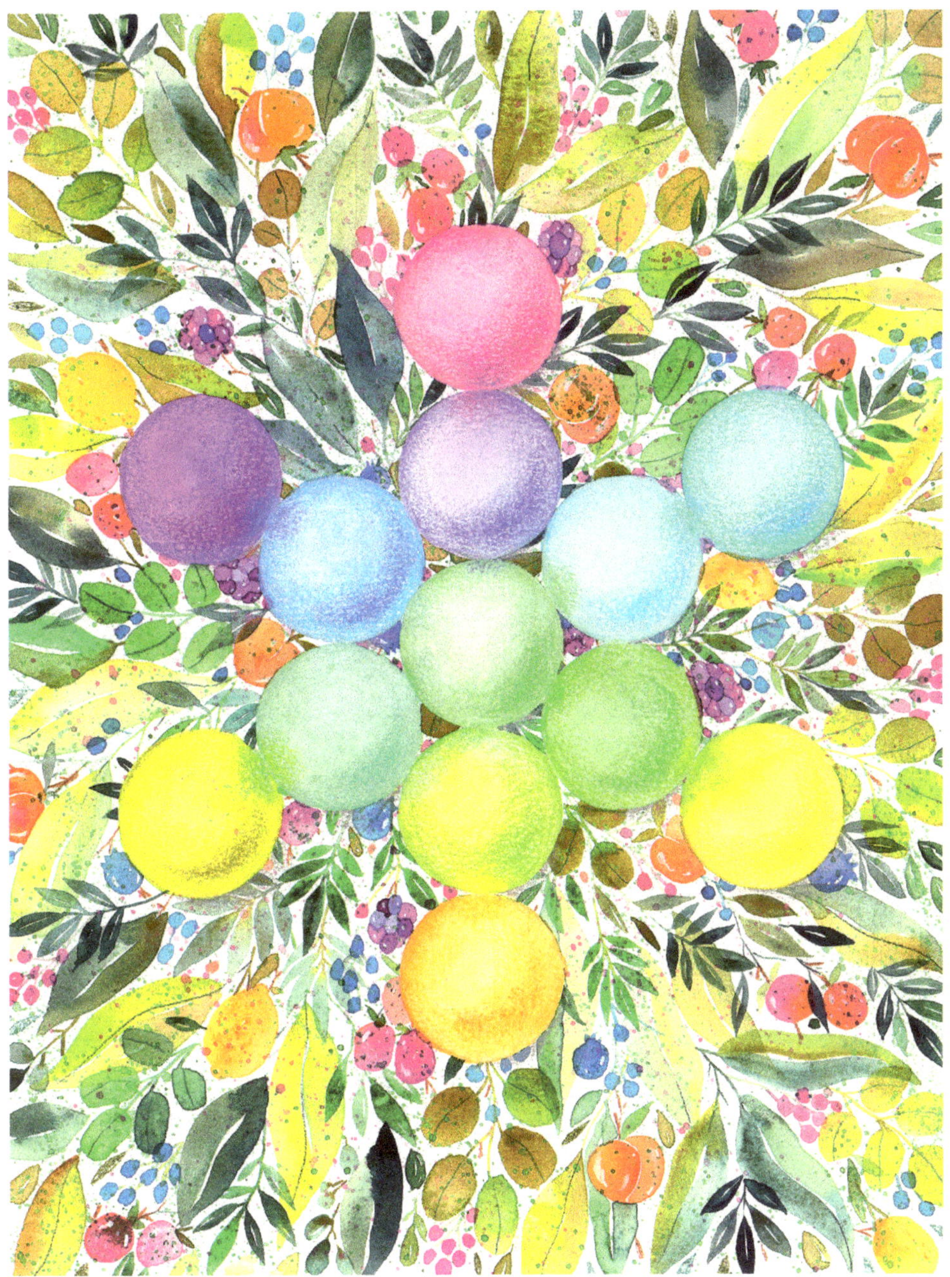

A tip for painting this particular style is to use masking fluid over your circles and paint freely around the geometric shape. I even added paint splatter over the entire composition while the masking fluid protects the circles. Once the loose foliage, fruit, and splatter design dried, I proceeded to remove the masking fluid and paint colorful circles. Then I used colored pencils to add shading to the circles to turn them into spherical shapes.

ARTISTIC EXPLORATION: ORGANIC SHAPES, MEDIUMS, AND COLORS

Artistic exploration is an important phase while creating sacred geometry artwork. Once you have the technical shape, let loose. Explore with organic shapes, mediums, and colors. This illustration is merely an attempt to expand your creative vision as to what you can make with your geometric shapes, as you can integrate them into your personal artistic style and use any medium your heart desires.

TREE OF LIFE PAINTING WITH OPAQUE PAINT ON BLACK PAPER

For this project, I am using Legion Stonehenge Aqua Black watercolor paper, but you can use any black watercolor paper. You can use opaque watercolor, gouache, acrylic, or a mixture of regular watercolor paint and white gouache for opacity. In this case, I am using pastel watercolors by White Nights, which are creamy and contrast nicely over a black surface. I am also using metallic and iridescent watercolors by Hydracolor, but any type of metallic medium will work.

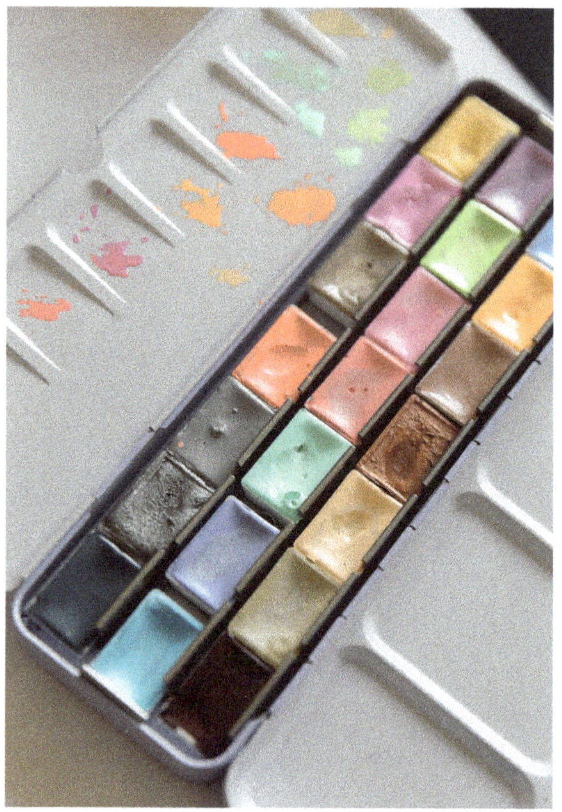

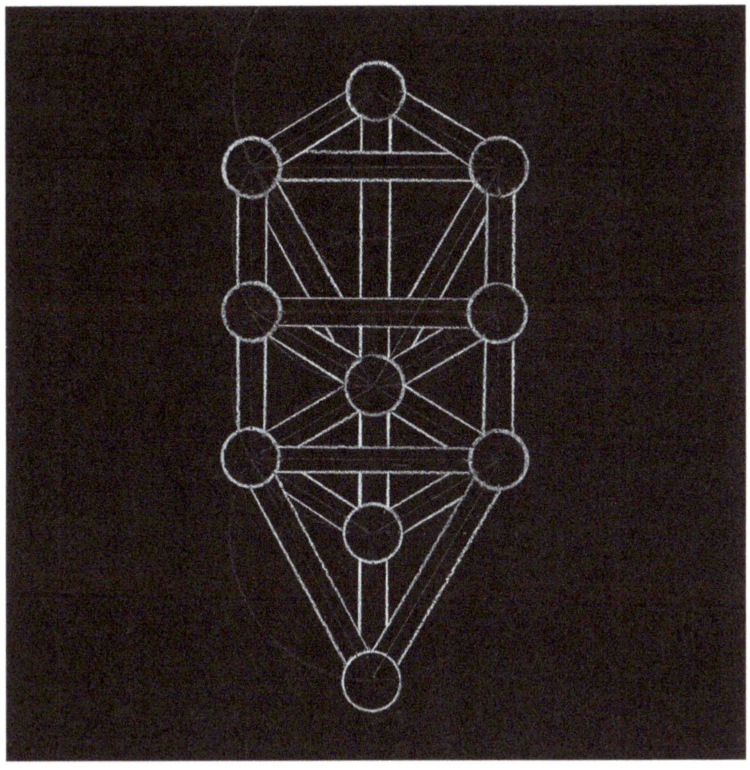

1 Trace a tree of life shape on black watercolor paper (see page 91). I find it easiest to trace the grid using a pencil, then use a white pencil to draw the final circles and lines.

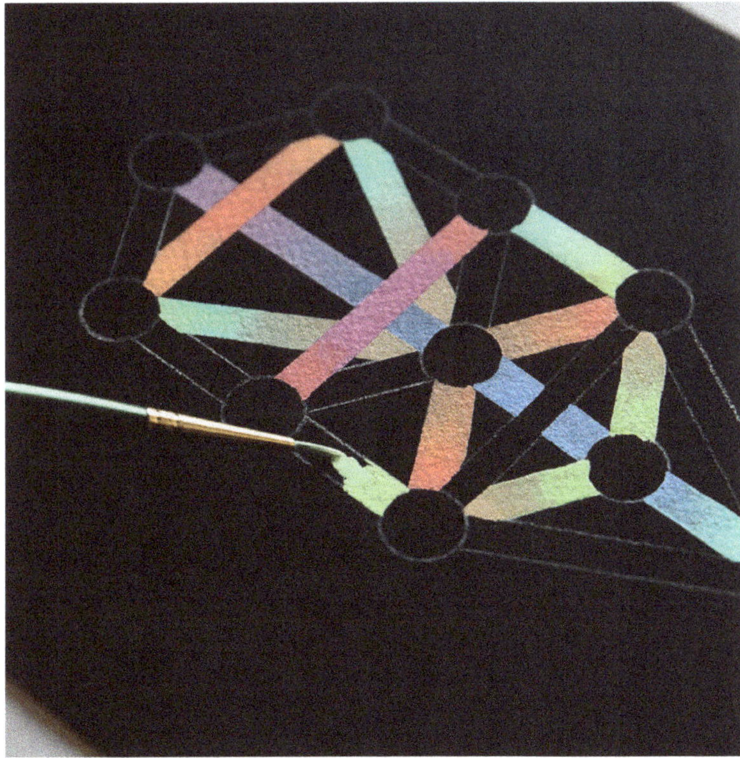

2 Paint the bars (paths) using your opaque medium. I am blending a couple of colors on each bar for an interesting effect.

(continued)

3 Let the paint dry completely.

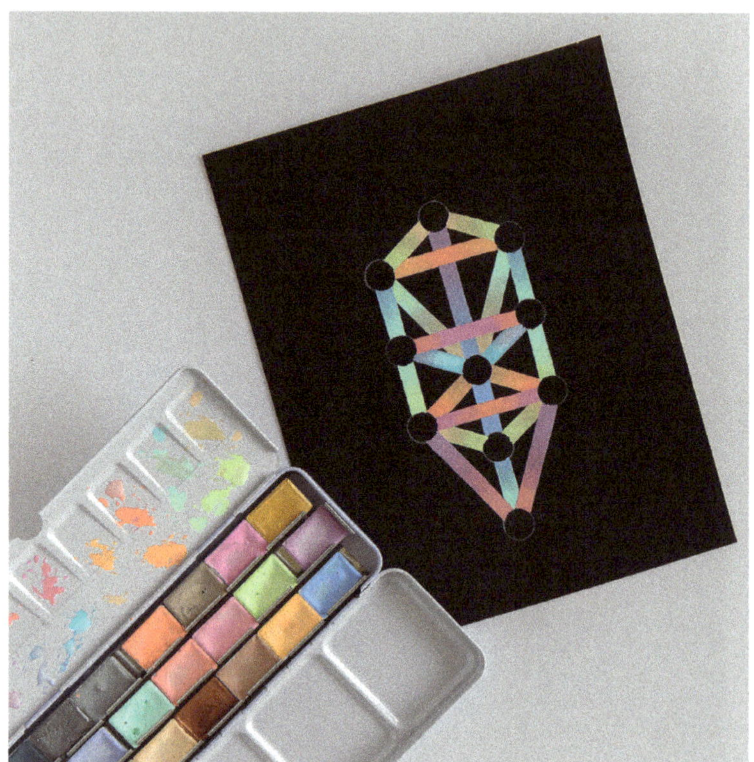

4 Paint the circles using the metallic medium to create a beautiful contrast.

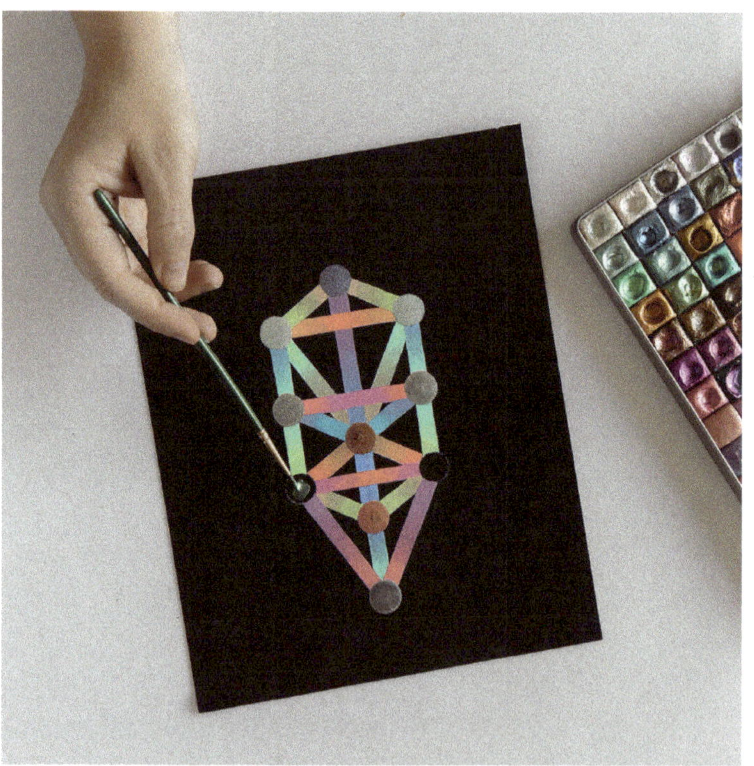

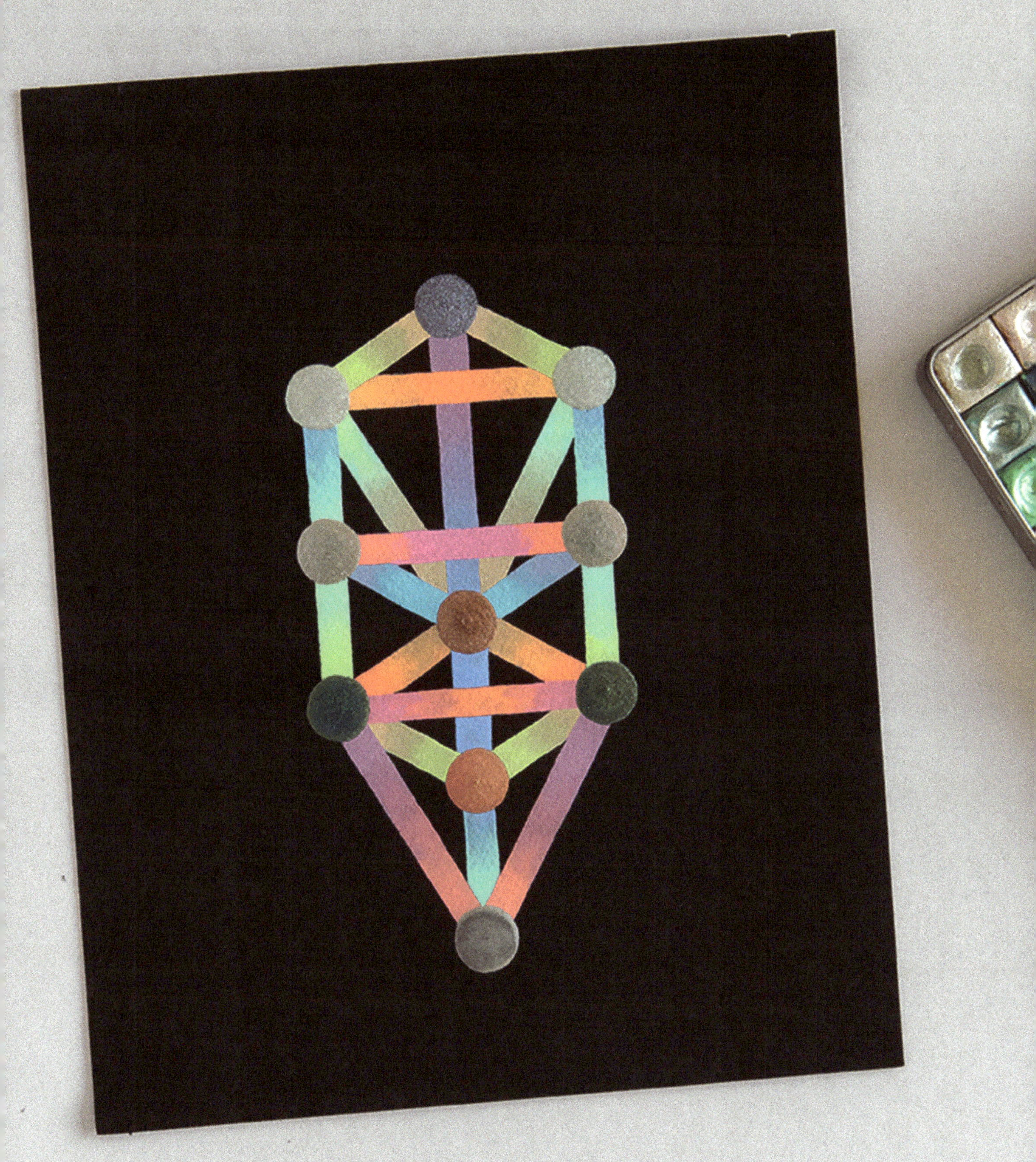

CRYSTAL GRID

All sacred geometry formations are widely used as guides to place special elements over, such as crystals, gems, or precious stones. This is a meditative practice that adds beauty and enchantment to your sacred space. In fact, there are many sacred geometry altar cloths available for this purpose, but I find it much more powerful to draw these shapes on my own.

Once your tree of life painting from the previous project is completely dry, place stones on the intersections. I place my stones intuitively, but if you want to dive deeper into this practice, I recommend learning about crystal meanings and formations. Each stone has its own power attributed to feelings, manifestations, and intentions. This practice is an art form of its own.

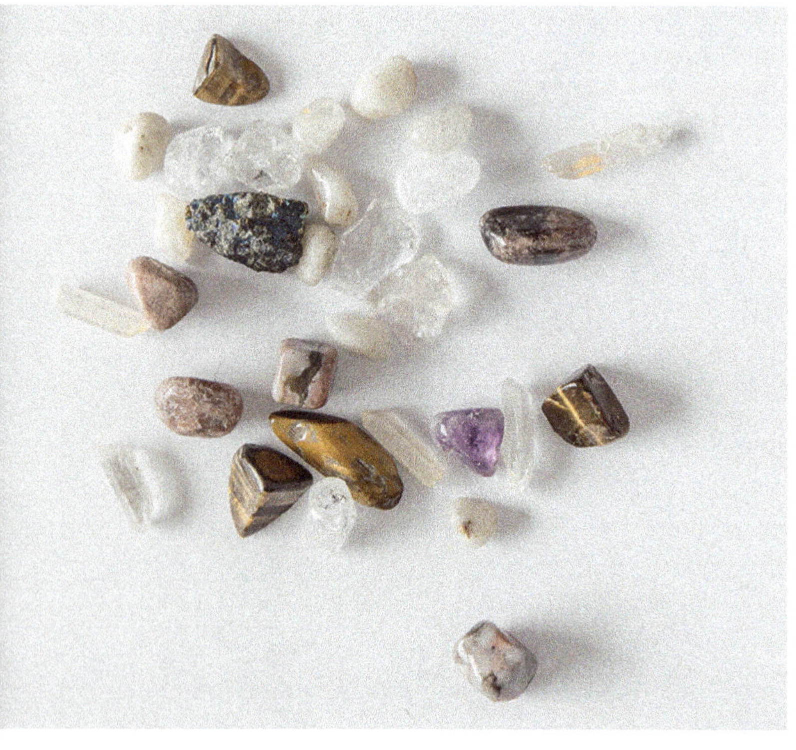

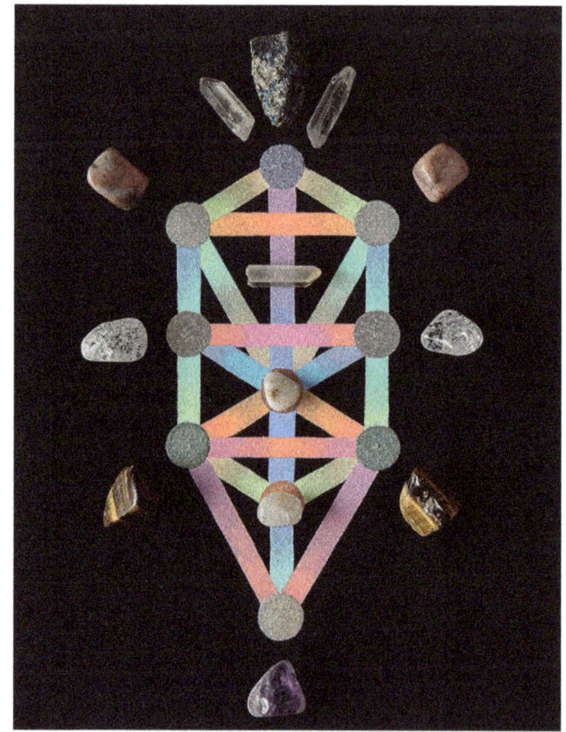

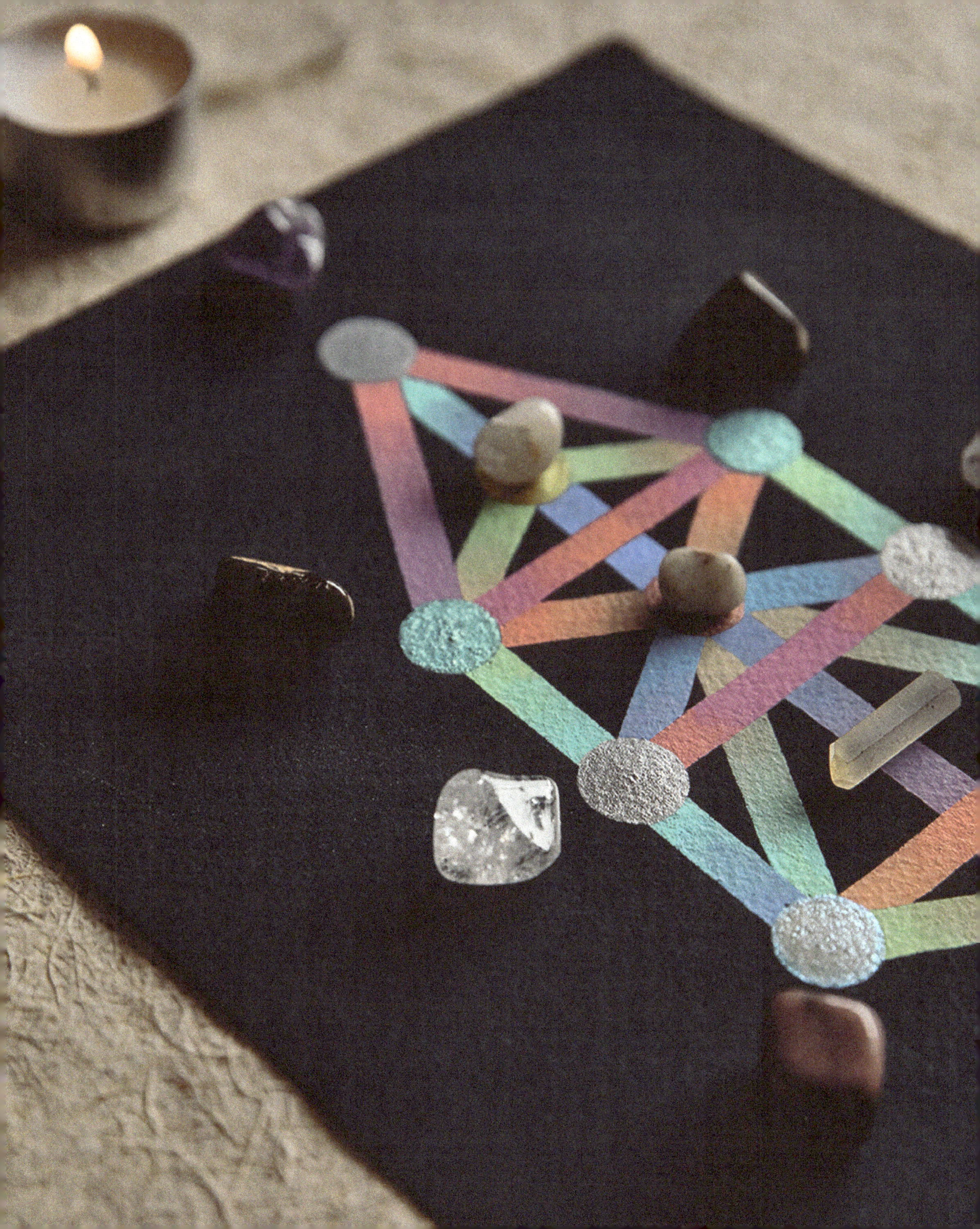

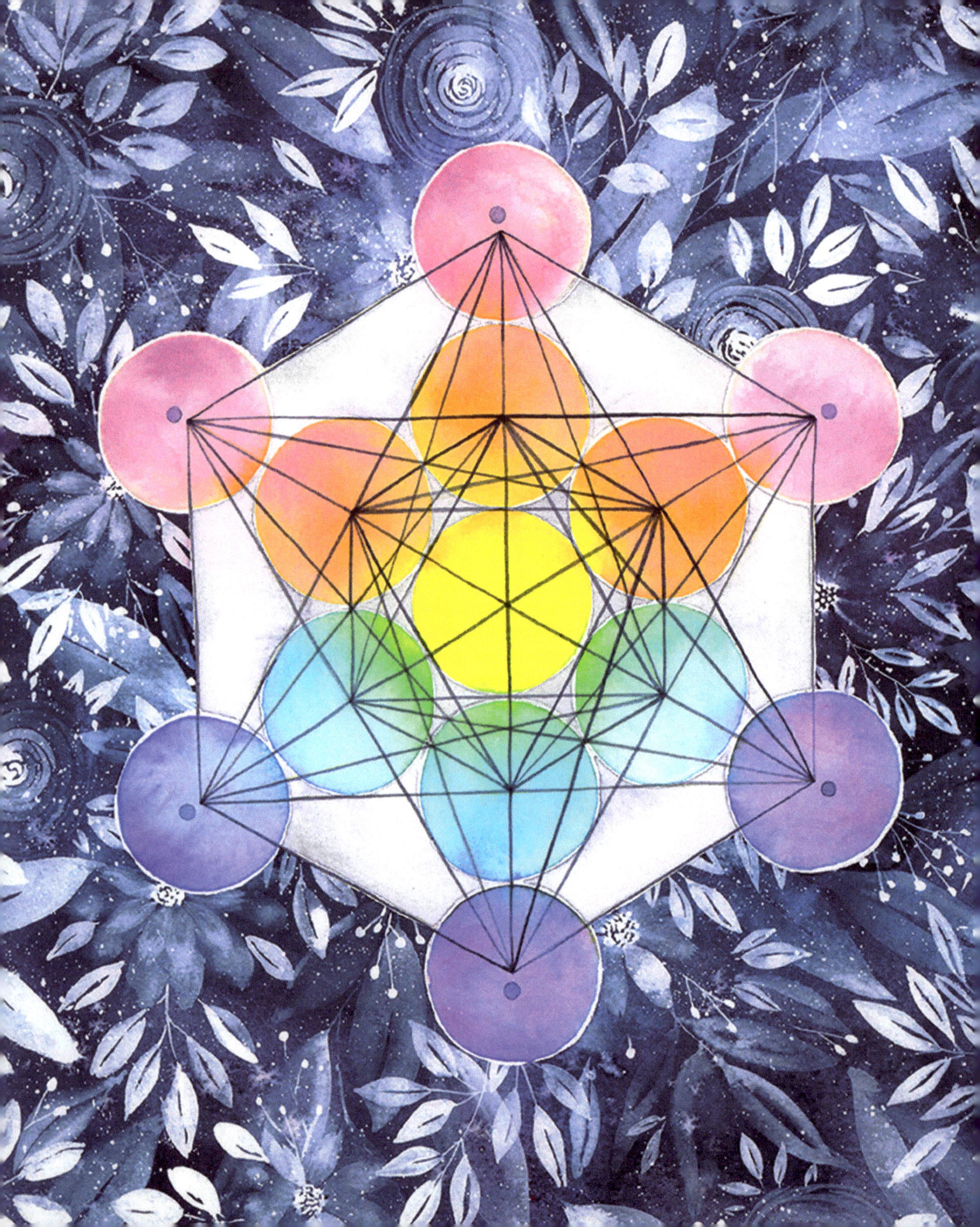

6

METATRON'S CUBE

Metatron's cube may appear to be quite complex at first glance, but if you've made it this far, it will feel quite natural to draw. Keep in mind that sacred geometry is a growing system; if you get ahead of yourself, you may get lost in the process. Make sure you've gotten the hang of previous formations before diving into this next phase.

THE POWER OF METATRON'S CUBE

This form is named after the archangel Metatron. It consists of thirteen circles, each of which has lines coming out of the center, extending to the center of the remaining twelve circles.

Medieval Italian mathematician Leonardo Pisano, also known as Fibonacci, is credited with the study of this figure. He is more commonly known for the famous Fibonacci sequence and the golden ratio.

METATRON'S CUBE: INTERPRETATIONS

Here are some symbolic meanings associated with Metatron's cube.

- Progression of the fruit of life shape
- Considered complex and majestic because of the ample variety of shapes found within this formation, specifically the Platonic solids
- Represents balance between female and male energy exemplified by the curves and straight lines

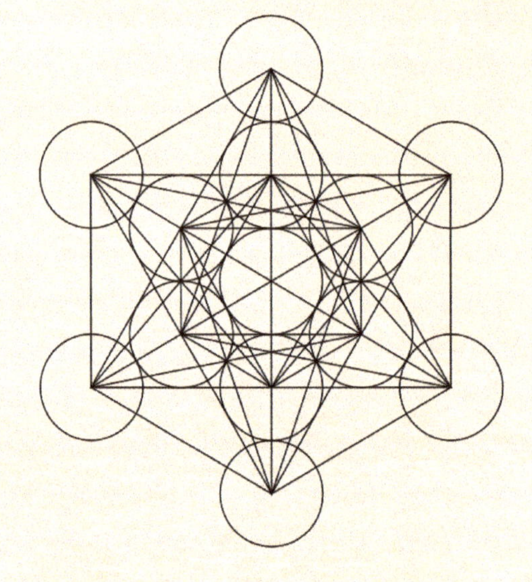

Drawing Technique

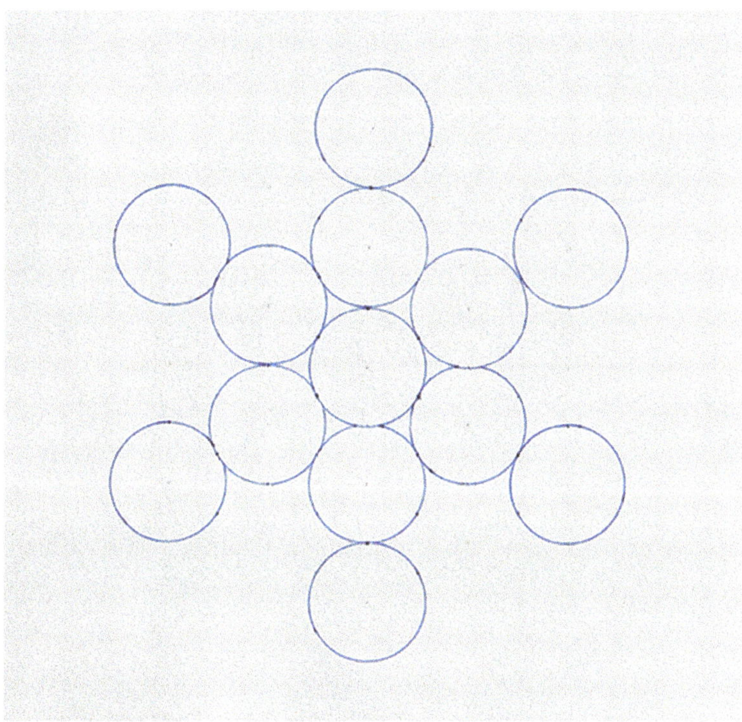

1 Follow the steps on page 95 to draw the fruit of life shape.

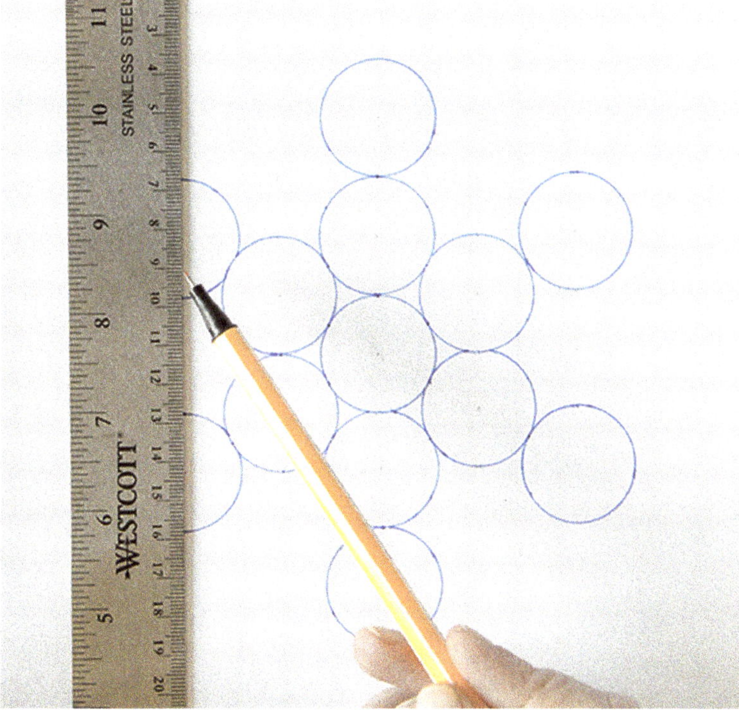

2 Using your straightedge, connect the center of each circle to the center of the remaining circles. Use the compass needle markings for these central points.

(continued)

3 Notice the pink lines: This is what your first circle's extending lines will look like. I find it easiest to begin connecting all the outer circles' centers first.

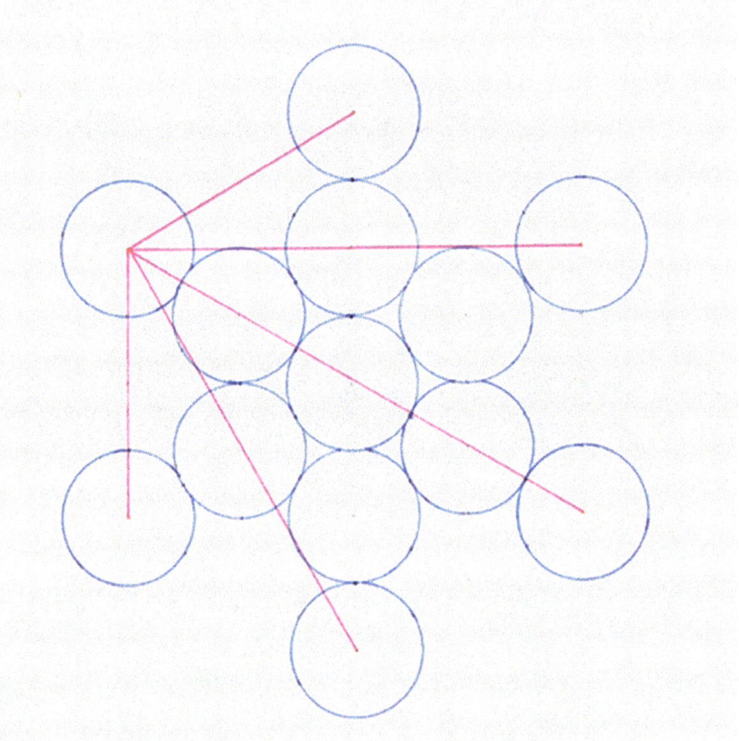

4 Continue connecting the center of your first circle with the remaining circles; here, I am using an orange pen to demonstrate these lines.

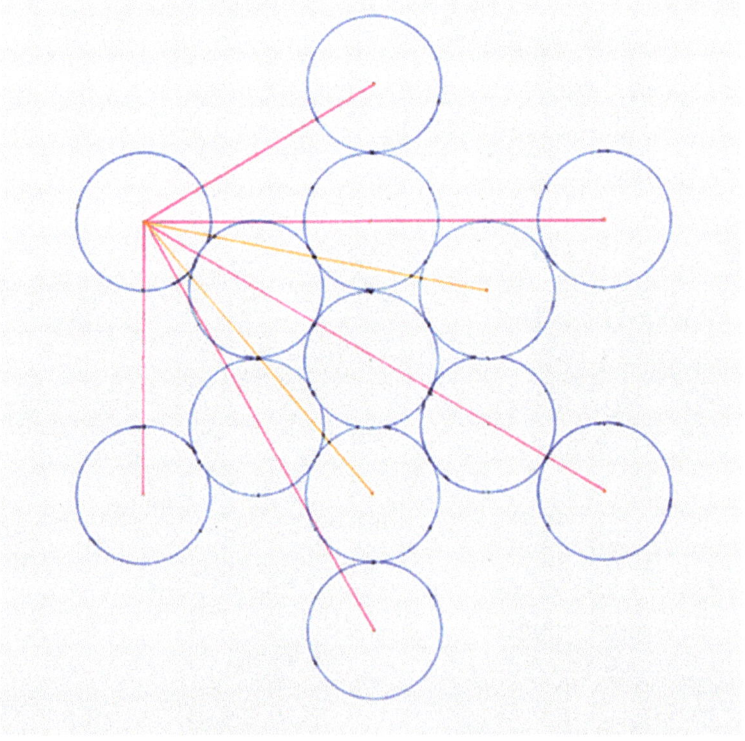

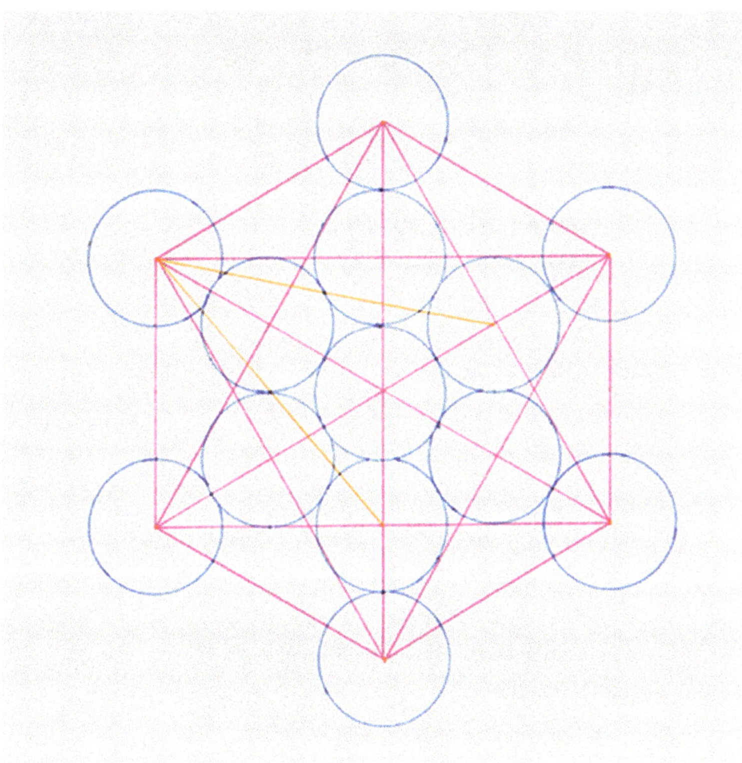

5 At this stage, I have connected the centers of all the outer circles for the hexagonal shape.

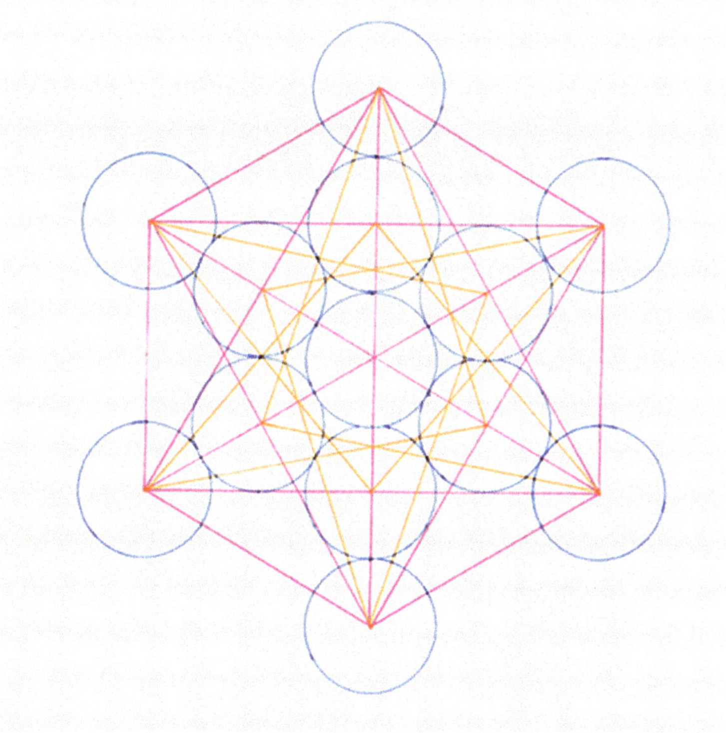

6 Repeat the connecting process with the rest of the circles. You have completed a Metatron's cube!

PLATONIC SOLIDS: SHAPES DERIVED FROM METATRON'S CUBE

The ancient Greek philosopher Plato believed he could describe the universe using five shapes. Geometric rules that apply to each Platonic solid include:

- All of its faces are the same size.
- All of its edges are the same length.
- All points fit in a sphere perfectly.

PLATONIC SOLIDS: INTERPRETATIONS

Here are some symbolic meanings associated with Platonic solids.

- Alchemy is thought to originate from these shapes.
- All Platonic solids can be found embedded in Metatron's cube.
- Plato theorized that a classical element (earth, water, air, fire, ether) was associated with each of these regular solids.
- Each solid is said to have a key function attached to it.

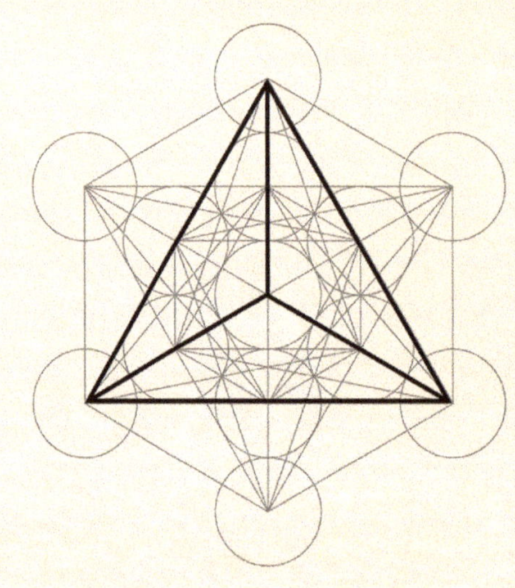

Tetrahedron
Element: Fire
Key Function: Manifestation

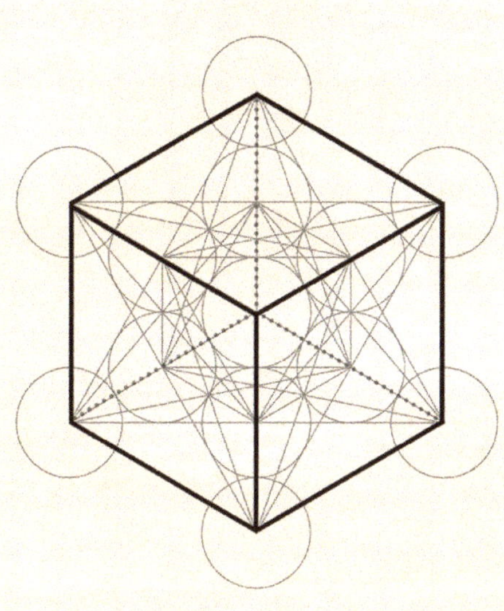

Cube/Hexahedron

Element: Earth

Key Function: Grounding

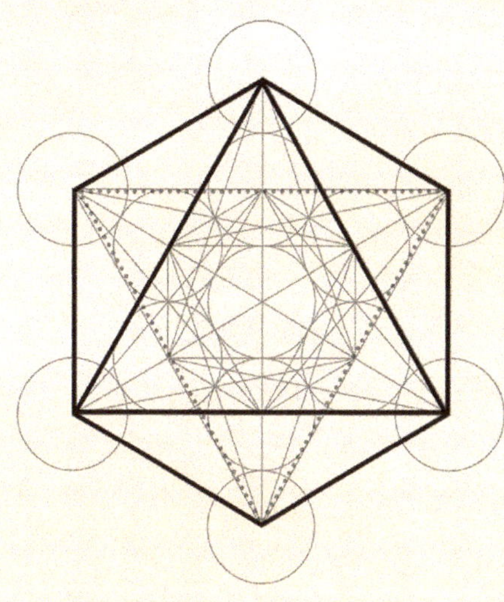

Octahedron

Element: Air

Key Function: Integration

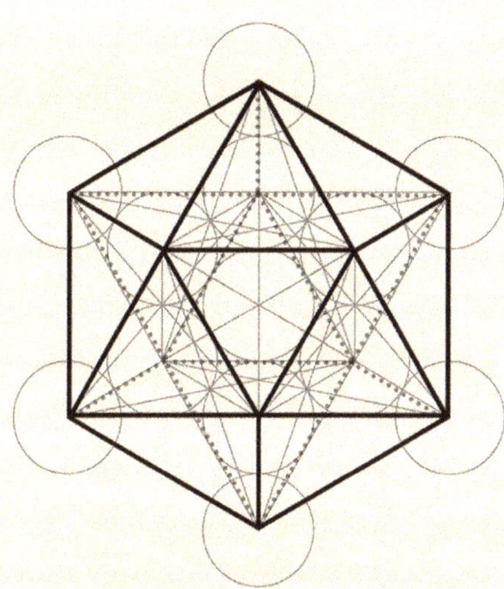

Icosahedron

Element: Water

Key Function: Transformation

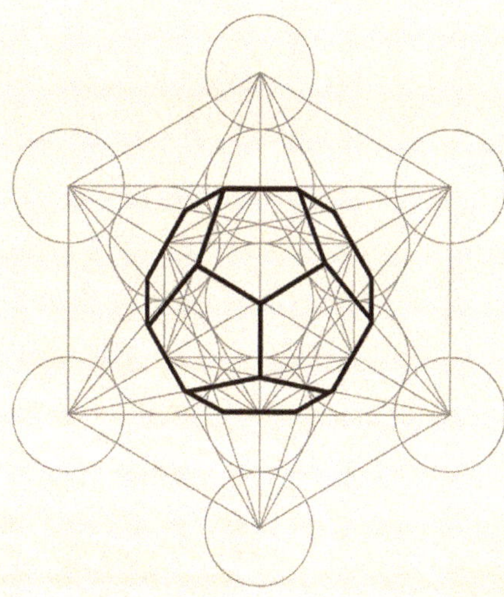

Dodecahedron

Element: Ether

Key Function: Ascension and mystery

Drawing Technique

Extracting the Platonic solids from Metatron's cube is quite simple and can be traced through observation, with the exception of the dodecahedron, which I will demonstrate step by step.

Observe the bold lines on the previous page in reference to the lighter gray lines to create your shapes.

While the rest of the Platonic solids are connected by the center points of different circles in Metatron's cube or even the fruit of life, the dodecahedron has just a couple of lines that are borne out of other intersections.

1 Begin with a complete Metatron's cube (see page 107).

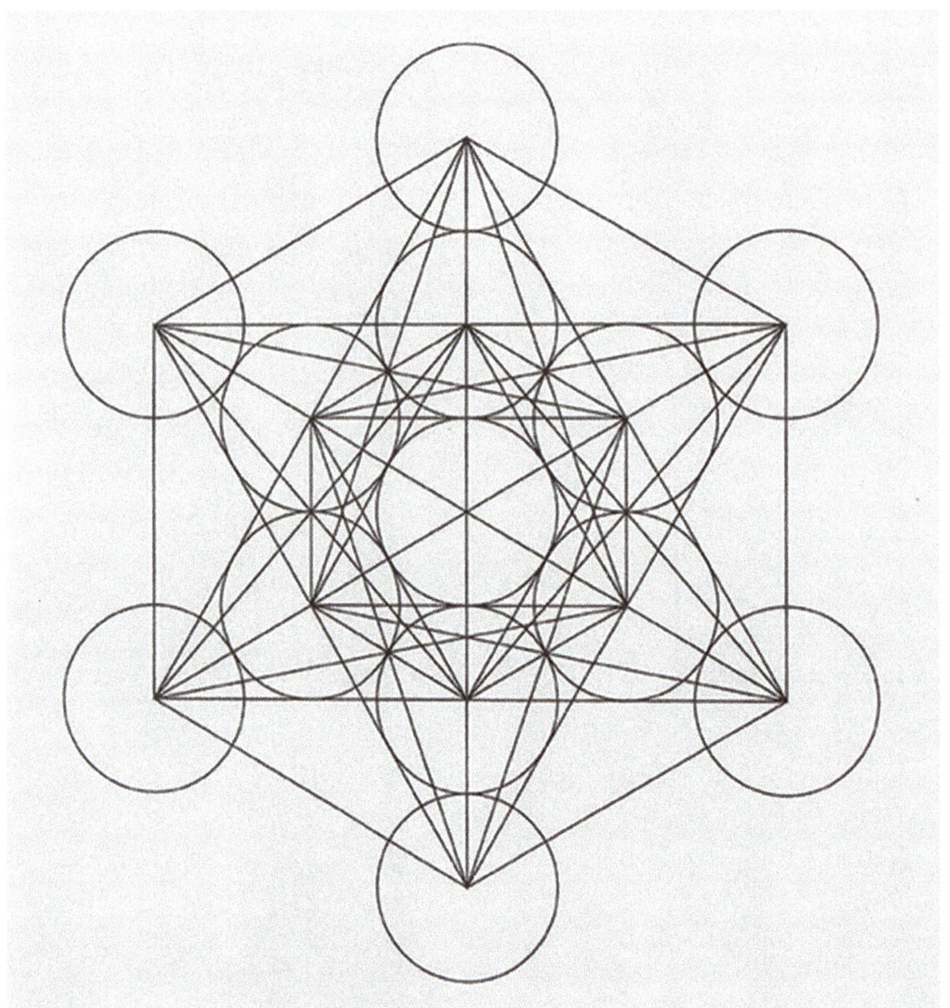

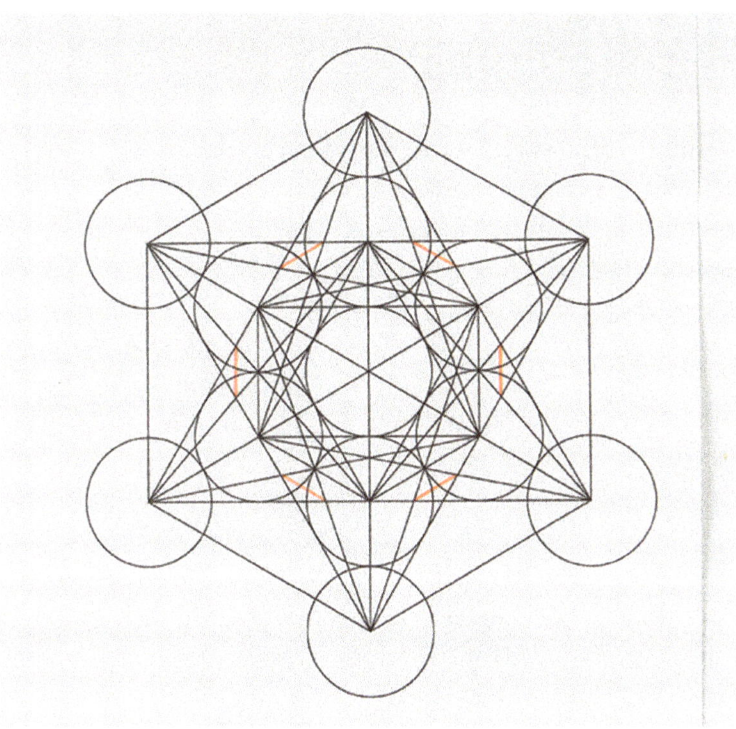

2 Note the orange lines, which are the indicators for the rest of the shape.

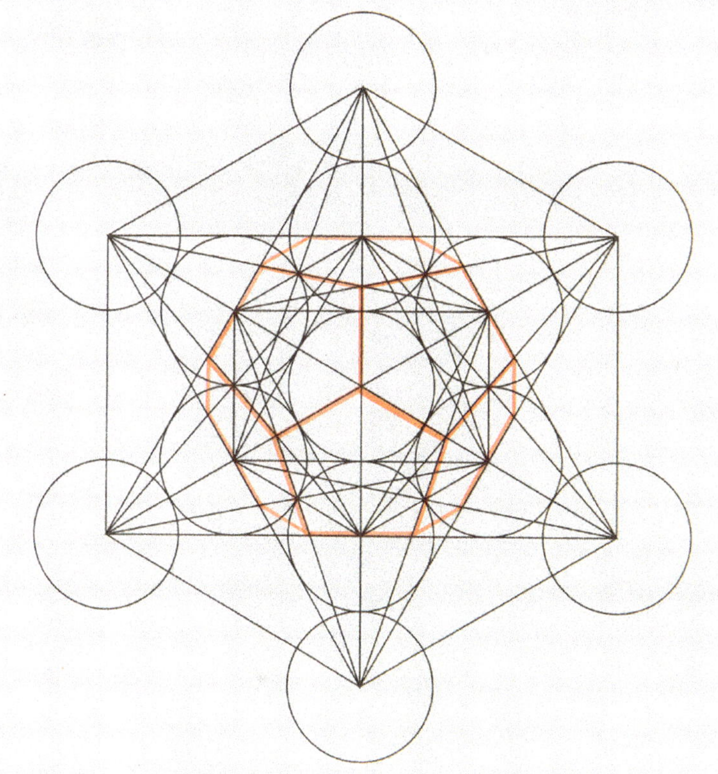

3 Continue to connect the lines from this point on, as demonstrated in this image. The lines will eventually connect in the center point of the original circle. You've made a dodecahedron!

ARTISTIC EXPLORATION: EMPHASIZING SPECIFIC LINES

What makes this type of art so interesting to explore is that ultimately the viewer can observe the shape without knowing all the steps and geometric alignments that took place to get to the final result. In the end, you decide which lines and formations to emphasize when it comes to your artwork. In this watercolor painting, I decided to keep the straight lines and painted an abstract landscape in the background.

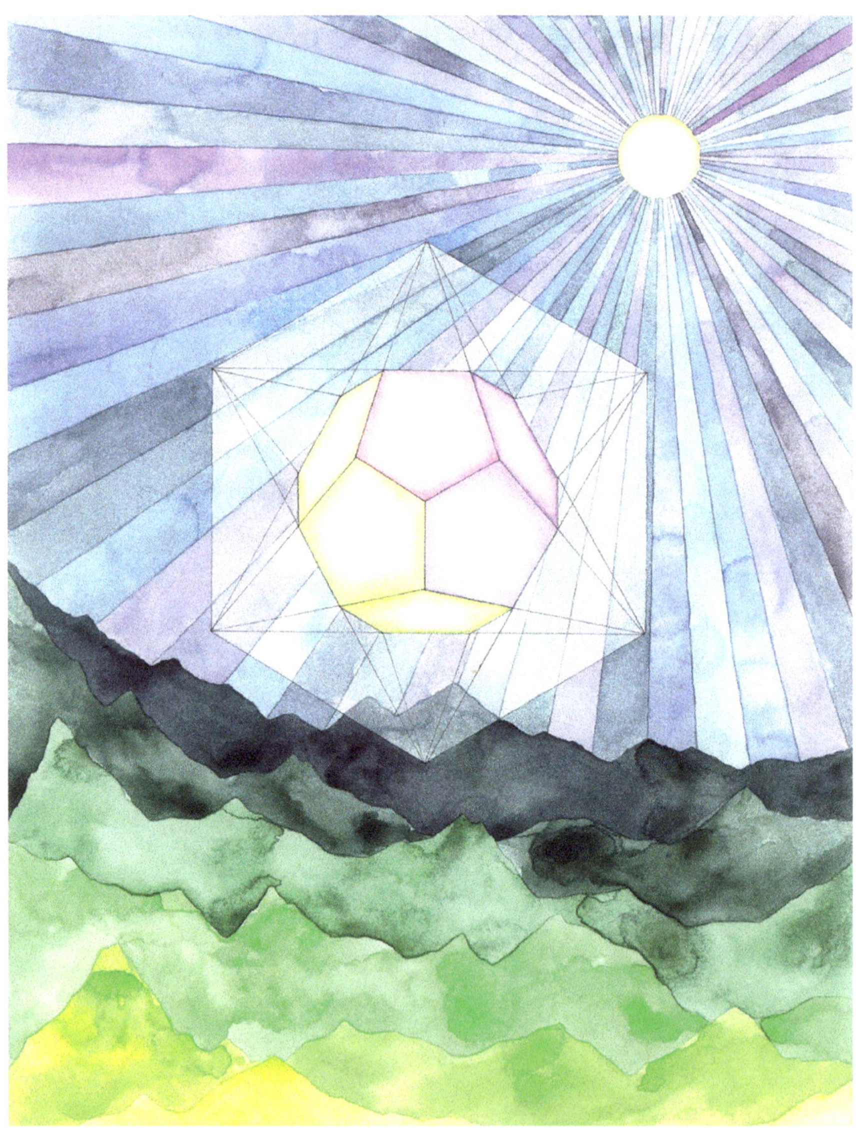

PLATONIC SOLIDS ON A SKY BACKGROUND

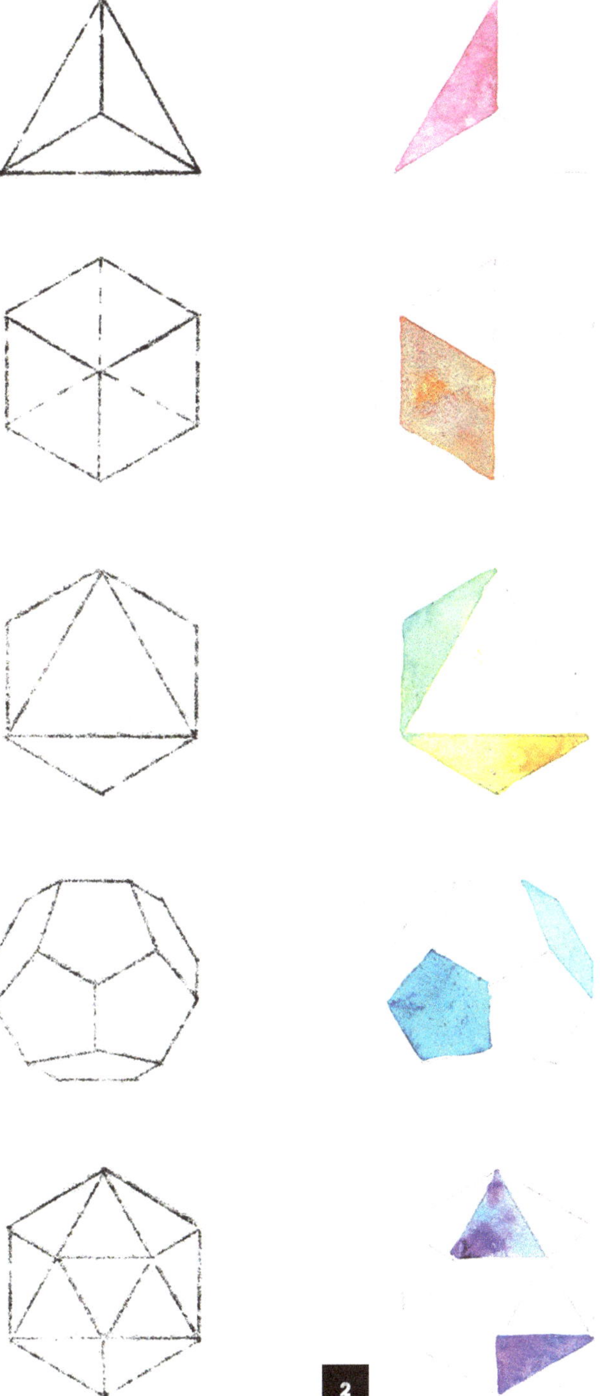

1 Trace the outlines of all five platonic solids on watercolor paper.

2 Paint selected areas of your shapes in a translucent watercolor mixture. I designated a certain color for each shape, but the color choices are up to you!

(continued)

3 Let those areas of paint dry completely to avoid bleeding and paint neighboring sides of each shape using a more saturated tone. In watercolor, we do this by adding more paint and less water to our mixture.

4 Continue with the rest of the areas, mixing it up a bit with tone and contrast. You can also add a bit of salt while the paint is still wet for an interesting effect.

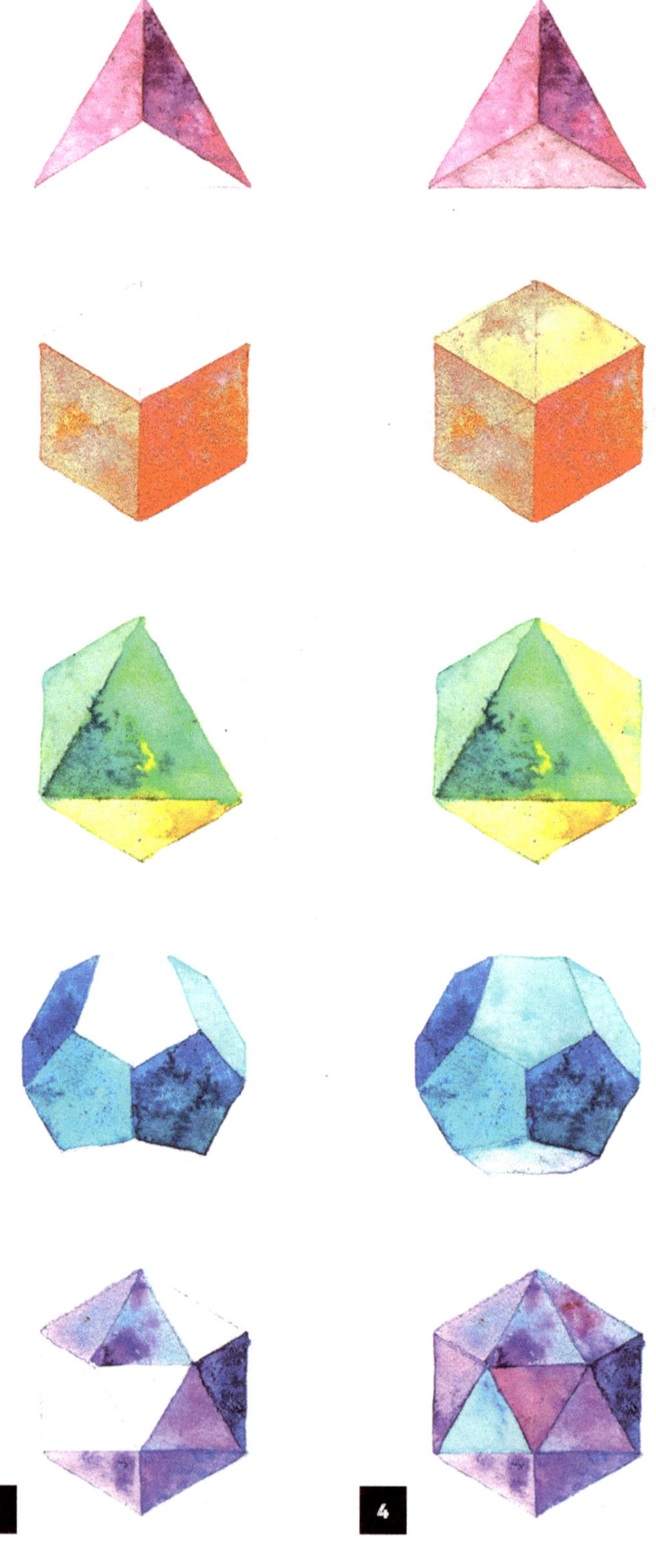

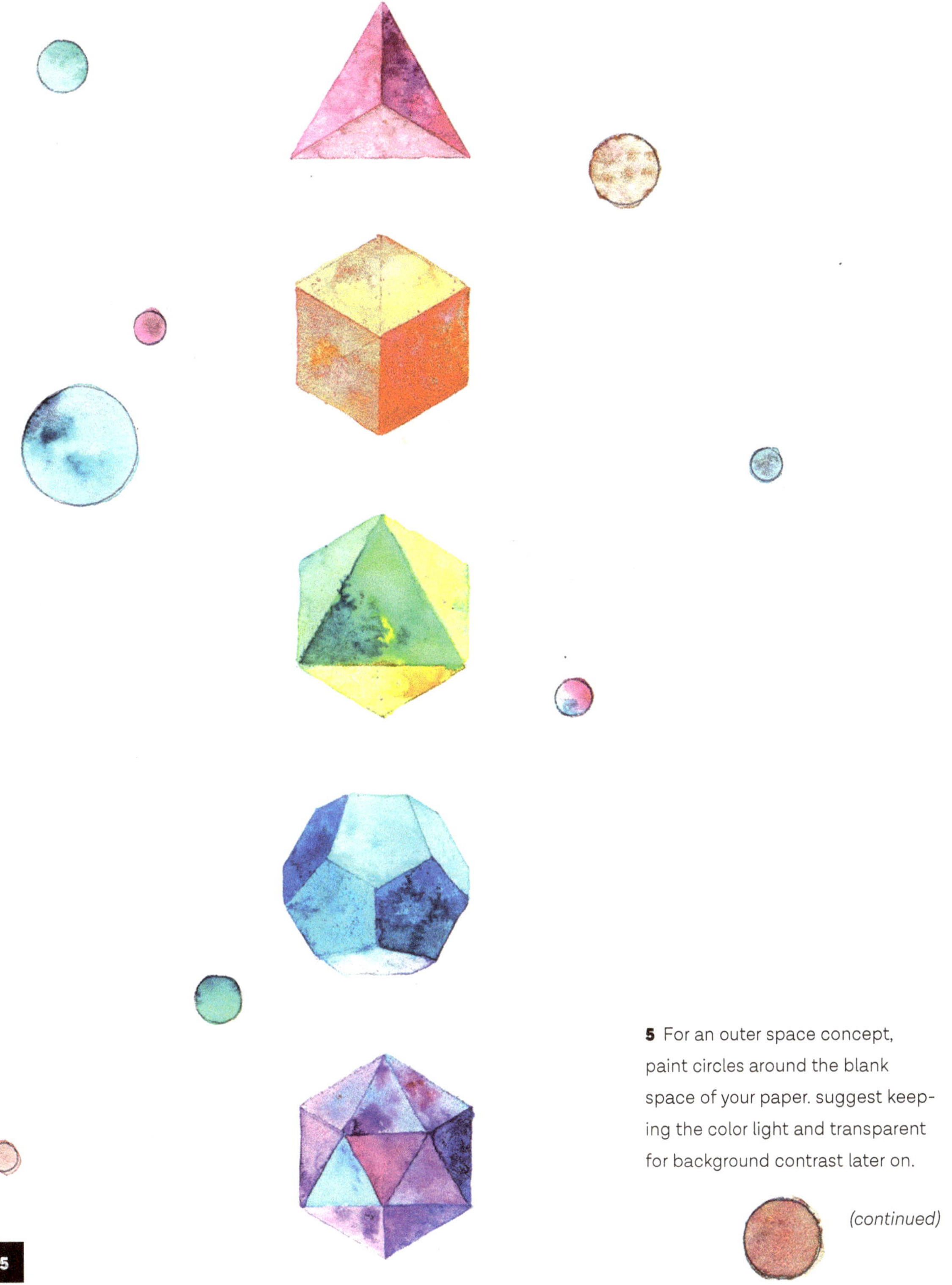

5

5 For an outer space concept, paint circles around the blank space of your paper. suggest keeping the color light and transparent for background contrast later on.

(continued)

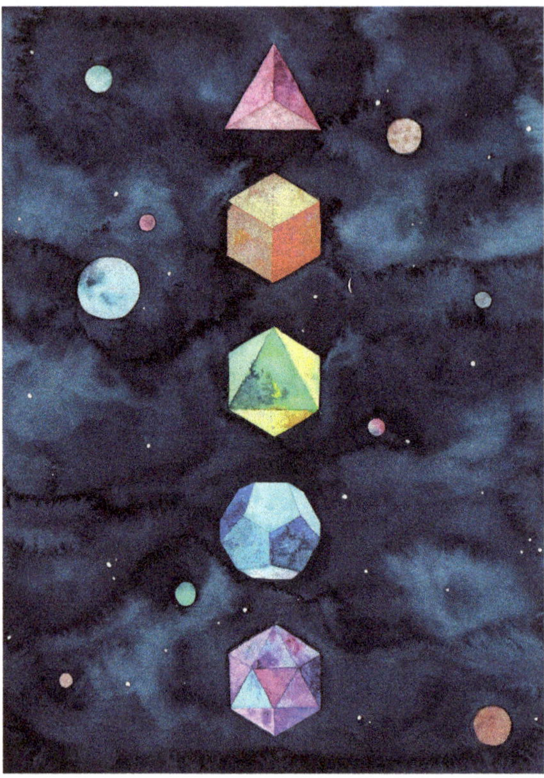

6 Now we paint our background! Notice how I left a few pockets of white dots and a mini moon to make use of the white paper.

TIPS FOR PAINTING DARK WATERCOLOR BACKGROUNDS

- Make quite a bit of paint mixture before you start painting. Seamless backgrounds are achieved by painting fast! You don't want to waste time by mixing in more water with paint throughout this process. The amount of paint you will need is relative to the size of your paper.
- To create a dark paint base with watercolors, you will have to use quite a bit of paint. In this example, I'm mixing up indigo tube paint and turquoise liquid watercolor. The consistency and creaminess of the tube form combined with the vibrancy of liquid watercolors is a good formula for achieving an abundant concentrated paint mixture. If you only have watercolor pans or cakes, lather up a lot of paint using your darker blues.
- Do not outline your shapes with watercolor beforehand, as this will just create a border that will dry before you paint the rest of the background. It's best to paint by sections, working your way around the blank space while painting around the previously painted shapes. Follow the edges of each shape and glide your paint to the edges.
- Make sure your foreground areas are completely dry before painting your dark background to avoid bleeding.
- Work fast and keep the edges of your painted sections moist to pick up where you left off, allowing the paint to blend.

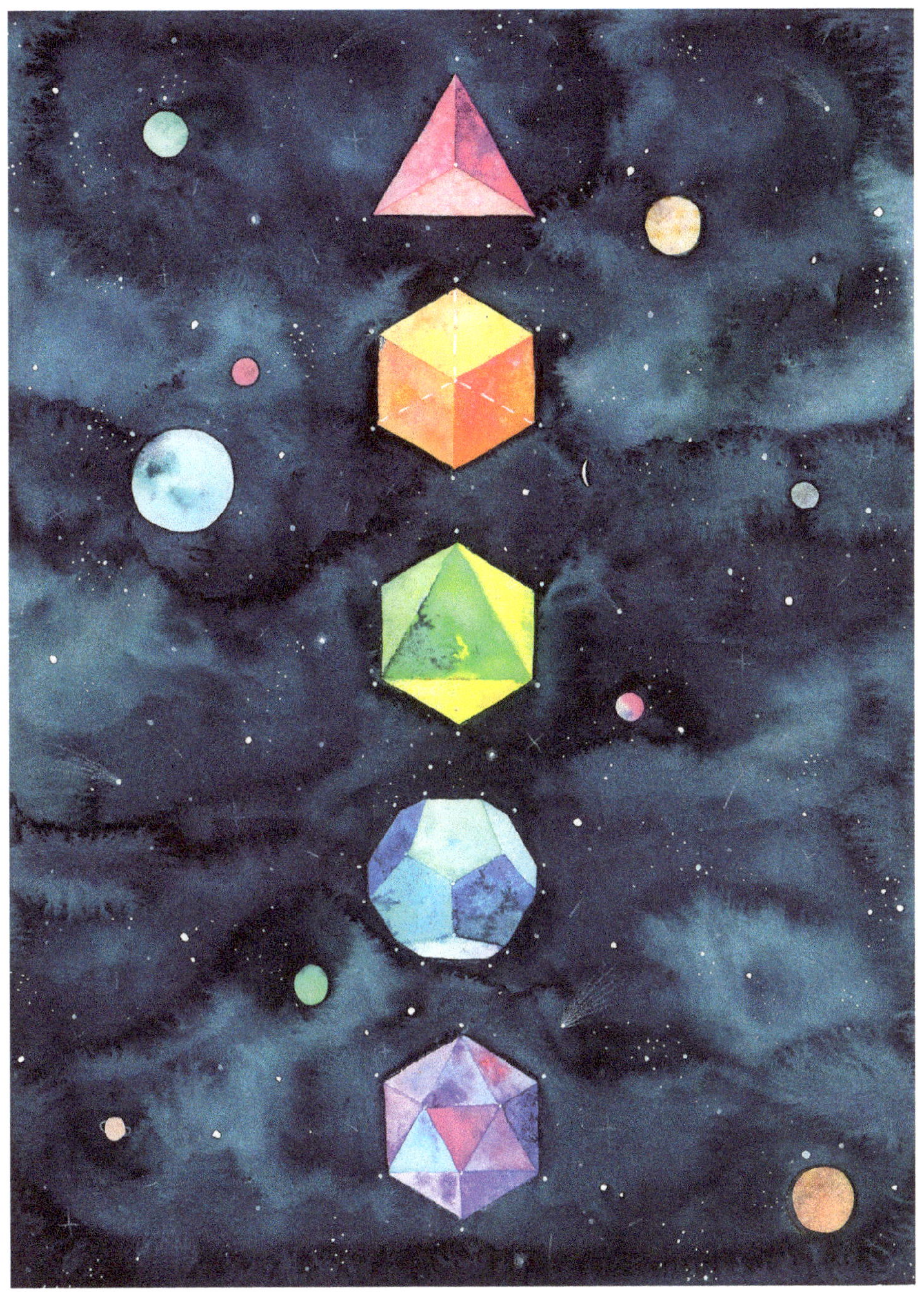

7 Add extra celestial details using the white medium of your choice. I'm using a Prismacolor white pencil for star clusters, shooting stars, and more dots.

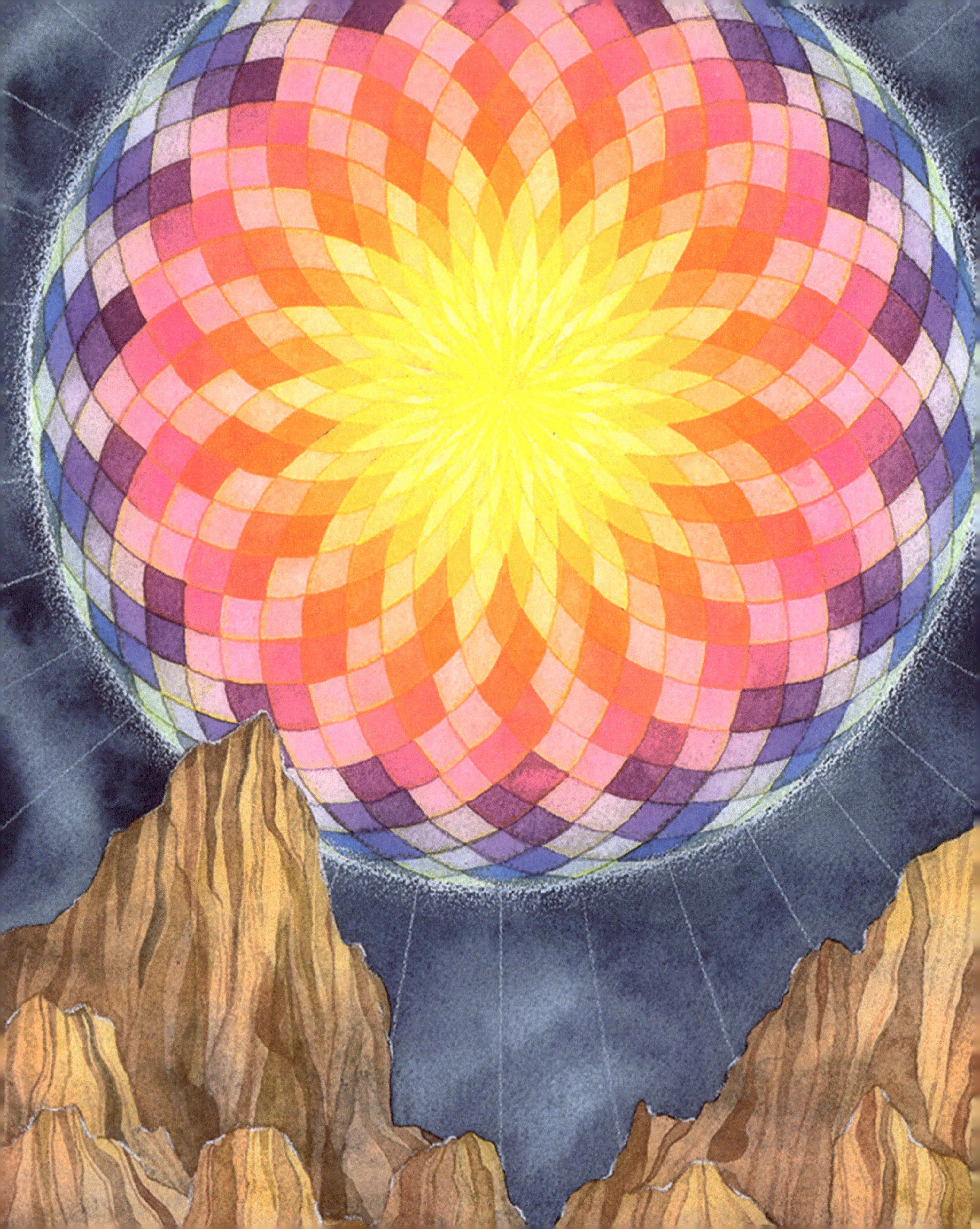

7

THE TORUS

The torus or vortex is an intriguing shape. Spiritual seekers travel to special locations around the globe to be in contact with these energetic spots, meteorologists study natural hurricane formations, and astronomers are discovering new findings related to black holes. As artists, this hypnotic shape is equally fascinating.

THE ENERGY OF THE TORUS

The torus is a two-dimensional representation of the toroidal flow, also known as the vortex in sacred geometry. When illustrated in three-dimensional form, it looks similar to a doughnut.

THE TORUS: INTERPRETATIONS

Here are some symbolic meanings associated with the torus.

- Resembles physical characteristics of a whirlpool.
- This ring of energy is often illustrated as the electromagnetic field surrounding every human.
- When drawn in two dimensions, this shape starts out as a seed of life.
- A gravitational vortex is studied by astronomers in relation to black holes.
- The center represents a tube or vacuum of light.
- Symbolizes energy when correctly aligned; it is continually cycling up, down, and around.

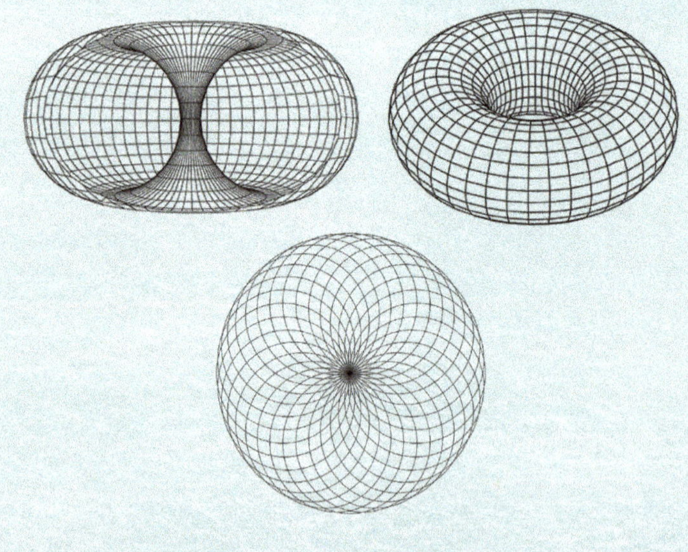

Drawing Techniques

There are two ways to draw the torus: the seed of life method and the protractor method.

TECHNIQUE 1: SEED OF LIFE METHOD

By this point, you will be familiar with the seed of life and how it grows onto itself when we begin to connect intersections.

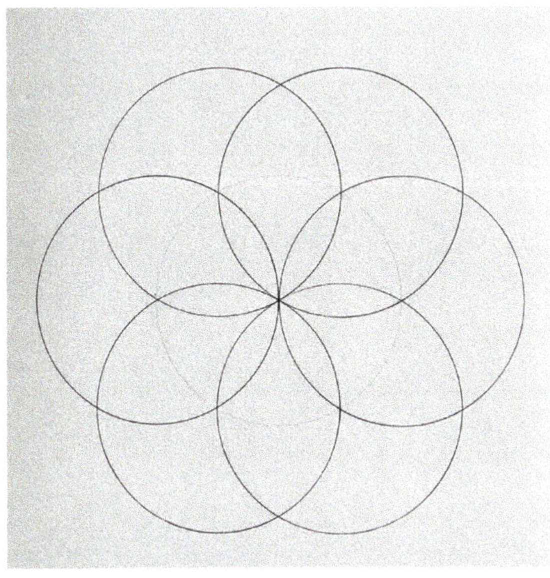

1 Draw a seed of life (see page 47). For best results, trace the middle circle using a pencil.

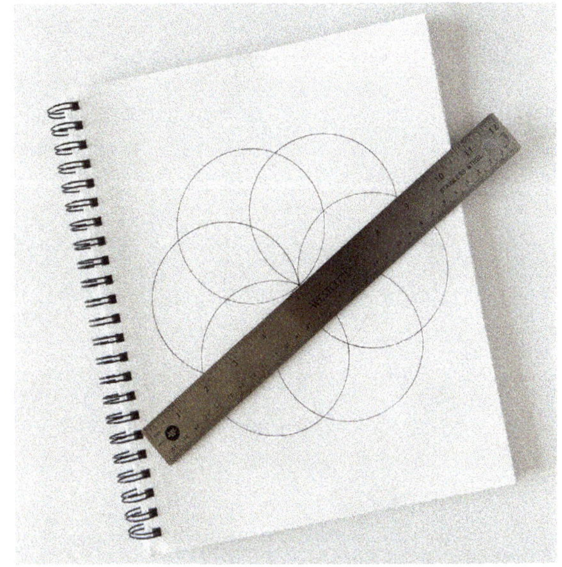

2 Using a straightedge, connect the two intersection points at opposite ends of your circles by aligning the intersections with your middle point.

(continued)

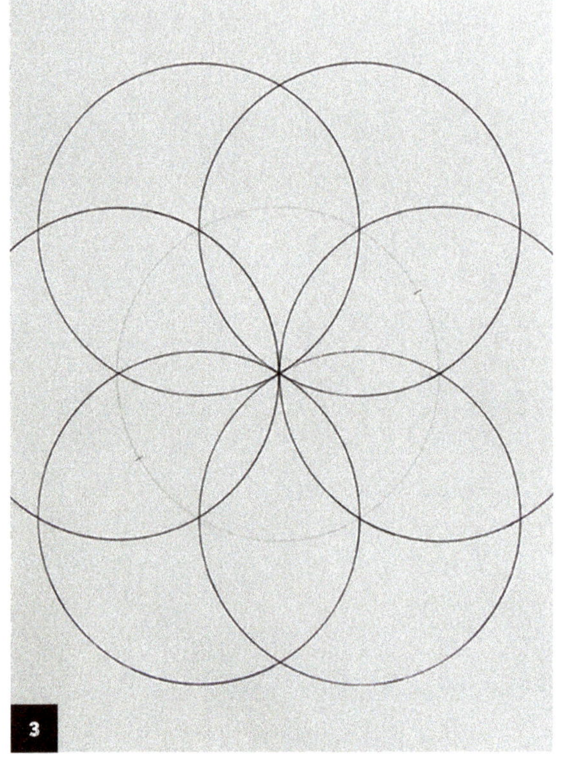

3

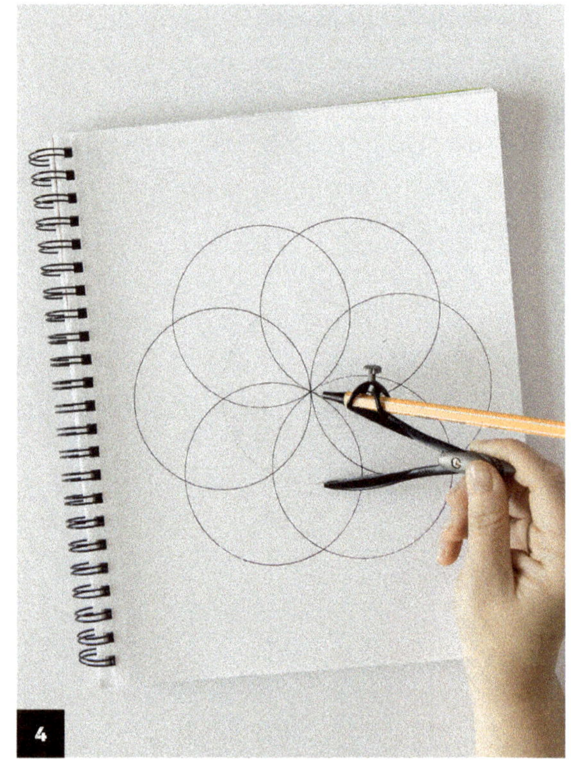

4

3 Mark the intersection points on your inner circle using a pencil. These lines are guides that you will erase later. Your drawing will now look like the image, and these points indicate the exact center of these sections of the inner circle circumference.

4 Continue this on all sides of your intersections, then place your compass needle at the center of each intersection and trace a new series of circles using the same aperture.

5 At this point, you will have two overlapping seeds of life or the twelve-petal mandala.

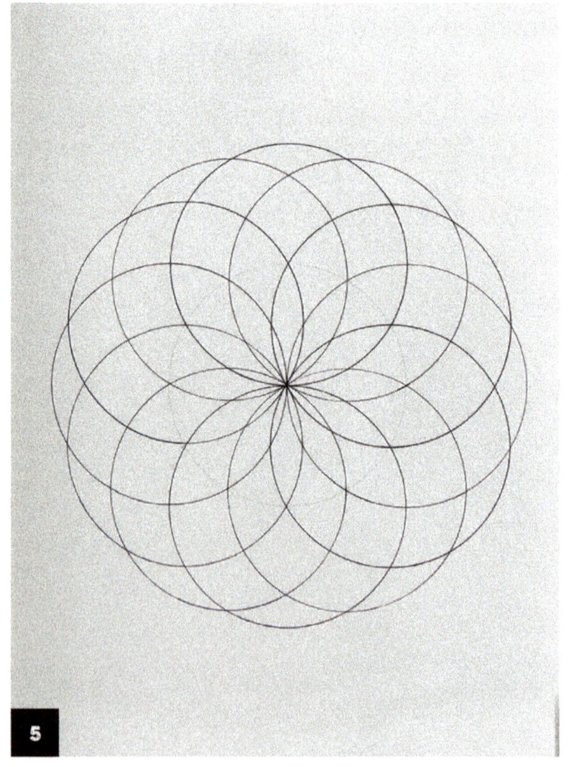

5

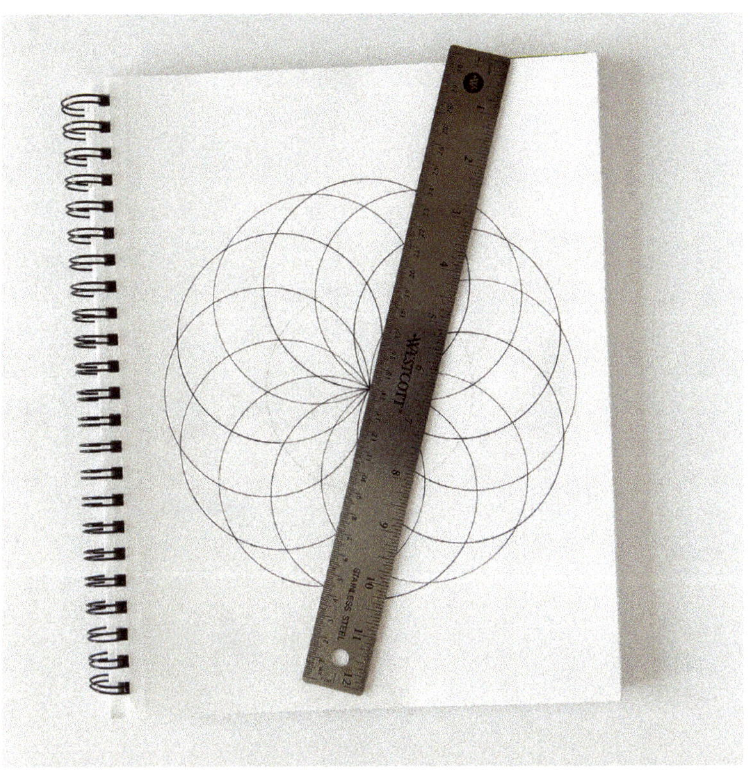

6 Now connect all the new intersections using the same method by placing your straightedge as shown.

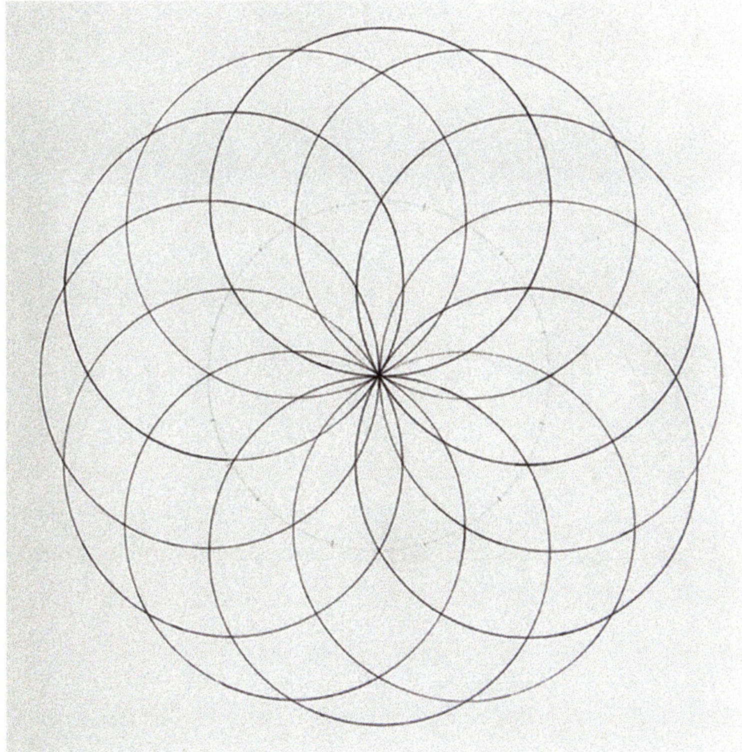

7 You will now have new markings for the rest of the circles.

(continued)

8 Draw another round of circles using these middle points as your centers. If you wish, you can continue going on for more rounds if the size of your shape allows.

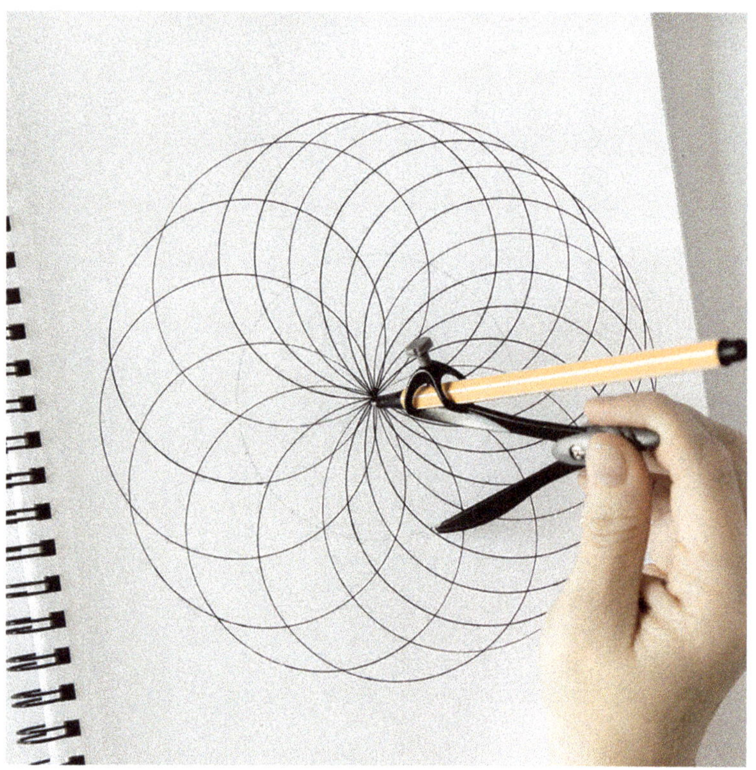

9 The torus is complete!

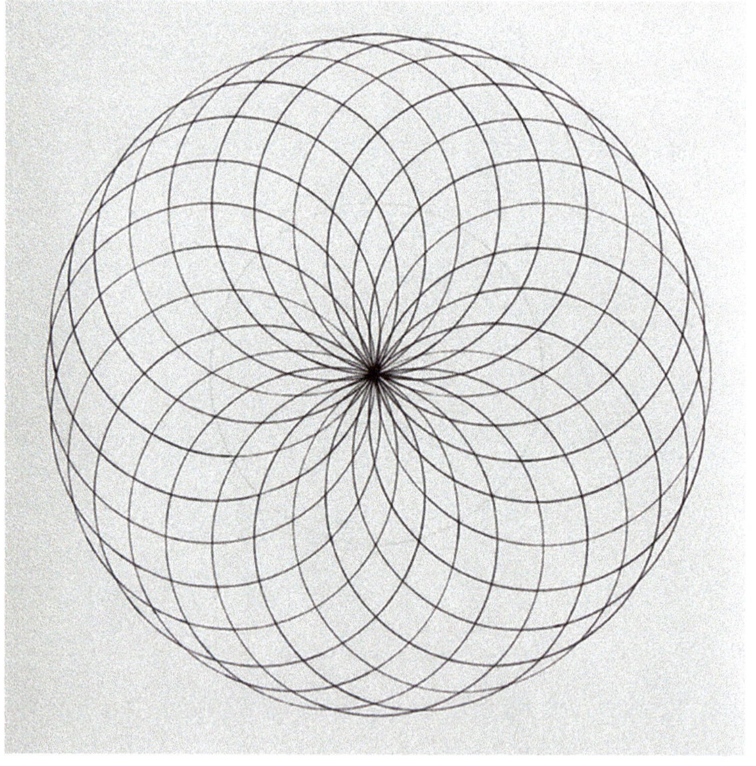

TECHNIQUE 2: PROTRACTOR METHOD

This other method of drawing a torus requires a protractor. Unlike the seed of life method, this way of drawing does not build up from the classic sacred geometry system, but the results are similar. I recommend trying both methods to see which one you prefer.

1 Find the center of your page and draw a cross shape using your straightedge.

2 Align your protractor with the center cross and create pencil markings every 10 degrees. Be precise.

3 Flip your protractor, align it with the center cross, and continue the markings on the other side.

(continued)

1

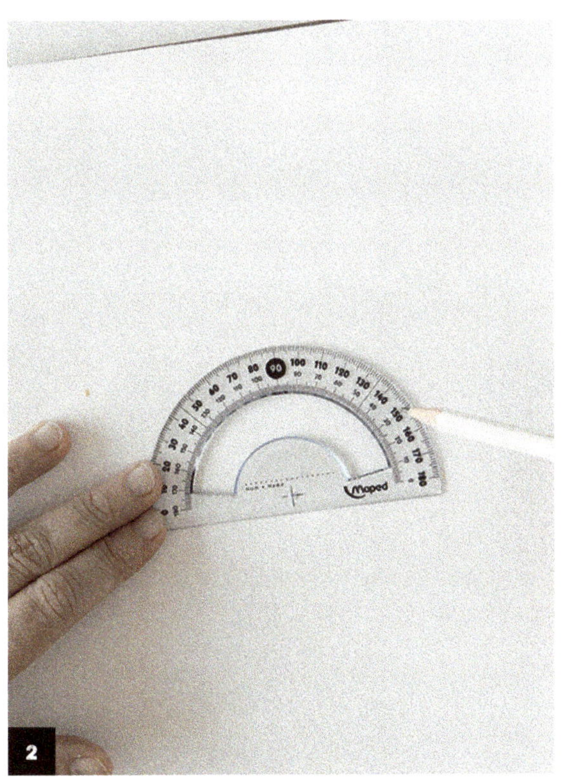

2

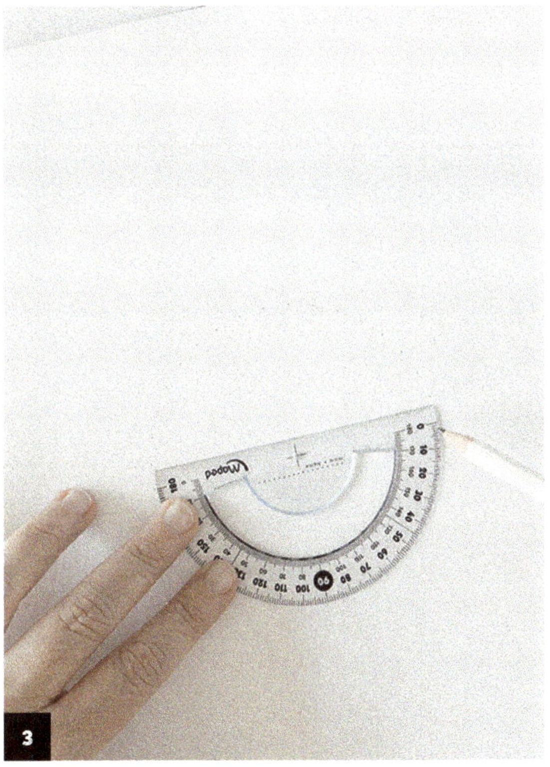

3

4

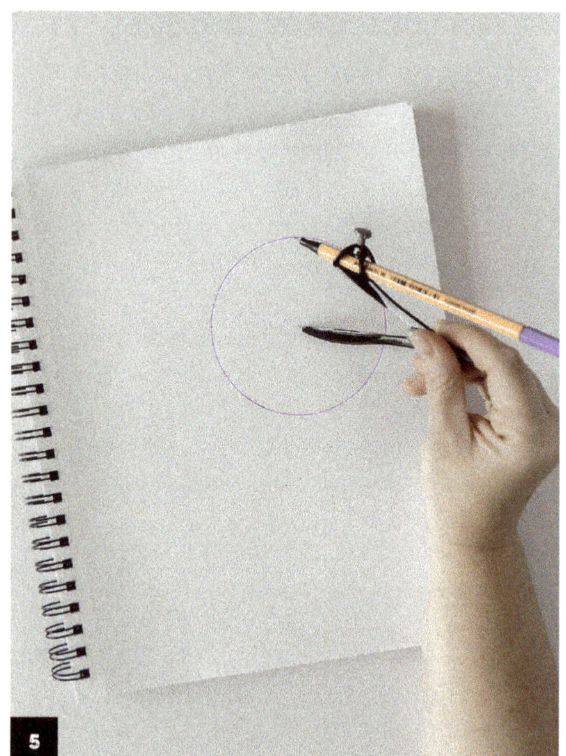
5

4 You will now have what looks like a circumference of pencil dots.

5 Set the aperture of your compass from the center of the middle cross to one of the pencil markings. Place the needle point on one of your protractor markings and trace a circle.

6 Continue this process until you have traced a circle at each marking.

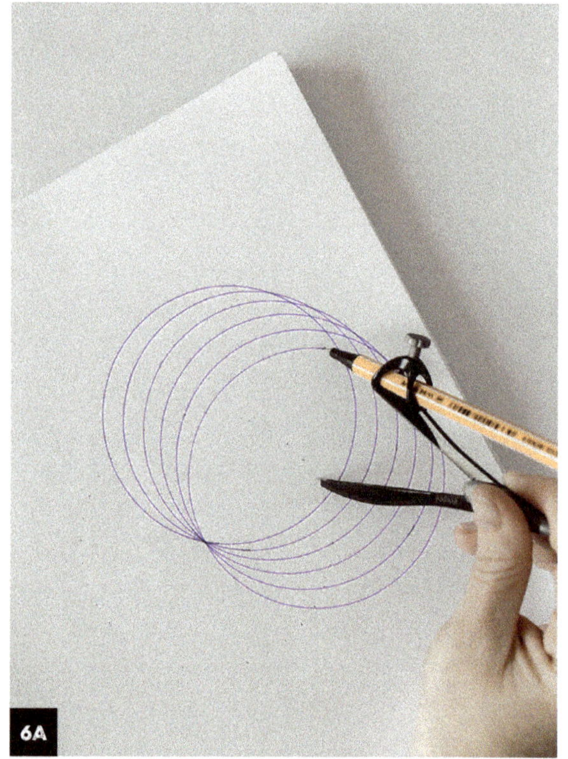
6A

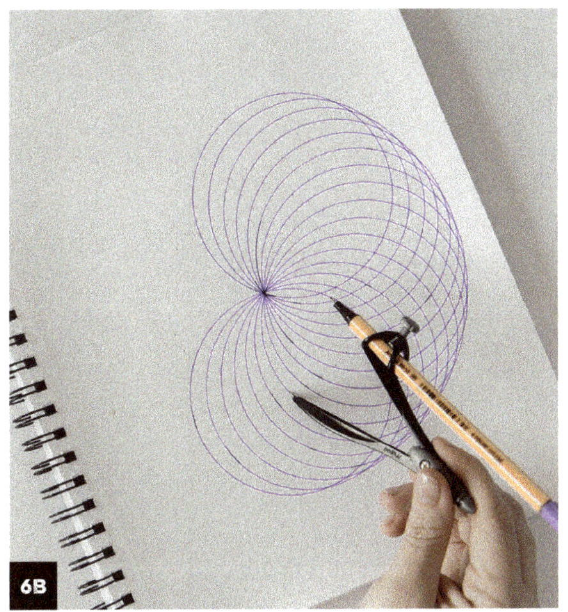

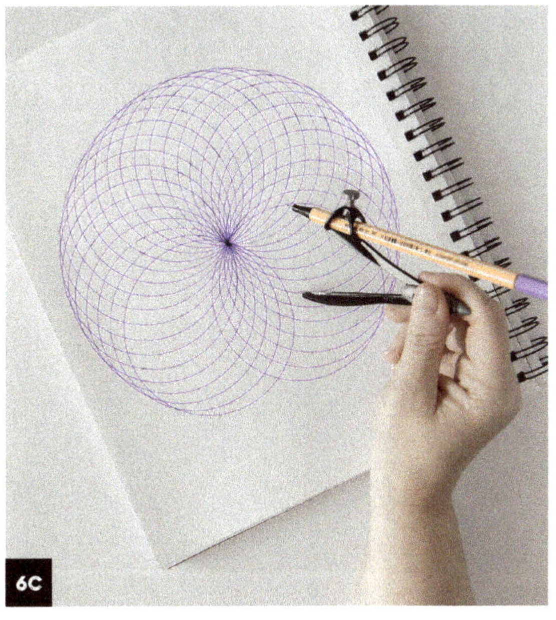

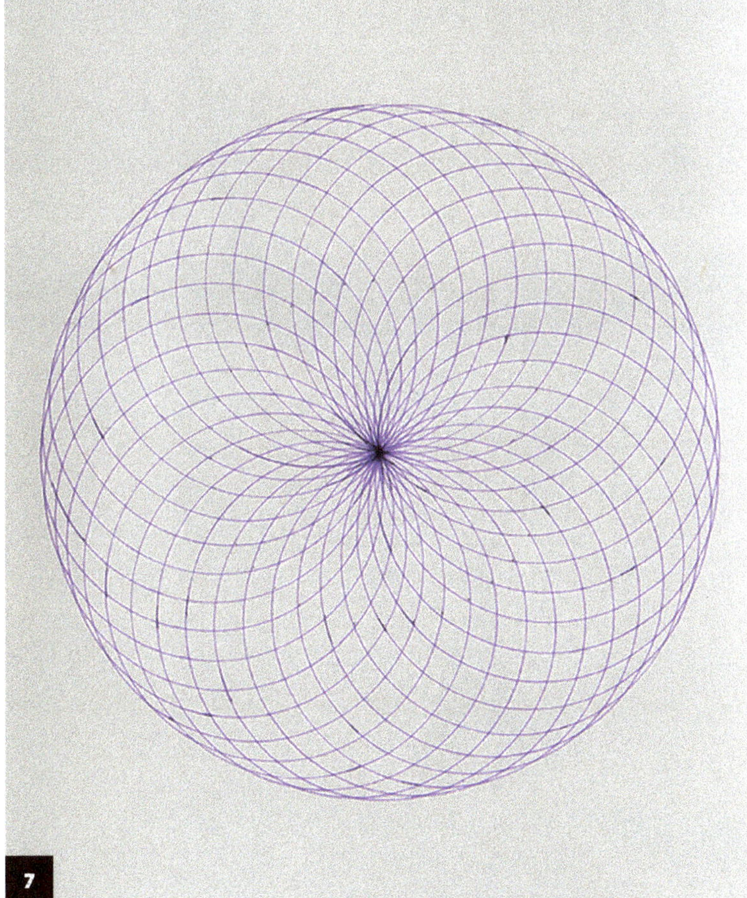

7 And you have a torus!

ARTISTIC EXPLORATION: ADDING AND SUBTRACTING LINES AND USING COLOR

There are many ways to artistically interpret the torus, such as adding more lines to enhance the drawing or omitting lines to simplify the form. Or you can add color, being strategic where you fill in the spaces to create a dramatic effect. Here are three projects for inspiration.

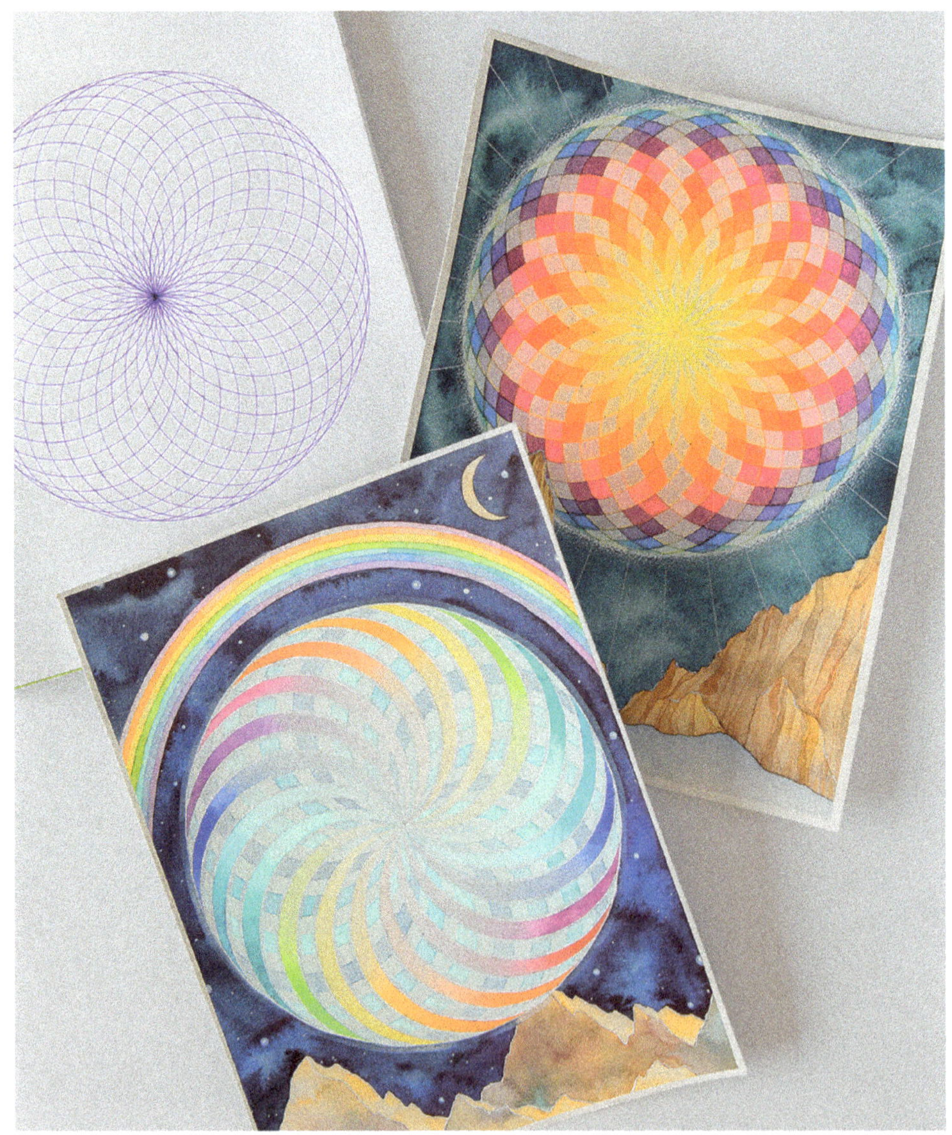

THE HYPNOTIC EYE

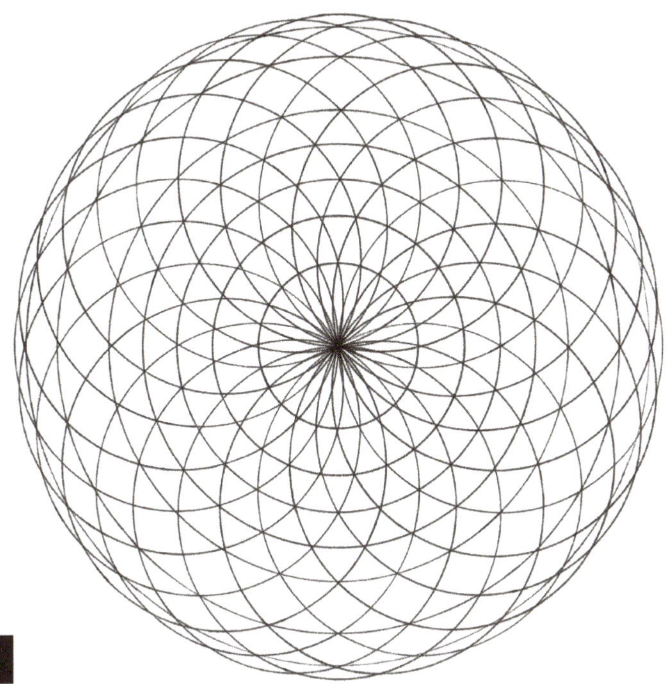

1

1 Once you have a torus shape, add more circles. Place your compass needle on the center point of the shape. Open the aperture to every intersecting point and trace a circle. The aperture will continue to open as your shape grows. You can trace a circle at each intersection or be selective.

2 For a clearer, more dramatic image, use a black marker to fill in chosen areas.

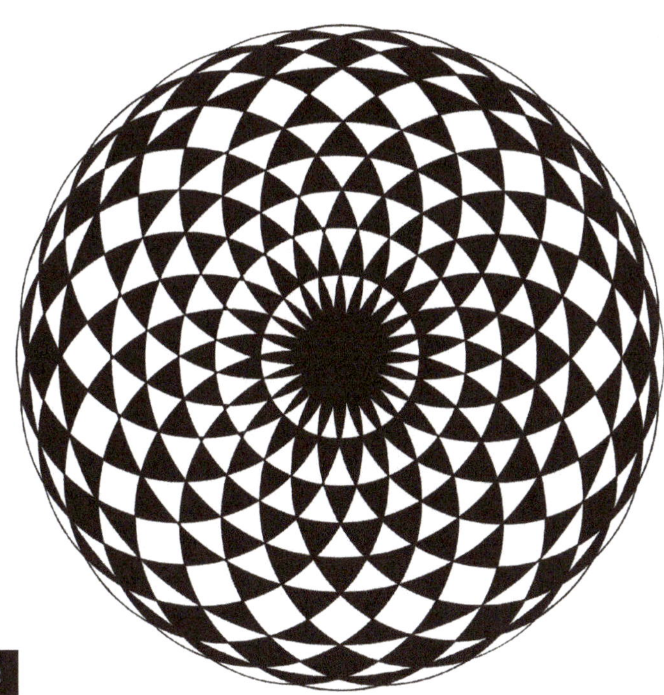

2

THE VORTEX

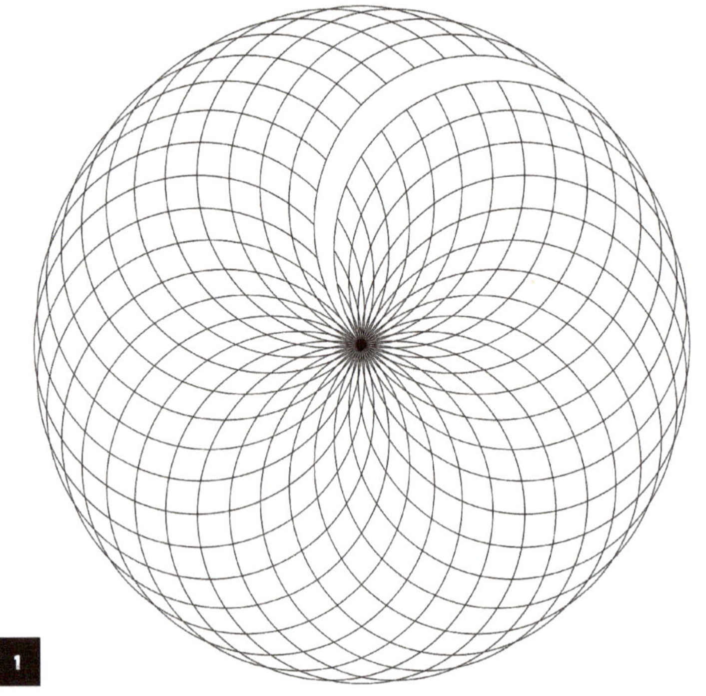

1

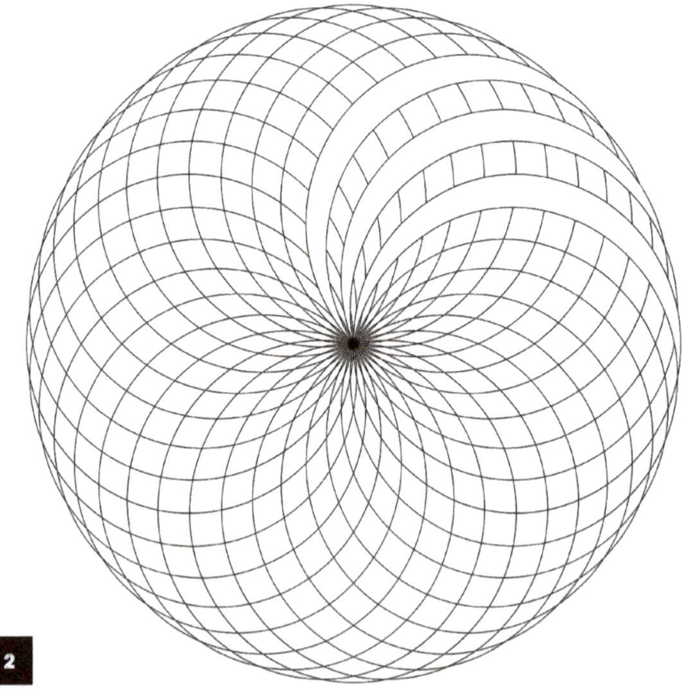

2

1 Another way to interpret the torus is by erasing lines to create a vortex effect. Trace your torus using a pencil and select an area to erase. Use this image as a reference.

2 Skip the neighboring area and erase the following one. Continue to do this until you have a vortex image. This creates a three-dimensional effect, similar to the doughnut reference (see page 122).

3 You can also use watercolor or another medium to create a celestial color spectrum effect.

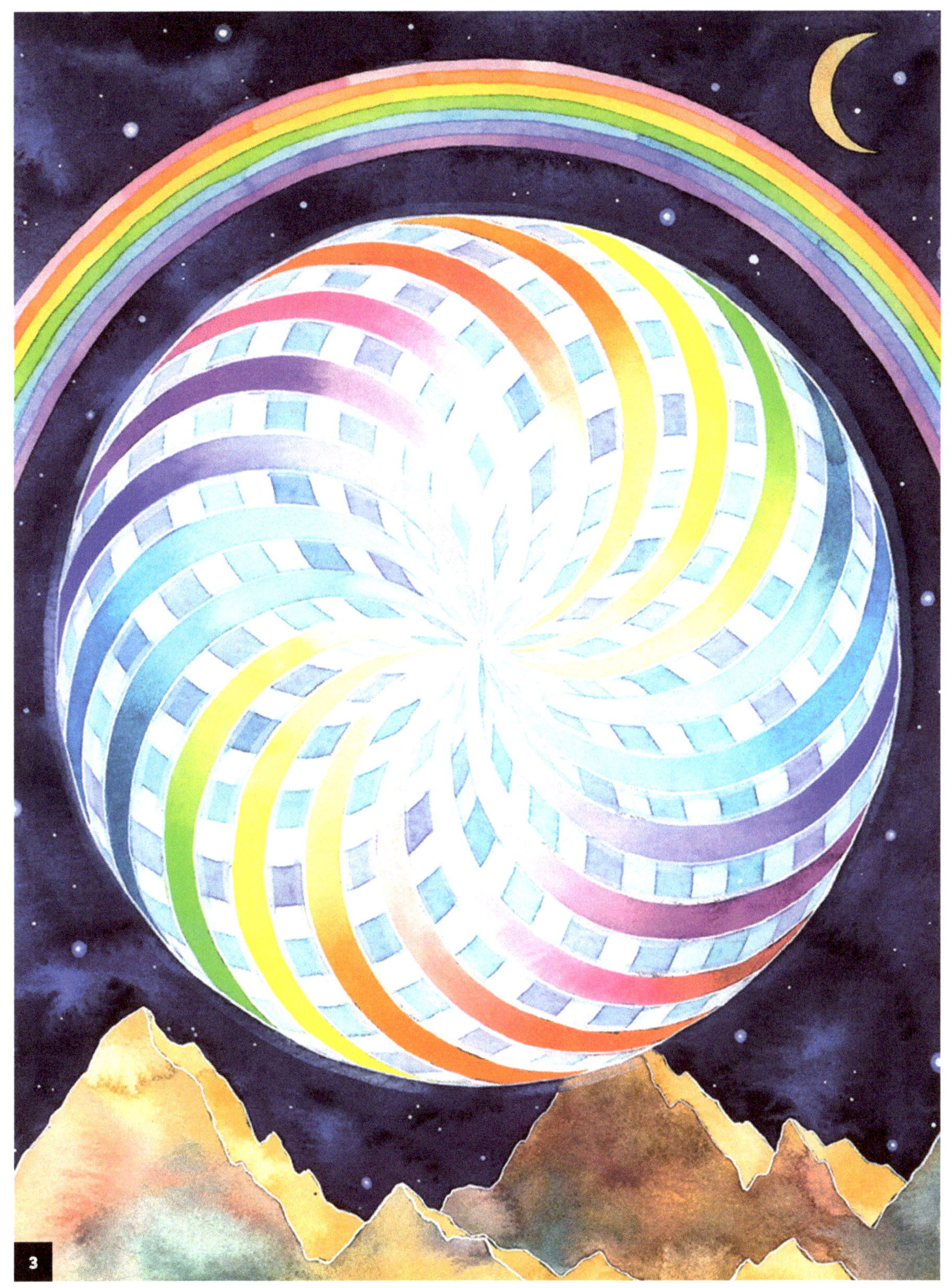
3

A BLENDED HYPNOTIC EYE

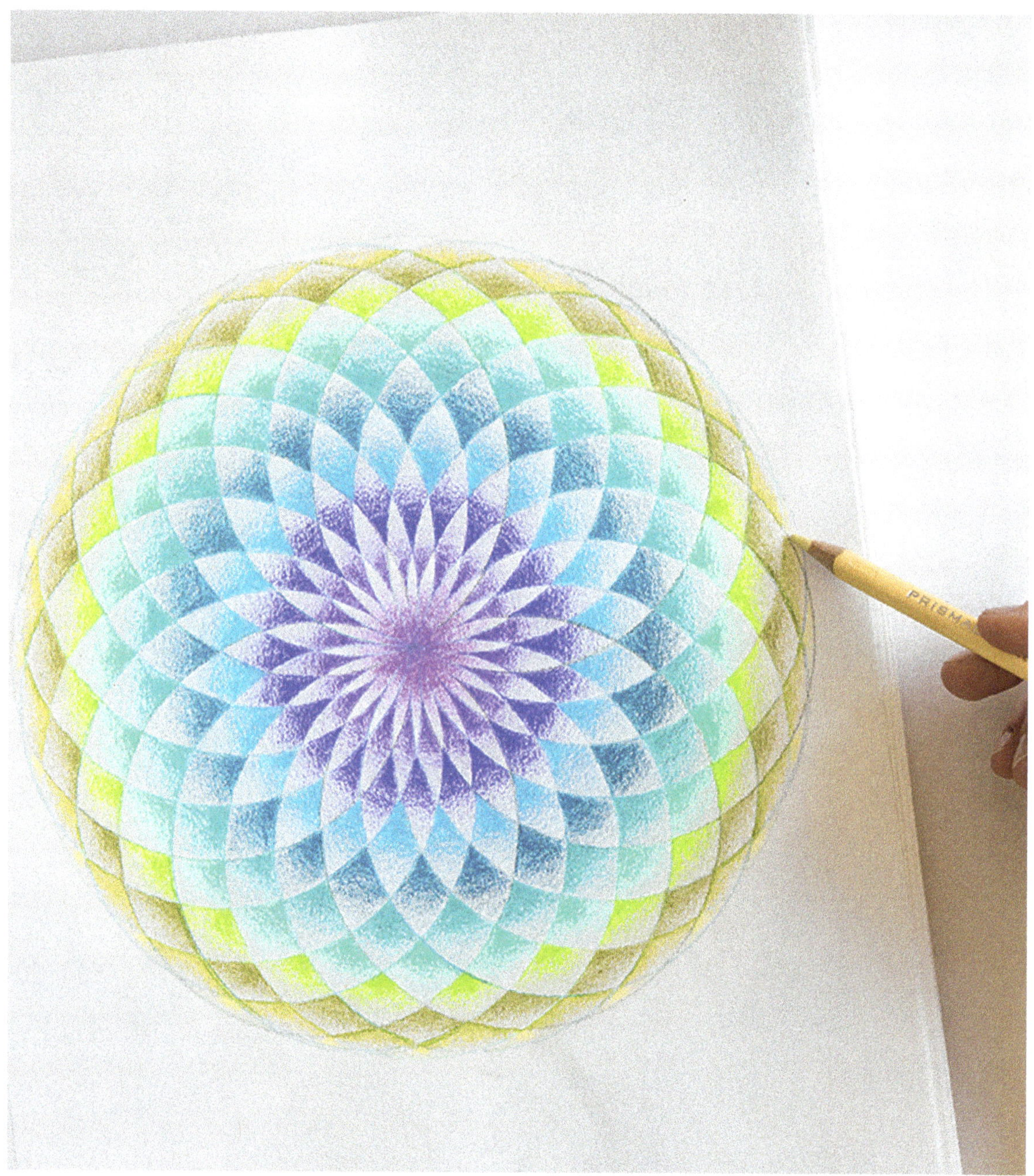

1 For a different artistic representation of the hypnotic eye, use colored pencils and blend from dark to light. Choose a color scheme and simply begin drawing each section. This process is quite therapeutic.

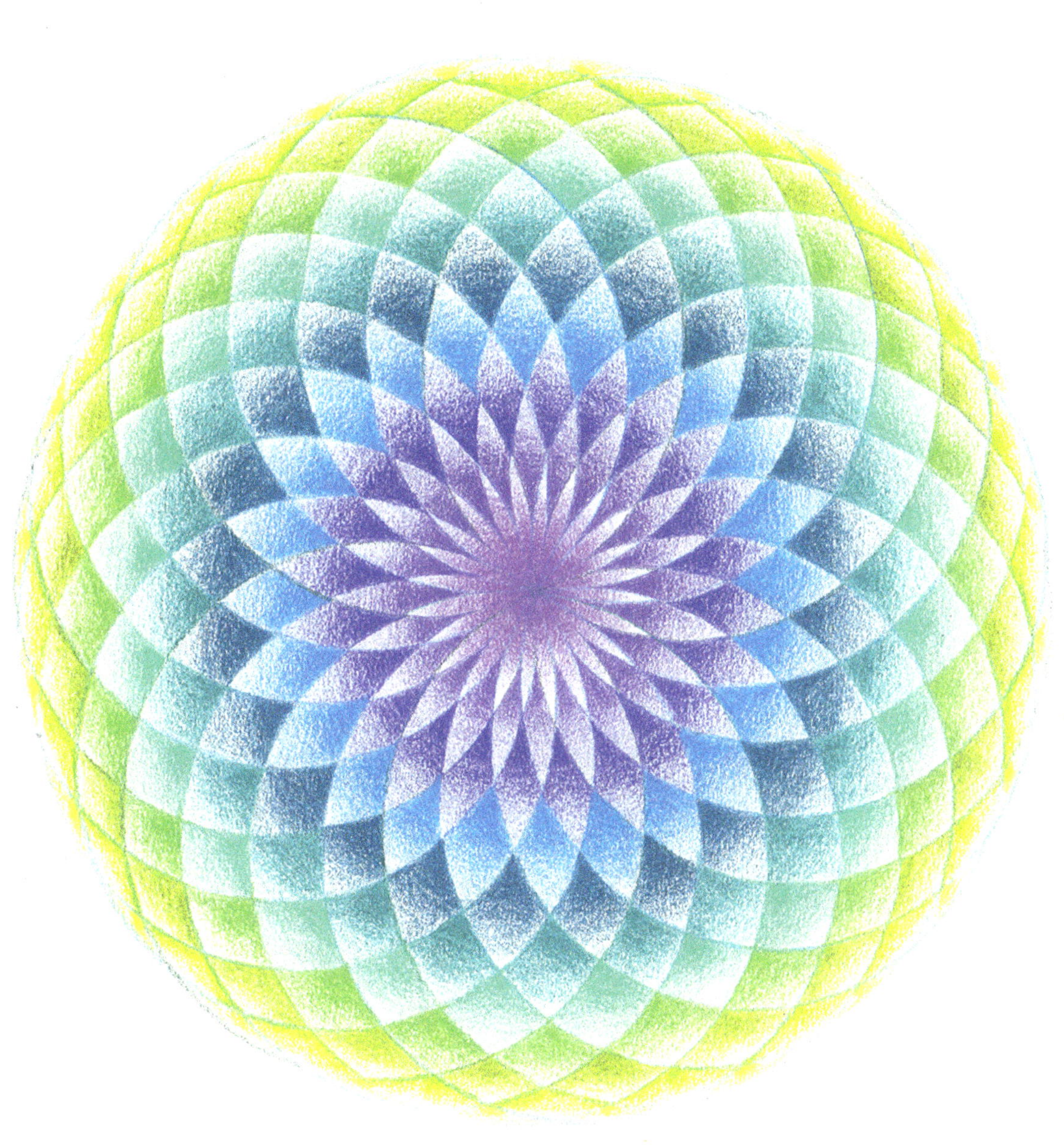

2 Keep going until you have filled in every section of the shape.

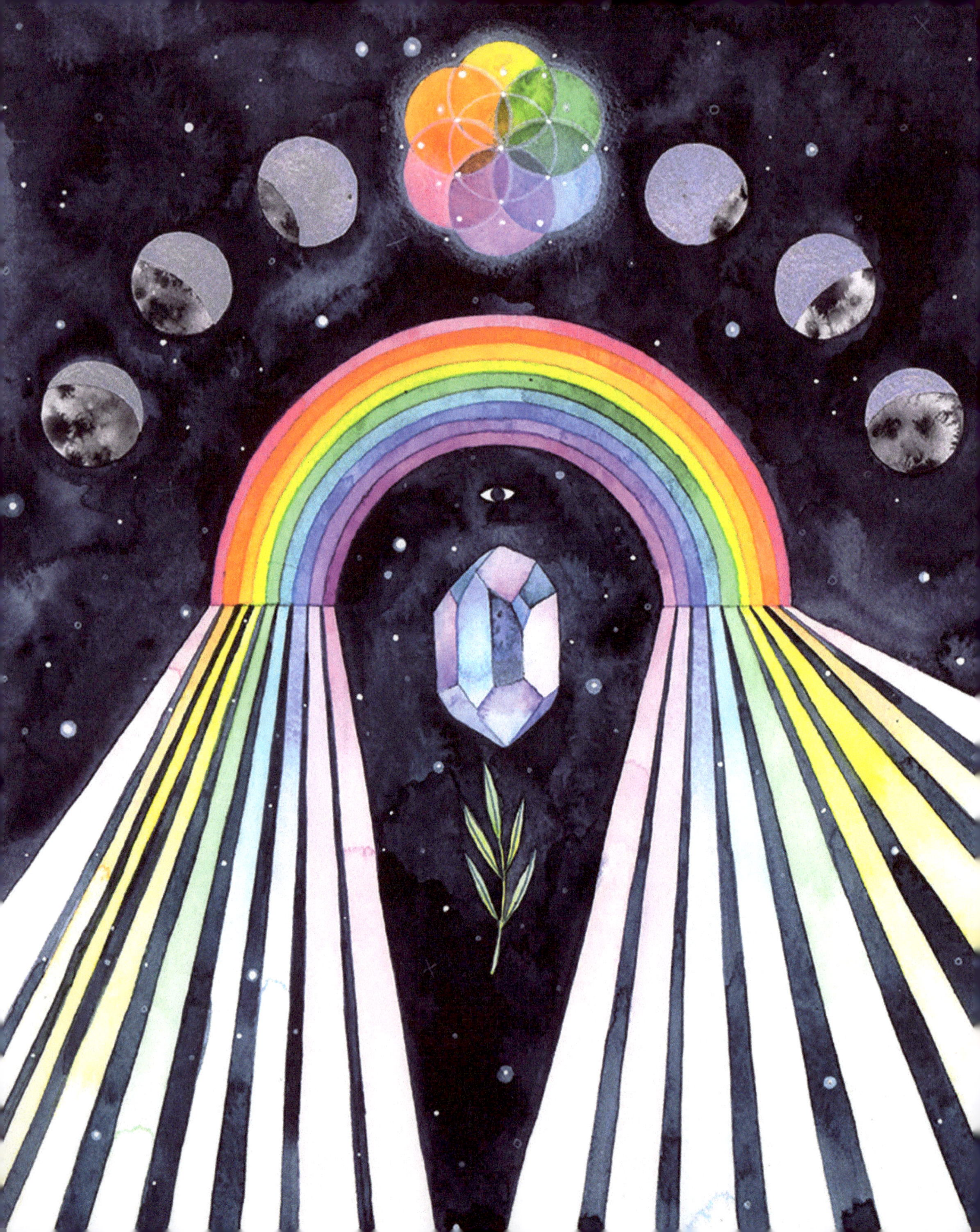

EPILOGUE

If you have found sacred geometry to be as captivating as I have, I invite you to continue your journey beyond this book. It can take you on many adventures and down all sorts of paths.

CONTINUE YOUR PATH OF EXPLORATION

The purpose of this book is to make sacred geometry accessible and demystify the basic shapes to get you started. While the content shared here focuses on the artist's experience, you may want to continue to research the topic or find other ways to give life to your geometric drawings. My intention is to spark inspiration and allow you to embark on a new journey of your own.

If you are intrigued by this, there are certainly a number of shapes and concepts you can continue to explore on your own. Here is a short list:

- Chakana
- Dance of Venus
- God's eye
- The golden ratio
- Vector equilibrium
- Yantras

Additionally, I invite you to expand your curiosity and even break some rules: Play with your compass and use your imagination to discover new formations within these curves and lines.

I wish you a happy journey, mindful relaxation, and many special moments in your creative practice!

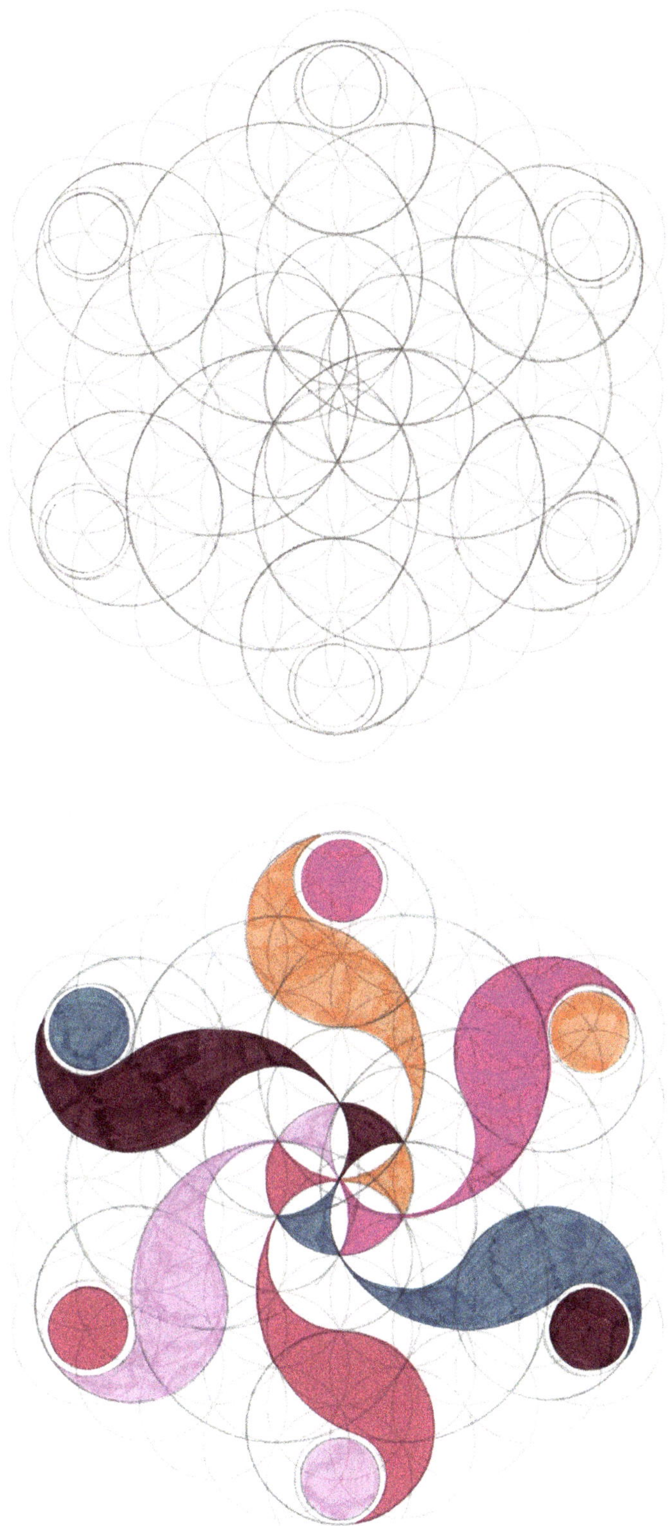

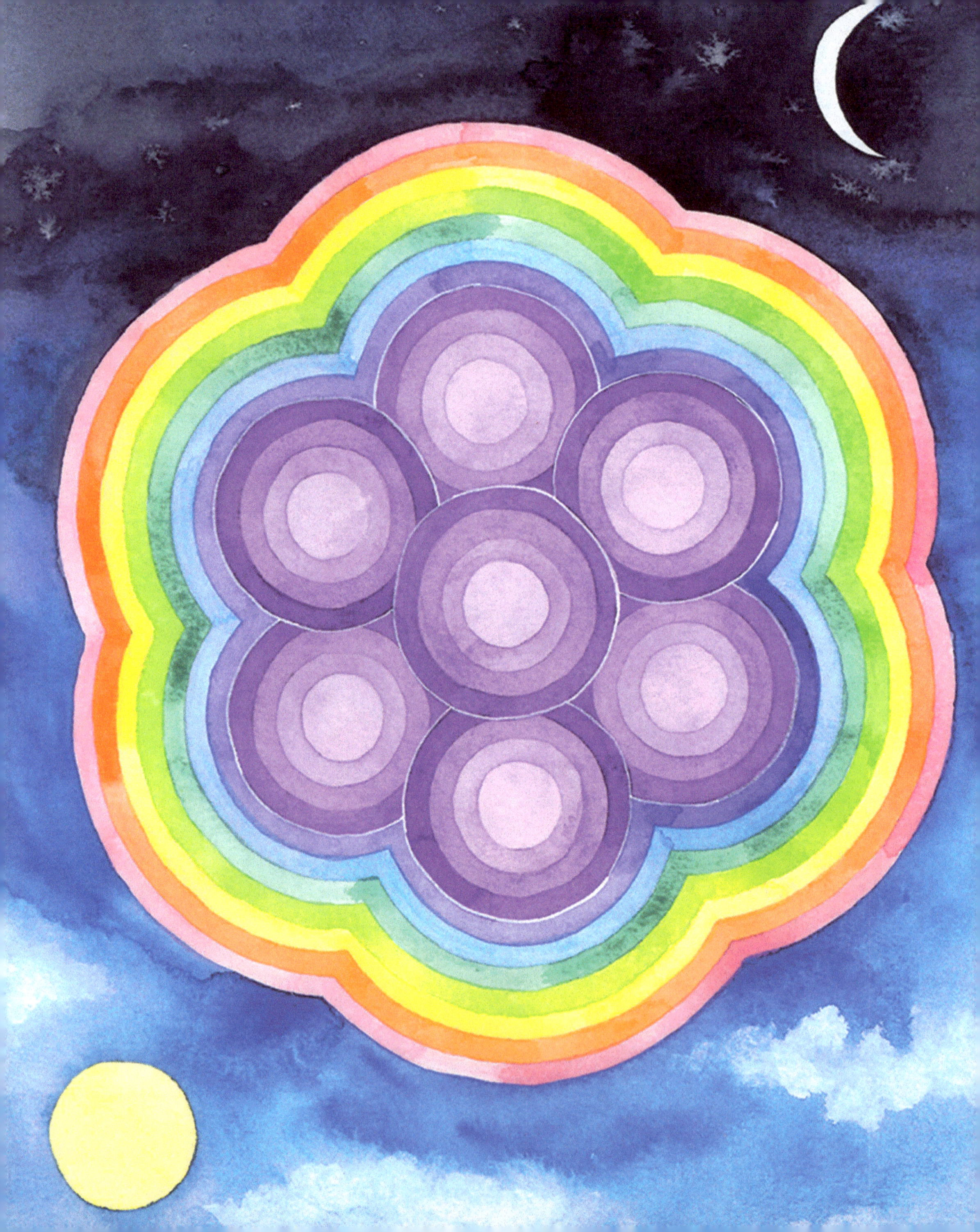

RESOURCES

For further watercolor instructions I highly recommend taking my online courses with Skillshare and Domestika.
skillshare.com/r/user/anavictoriana
domestika.org/en/anavictoriana

If you would like to continue your artistic journey and attend in person workshops and retreats, please visit the following website.
anavictoriana.com/learn

For more information on supplies used in this book, visit the following websites.

Winsor & Newton
winsornewton.com/row

Princeton
princetonbrush.com

Canson
en.canson.com

Kremer Pigmente
kremerpigments.com

HydraColour
etsy.com/shop/HydraColour

Sennelier
sennelier-colors.com

Daniel Smith
danielsmith.com

Legion Paper
legionpaper.com/stonehenge

Holbein
holbeinartistmaterials.com

Prismacolor
prismacolor.com

Caran d'Ache
carandache.com/ch/en/

Faber-Castell
faber-castell.com

White Nights Pastel Watercolours
stpetersburgwatercolours.com

ACKNOWLEDGMENTS

I would like to thank my editor, Joy, who trusted me with this unconventional topic. After collaborating on four books together, I have nothing but kind words for the entire Quarto team.

This book was written throughout my pregnancy and during the early days of postpartum. As any new mother knows, these days can be quite overwhelming. We are so in love with our baby, and if it had not been for my husband, I wouldn't have had the space to write this lovely book that means so much to me. I will always be grateful for his complete support and devotion.

As always, a special thank you to my family. Art has always been my path, and their encouragement has meant the world to me.

Lastly, none of this would be possible if it weren't for YOU. A special thank you to all my students and readers. It has been a true joy to share my love of painting with you. Your enthusiasm keeps me motivated, and I hope to continue sharing this with you for many years to come.

ABOUT THE AUTHOR

The author of *Creative Watercolor, Color Harmony for Artists,* and *Creative Watercolor and Mixed Media,* **Ana Victoria Calderón** is a Mexican/American watercolor artist and teacher with a bachelor's degree in Information Design and continued studies in Fine Arts. Her licensed artwork can be seen in retail outlets throughout the United States and Europe on a wide variety of products. Ana teaches in-person workshops and hosts creative retreats in the Mexican jungle and summer watercolor retreats around the world. She has more than half a million students combined on Skillshare, where she is a Top Teacher, and Domestika. See more of Ana's work on Instagram (@anavictoriana), YouTube (Ana Victoria Calderon), and Facebook (Ana Victoria Calderon Illustration). She lives in Mexico City, Mexico.

INDEX

To my magical daughter Sabrina,
who was growing inside me as I wrote this book.

Quarto.com

First Published in 2022 by Quarry Books, an imprint of The Quarto Group,
100 Cummings Center, Suite 265-D, Beverly, MA 01915, USA.
T (978) 282-9590 F (978) 283-2742

EEA Representation, WTS Tax d.o.o.,
Žanova ulica 3, 4000 Kranj, Slovenia.
www.wts-tax.si

Quarry Books titles are also available at discount for retail, wholesale, promotional, and bulk purchase. For details, contact the Special Sales Manager by email at specialsales@quarto.com or by mail at The Quarto Group, Attn: Special Sales Manager, 100 Cummings Center, Suite 265-D, Beverly, MA 01915, USA.

ISBN: 978-0-7603-7453-5

Digital edition published in 2022
eISBN: 978-0-7603-7454-2

Library of Congress Cataloging-in-Publication Data is available

Page Layout: Megan Jones Design
Photography: Maureen M. Evans

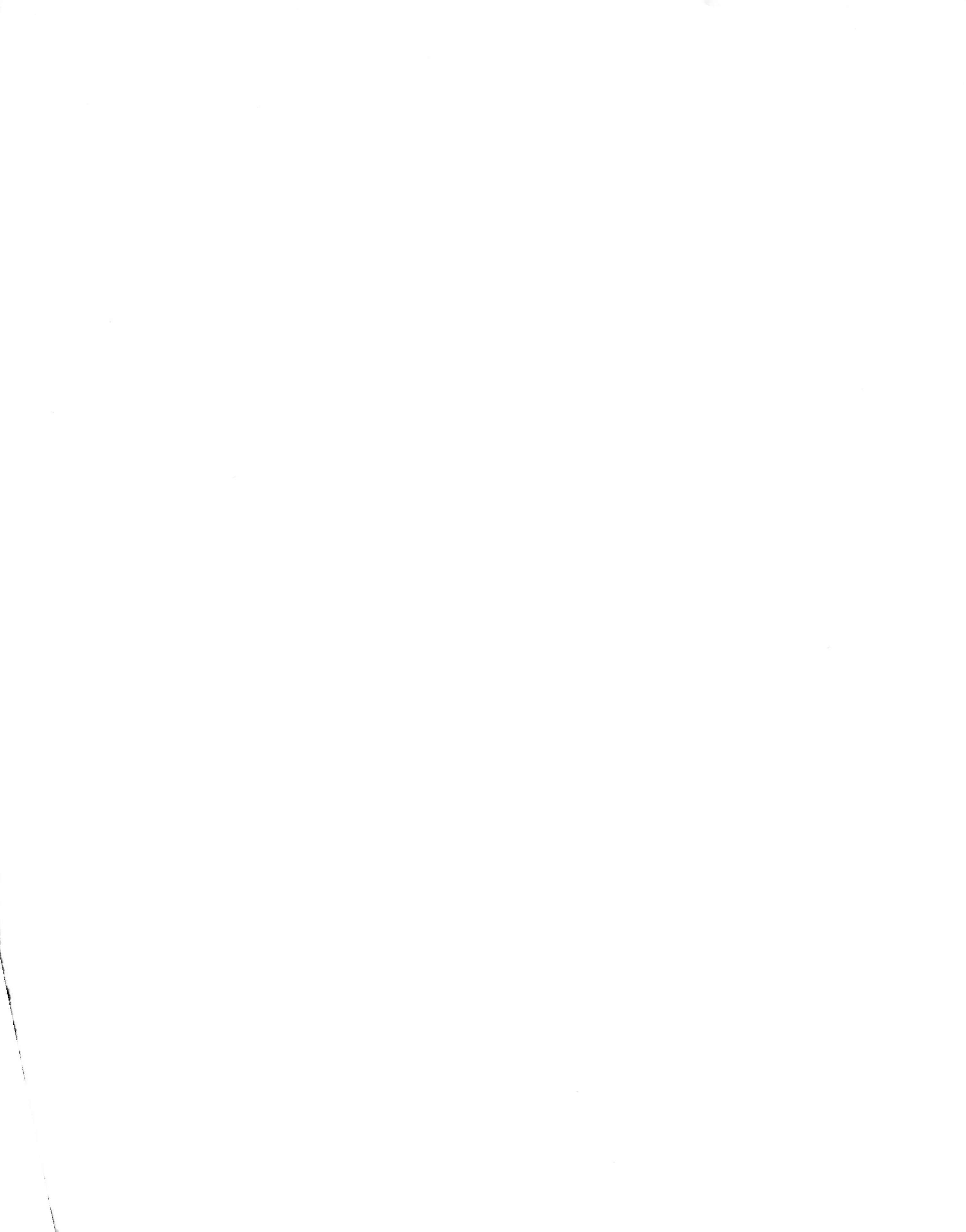

www.ingramcontent.com/pod-product-compliance
Lightning Source LLC
LaVergne TN
LVHW071358100626
840831LV00006BA/6

9780760374535